KING PŌTATAU

Te Wherowhero

George French Angas
AA 8/6/35 G.F. Angas Collection, South Australian Museum Archives.

KING PŌTATAU

An Account of the Life of

PŌTATAU TE WHEROWHERO

the First Māori King

By

PEI TE HURINUI

The Polynesian Society Memoir No. 55.

First published in 1959 by The Polynesian Society (Inc.)
Reprinted in 2010, 2025 by Huia Publishers and The Polynesian Society (Inc.)

Huia Publishers
39 Pipitea Street, PO Box 12280
Wellington, Aotearoa New Zealand
www.huia.co.nz

The Polynesian Society
c/- Māori Studies
The University of Auckland
Private Bag 92019, Auckland
New Zealand

ISBN 978-1-86969-423-4

Copyright © The Polynesian Society (Inc.) 2010
Cover image: *King Potatau* – painting AA 8/6/35, GF Angas Collection,
South Australian Museum Archives.

This book is copyright. Apart from fair dealing for the purpose of private study,
research, criticism or review, as permitted under the Copyright Act, no part may be
reproduced by any process without the prior permission of the publisher.

A catalogue record for this book is available from
the National Library of New Zealand.

Original edition published with the support of the
New Zealand Lottery Grants Board and Creative New Zealand.

Reprinted with the support of Te Takarangi,
Te Rōpū Whakahau and New Zealand Libraries Partnership

DEDICATION

This volume is humbly dedicated to
The House of Pōtatau

Ko Waikato te Awa;
Ko Taupiri te Maunga,
Ko Te Wherowhero te Tangata.

Waikato is the River;
Taupiri is the Mountain,
And Te Wherowhero is the Man.

The Author

PREFACE

By The Author

This history of Pōtatau Te Wherowhero deals with all the outstanding events of his life. The period covered is from about the year 1775 to his death in 1860. In early life he was known by the name of Te Wherowhero, which name we have adopted for Book One of this volume. Later he was given the name of Pōtatau; and it was as King Pōtatau Te Wherowhero he was proclaimed the first Māori King.

In presenting this work as a contribution to New Zealand history we hope that note will be taken of it together with other accounts. The allocation of the responsibility and the assignment of blame for the events that led up to the Māori Wars of the Eighteen Sixties, which synchronised with the setting up of the Māori King and which have been generally assigned to the Māori King Movement, should be reviewed in the light of the facts given in this account.

Several facts have been recorded by European writers on this subject; notably Sir John Gorst, a fair-minded and cultured English gentleman, and quite a library could be assembled. Many of the outstanding actors: governors, statesmen, soldiers, churchmen, administrators, and Māori Loyalists have had their stories told. These records reveal the perplexities, misunderstandings and difficulties of the times.

History can be too severe in its judgement, and it is our purpose in this volume to place on record and make available to future historians material upon which they can gauge the stress and strain under which, leading Māori actors or "rebels", so called, played their parts. We have tried to throw light into the recesses of the Māori mind and over the tribal background of the times, and to reveal the motives which actuated the Māori chiefs in the setting up of a Māori King. The data on which it is based was the result of a painstaking quest and an eager desire to acquire knowledge of the traditions of our Tainui people.

Since the writing of the book was completed on the 4th of June, 1945, all the elders listed at page 279 have passed away. In the course of our investigations, we compiled a table of dates of the five Māori Kings as follows:

MĀORI KINGS	WHAKAWAHINGA OR RAISING-UP	DATE OF DEATH
Pōtatau	2/5/1859	25/6/1860
Tāwhiao	5/7/1860	26/8/1894
Mahuta	14/9/1894	9/11/1912
Te Rātā	24/11/1912	1/10/1933
Korokī	8/10/1933	

Before the Centennial celebrations for the founding of the Māori King Movement, which was held at Ngāruawāhia on the 2nd of May, 1958, the author argued with the Tainui elders that the centennial date should be the 2nd May, 1959. We found ourselves in a minority. We have since made a further search and discovered evidence in Rusden's *History of New Zealand* that the 1959 date was after all the correct centennial year. In the year 1858 for instance the name "*Matua*" (father) was favoured by a large section of the Waikato people. The record of the 1859 date is given in Volume II of Rusden's book (1895: 100-101) from which we quote:

> Donald McLean went to the meeting at Ngaruawahia with Wiremu Nera (earlier known as Te Awataia). The main object was to confirm Potatau as king and to erect his flag. War dances were indulged in with savage delight as the lower Waikato and Manukau natives landed from their flotilla of canoes.... The majority of the meeting staunchly supported the King movement. Some were moderate adherents. Some opposed it as likely to lead to a war of races.... McLean's speech (not recorded by Rusden), unfinished at night, was to be resumed in the morning, but the Maoris were slow to assemble, and as McLean heard that the flagstaff was to be reared that day—a ceremony he desired not to see—he bade farewell to Potatau. The flagstaff was erected (29th May) and named after Potatau's ancestor Te Paue (sic)—Tapaue. Potatau on that day spoke publicly for the first time, and spoke in friendly terms of the English.

Confirmation of the date of death of Pōtatau, which was also the subject of argument prior to the Centennial celebrations, was recorded by Rusden in the same volume:

Two days before the attack on Puketakauere (in Taranaki, at the southern end of the town of Waitara) Potatau died.... The son of Potatau, called at the time Matutaera, but who subsequently took the name of Tawhiao, was chosen king. (*ibid*: 110).

The fight at Puketakauere which resulted in the repulse of the British forces by the Māori, principally of Ngāti Maniapoto under Rewi Maniapoto, took place on the 27th of June, 1860:

> Major Nelson with 348 of all ranks... after a severe and gallant conflict, he was obliged to retire with a loss of 30 killed and 34 wounded (*ibid*: 109).

This engagement is mentioned in Chapter 9 of this volume:

> Upon the Maori Kingship, more than any other party, the responsibility has been cast for the Maori Wars of the Sixties and all that flowed from that unhappy chapter in New Zealand history. The most unhappy period was still in the laps of the gods during the time covered in this account, but a good deal of propaganda had already been built up against the Maori King Movement. In these transactions the Maori was at a decided disadvantage. The Press was out of touch with the Maori world and was generally hostile. The Maori himself failed to appreciate the need for recording his side of the case, and he was for the most part a harassed actor in a moving drama which had aspects in it of a Greek tragedy. In the light of knowledge given to him at the time he emerged from the maelstrom with honour; he lived and fought courageously and came through an agonising struggle with his head unbowed; and it must not be forgotten that barely twenty years separated Te Wherowhero from the old-time way of life of his people at the time he died in 1860 (*ibid*: 228-229).

To all my Tainui elders I pay my tributes for making it possible for me to write this account. I have listed their names at page 279 of this volume. The late Princess Te Puea was most helpful, and I am most thankful to her for entrusting to my care much of the valued records of the *Kāhui Ariki* (The Māori Royal Family).

I salute the fifth in succession of the Royal House of Pōtatau, King Korokī.

PEI TE HURINUI

"Te Horanga-pai"
Te Puru ki Tūhua,
Taumarunui.
6th November, 1959.

EDITOR'S NOTE

The first edition of *King Potatau* by Pei Te Hurinui was published by the Polynesian Society in 1959. It was widely sought and has been out of print for some time.

In 2006 the Māori Queen, Queen Te Atairangikaahu, suggested to the Polynesian Society that a second edition of this important work should be made.

After the Queen's death later that year, the Society sought the approval of the present Māori King, King Tūheitia, and this was gladly given. An editor and funding were sought and found in 2008 and a publishing partnership was initiated in early 2009.

The first concern of the Society and of the Editor has been to preserve the integrity of Pei Te Hurinui's original, significant work. Changes have been made only to correct the noted errata and other minor errors, to ensure consistency throughout the text, for example, in placement of Māori before English in *waiata*, and in matters of format, and to complete the bibliography. Macrons have been introduced to conform to current linguistic practice. These have been placed on all common Māori words and on personal and place names where they have already been accepted in other authoritative works.

I would like to thank Jane McRae for checking my editing, Anne Wydenbach for drawing the whakapapa and Hamish Macdonald for designing the layout. I am also grateful to Steven Innes, Special Collections, University of Auckland Library and Jocelyn Chalmers, Librarian, Research Centre, Alexander Turnbull Library for their help in completing the bibliography.

Jenifer Curnow,
Hon. Research Fellow,
Department of Māori Studies,
University of Auckland.

TABLE OF CONTENTS

Preface vii
Editor's Note xi

BOOK ONE

Te Wherowhero (The Lord of Waikato) 1

Chapter 1	Te Rauangaanga	2 - 22
Chapter 2	The Pathway of Tūrongo	23 - 30
Chapter 3	The Priestly Scholar	31 - 40
Chapter 4	Te Rauparaha	41 - 56
Chapter 5	The Battle of Kāwhia	57 - 77
Chapter 6	Te Arawī and the Flight from Kāwhia	78 - 90
Chapter 7	An Epic Duel	91 - 108
Chapter 8	A Severe Defeat (Mātakitaki)	109 - 116
Chapter 9	Ōrongokoekoeā	117 - 126
Chapter 10	A Romantic Interlude	127 - 140
Chapter 11	Settling of Accounts	141 - 147
Chapter 12	The Stars Look Down	148 - 172

BOOK TWO

Pōtatau (The First Māori King) 174
Introduction to Book Two 175

Chapter 1	The Genesis of an Idea	176 - 181
Chapter 2	The Chiefs and Tribes Deliberate	182 - 185
Chapter 3	Search the Land, Search the Sea	186 - 191

Chapter	4	The Pro-consul and the Bishop	192 - 196
Chapter	5	The Well-spring of Tears	197 - 202
Chapter	6	The Birds of Strong Flight	203 - 209
Chapter	7	The King is Raised-up	210 - 217
Chapter	8	The Storm Clouds of War	218 - 221

BOOK THREE

Mana Motuhake (Spiritual Prestige Set Apart)	222
The Māori Kings' Coat of Arms	223

Chapter	1	Waikato	225 - 234
Chapter	2	Religion	235 - 263
Chapter	3	Father and Son	264 - 266
Chapter	4	Haere rā! (Farewell)	267 - 276

Bibliography	277 - 279
General Index	283 - 300
Index to Genealogical Tables	301 - 303

BOOK ONE

TE WHEROWHERO

Te Ariki o Waikato

The Lord of Waikato

TE RAUANGAANGA

The Chieftain Warrior

O River!
Give me great Strength —
Strength to haul this Mighty *Kauri*...

From "The Battle Song of Te Rauangaanga"

CHAPTER 1

TE RAUANGAANGA
The Chieftain Warrior

I

Te Wherowhero was the elder son of Te Rauangaanga, the warrior chieftain of the Waikato confederation of tribes. From dates in the missionary records of the various episodes in which Te Wherowhero figured, we have arrived at 1775 as the approximate year of his birth. He was, on this reckoning, about eighty-five years of age at his death in 1860.

On his paternal side Te Wherowhero was sixteenth in direct male line of descent from Tamatekapua, the famous commander of the Arawa Canoe which sailed from Tahiti in the Society Group and arrived in Aotearoa (the North Island) about the year 1350 A.D. As the genealogical table at the end of this chapter shows, he could also claim kinship with every important tribe in New Zealand. It would take a volume in itself to give all his lines of descent, and the table referred to above is based on a selection made almost at random. The only other chieftains of his time who could vie with him in this respect were the paramount chiefs of Taupō, Te Heuheu Tūkino (Te Heuheu II) and his younger brother who succeeded him, Iwikau (Te Heuheu III).

In the selection of a leader, the Māori invariably chose after a careful scrutiny of the *whakapapa* or genealogy. The Māori was a firm believer in heredity and he had, to his mind, good grounds for his belief. As a genealogist of the first order he had made a close study of the subject and could quote innumerable instances of the tendency of like to beget like. Apart, therefore, from any intimate knowledge of the character, behaviour and achievements of any candidate for high office, or as a suitor for a maiden's hand in marriage, the Māori, after a recital of a man's genealogy had been given, would soon sum up his worth. More often than not, after assaying the demerits and fine points in a *whakapapa*, the Māori made an accurate valuation. In these modern days the Māori is influenced by other factors introduced by the Pākehā or European. It remains to be seen whether the present methods will measure up to the centuries-old Polynesian ideas.

II

Te Rauangaanga, at about the time Te Wherowhero was born, had become the war leader of the Waikato tribes. On the epic battlefield of Hingakākā, near Ōhaupō, Te Rauangaanga had led Waikato and Maniapoto warriors in the greatest battle in the annals of Aotearoa.

Pikauterangi, a Tainui chief of the coastal tribes inhabiting the Marokopa river district, aggrieved over the division of a fish harvest, had recruited an army of upward of 10,000 men from the southern and eastern tribes of the North Island. The southern section had marched unexpectedly into Maniapoto country at the southern end of the Tainui territory, and had been joined by the eastern forces some distance north of Ōtorohanga. With the rebel Pikauterangi in command, the invading army marched over the wide and rolling country northward and toward the junction of the Waipā and Waikato rivers. They crossed the Pūniu and moved into the fertile lands around Ōhaupō and Rangiaohia, dotted with myriad lakes and marshes. Their route would take them directly to the wide and fertile plains in the heart of the Waikato country.

Wahanui,[1] the Maniapoto leader, had made contact with an advance party of the southern section of Pikauterangi's army near Ōtorohanga. With a hastily organised contingent of his tribe Wahanui immediately set off to join up with the Waikato. He had, at the same time, sent fleet-footed messengers to give warning of an impending invasion of the Waikato and also to give an estimate of the size of the invading army.

III

It was thought that with a large force under him, Pikau' would not choose to come through by devious ways. Te Rauangaanga and his war-leaders therefore decided that the invading army must be opposed in the Ōhaupō lake country, as this locality offered the most favourable defensive position. Pikauterangi was not to be allowed to penetrate too far into the Waipā and Waikato land. The place decided on was among the lakes at Ngāroto.

The mobilisation of the fighting men was hurriedly arranged, and on the eve of the battle 3,000 warriors were assembled and had taken up their battle stations at Te Mangeo, the place chosen for the battlefield. Alarming reports had now reached Te Rauangaanga that Pikauterangi's army had grown considerably and that he was leading the largest force of fighting men in the history of Māori warfare. Wahanui, who had of course broken off contact with Pikauterangi before the arrival of the Eastern force (which section made up nearly half of Pikauterangi's army of 10,000 men), had estimated the hostile army at about half of its full strength.

IV

Late in the afternoon of a summer's day, about the year 1790, Pikauterangi and his army halted at Te Mangeo in full view of Te Rauangaanga's position. Advanced patrols of the invading army had previously approached to reconnoitre and hurried back to the main body. The leaders of these patrols had made a fairly accurate appraisal of the forces under Te Rauangaanga, and had duly reported to Pikauterangi and the other leaders of his army. Pikauterangi was pleased with the news. "Tomorrow," he said, "the proud Waikato and the vain Maniapoto will meet their match!"

As night fell and in the still air of a moonlit sky, Pikauterangi, pleased with the prospects of the coming battle, sang his battle song:

TE WAIATA A PIKAUTERANGI

Whakarongo!
Whakarongo rā ki te hau e tangi mai nei!
Kei whea? Kei whea?
Kei te aro,
Kei te tua!
Tikina taku ika
Ki Te Moana nui a Kiwa,
E takoto mai nei;
He koronga.
He koronga nōku
Kia tae au ki ngā uru kahika
Ki ō uru, ki ō awa—
Ki ō kata noa mai,
E te kihikihi ka taka i te pae;
Ka taka i te pae!
Kiki pounamu e tangi ana ki tōna whenua,
Ka tupuria nei e te māheuheu.
Tangi kau ake te mapu, ē ē!

PIKAUTERANGI'S BATTLE SONG

1   Hearken!
O hearken unto the song that comes on the wind!
Whence comes it? Whence comes it?
It comes from the front,
5   It comes from behind!
And we are proceeding to fetch my fish
From the Great Sea of *Kiwa*,
That lies o'er yonder;
This is a consuming desire.
10   Indeed, my consuming desire is
That I should reach these *kahika'* bushes
These, your bushes and your rivers—
Ye, who did laugh derisively,
Know ye, that now the cicada hath come o'er the horizon!
15   Indeed, it hath come o'er the horizon!
And I am like unto the mute greenstone
That grieves for its own abiding place;
The place that is now o'ergrown with weeds. And I sigh deeply,
Ah me!

(See Notes at end of chapter.)

Te Rauangaanga and the two armies listened. Here and there the keen ear of Te Rauangaanga detected an *iri-rangi* (a false note or a perceptible break when singing in a high-pitched voice). This betrayed to Te Rauangaanga's practised ear that Pikauterangi was labouring under some mental strain. "If he is unduly elated," commented Te Rauangaanga, "our battle plans on the morrow will confound him!"

That night Te Rauangaanga had his final council of war with the veteran Wahanui, and with the younger leaders, Tiriwa, Tipi, Huahua and the other tribal leaders. Wahanui suggested, and it was resolved, to resort to a ruse so as to deceive the enemy as to their smaller numbers. The latest count had shown that Te Rauangaanga's army numbered a few more than the 3,000 previously counted. In accordance with Wahanui's plan, during the night conspicuous white *toroa*[2] feathers were issued to several of the lesser chiefs, to be worn on the following day. Feathers were also fastened to the tops of the fern and scrub in specially selected areas. By dawn next day, the surrounding slopes seemed to be alive with a considerable number of figures with white plumes waving in the morning breeze. And each plume represented, to Pikauterangi and his men, at least some tribal warrior of note.

V

Wahanui, the Maniapoto leader whose prodigious deeds of valour on many fields of battle had become legendary, had decided to hand over command of the Maniapoto contingent to his younger kinsman Huahua.[3]

Te Rauangaanga arranged the battle stations. He took the centre, with Wahanui as chief-of-staff and with Tipi as a fighting leader second-in-command. The centre force comprised 1,600 men made up of a composite force representing Te Rauangaanga's own tribe of Ngāti Mahuta from the Waahi lake district; the lower Waikato river tribes of Ngāti Tipa and Ngāti Tamaoho; Ngāti Te Ata of Waiuku; Ngāi Tai of south Tāmaki isthmus; and a contingent of Ngāti Whātua from the Kaipara district. On the left flank was Tiriwa with the Hikairo and Apakura tribes, and Ngāti Hourua and other central Waikato tribes, numbering in all 900 men. Huahua, on the right flank, had a force of the cream of the dashing and intrepid Maniapoto tribe, 500 strong.

Pikauterangi, with his army drawn up in battle array, hesitated when he perceived what he took to be a formidable force opposed to him. In the lull, Te Rauangaanga rose from the midst of his army, and in a loud sonorous voice he chanted his battle song.

THE BATTLE SONG OF TE RAUANGAANGA

E Awa, e!
Ka tō te tō o te Kauri;
Ka tupu te pukatea i te wai;
Ko ngoungou te iwi o te tau;
Ka ruperupe te kererū,
Ka waru te kao,
Ka patu te rou,
Ka reka te kao-miti:
Ā! i aha hā!

FREE TRANSLATION

O River! [4]
Give me great strength—
Strength to haul this mighty *Kauri* [5]
Let the *pukatea*[6] in thy waters grow,
Like the softened bones of yesteryear [7]
Are those, the recumbent tribes!
But the dauntless ones are here; [8]
And let the morrow bring:
The chortling of the *kererū*,[9]
The sound of *kao*[10] a-scraping,
And the beating of the *rou*— [11]
Ah! sweet, indeed, will be the eating;
The eating, the *miti*[12] of the *kao*!

VI

The opposing armies listened in profound silence to the stirring chant of the great Waikato leader. His bold and commanding appearance, his resonant tone of voice, and the pregnant words of his battle song struck cold terror into the hearts of Pikauterangi and his men. The Waikato and Maniapoto were like men inspired. Huahua, Tipi, and the other young braves were elated. Huahua was so eager to get to grips with the enemy that he called out to Tiriwa: "*Tiriwa, ē! Māu te titi; māku te whewhera!*" (O Tiriwa! You apply the wedge and I'll open tip the crevice!) From the lower ground on the left flank Tiriwa called back, "*Māu anō tau titi; māku anō tāku whewhera!*" (You apply your own wedge; I'll open up a crevice of my own!) This by-play of words between Te Rauangaanga's lieutenants referred to the battle plans of the night before, when Huahua and Tiriwa had each urged that his section should attack in the *kawau-mārō*, or wedge formation, and divide the opposing army in two. Though not so intended this passage of words between Huahua and Tiriwa had the result of confusing Pikauterangi as to what was to be the initial move and it was at this point that Te Rauangaanga decided to execute the offensive strategy planned during the previous night.

Te Rauangaanga had expected Pikauterangi to make a frontal attack and had chosen the ground with this in mind. Huahua on the right flank and on rising ground was protected on the right by a steep bank overlooking a lake, while Tiriwa's force on the flat below had marshy and scrub-covered land to guard its left flank against any enveloping move by the enemy's right flank.

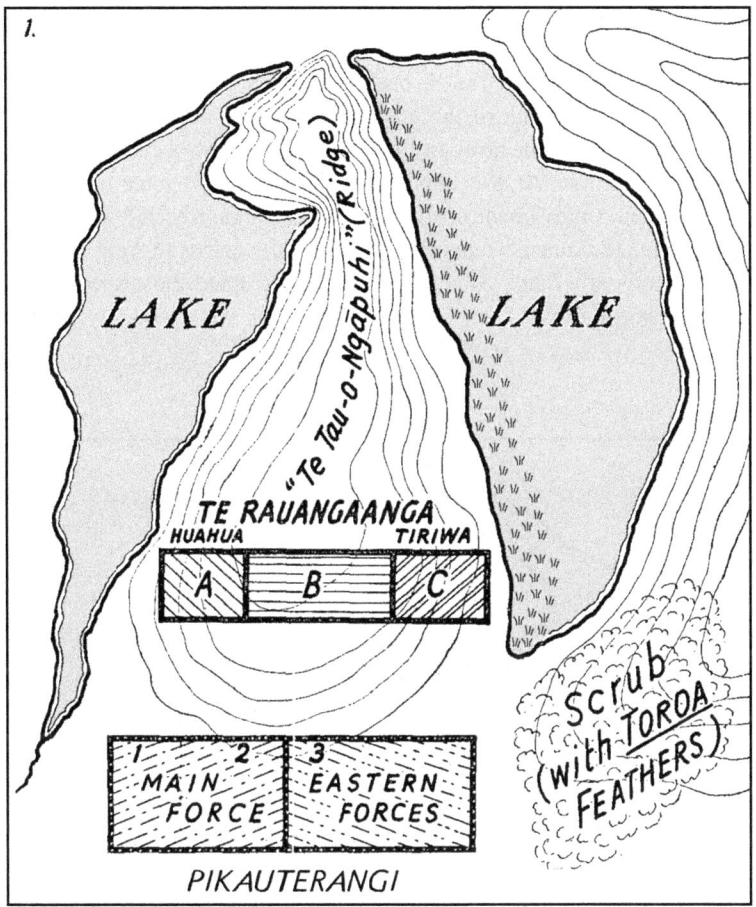

BATTLE OF HINGAKĀKĀ—FIRST PHASE

VII

As the enemy had made no move Te Rauangaanga indicated to Wahanui to give Huahua the signal to open the attack. Wahanui thereupon gave the time-honoured command, first given by their ancestor Maniapoto: "*E Hua', ē! Tukua i te kawau-mārō. Kōkiri!*" (O Hua'! Let it be the swoop of the cormorant. Leap forth!) At the same time Te Rauangaanga moved up part of his centre from the lower ground and drew back the left flank under Tiriwa to the position in the centre, from where he had moved part of the centre on the higher ground. While these movements were being executed Huahua had opened the attack on Pikauterangi's army.

The impetuous rush of Huahua's warriors, aided by the sloping ground, came as a crushing blow on the opposing flank of the enemy. The enemy's left flank reeled back, and toward its centre. Presently, the shattered left flank of the enemy was inextricably mixed with the centre. One half of the army of Pikauterangi was now a confused crowd of struggling men. As previously arranged, Huahua's force then began an enveloping movement on the enemy's disorganised left and, at the same time, Te Rauangaanga charged diagonally across to what was now the enemy's left flank. This blow further disrupted the disposition of Pikauterangi's army.

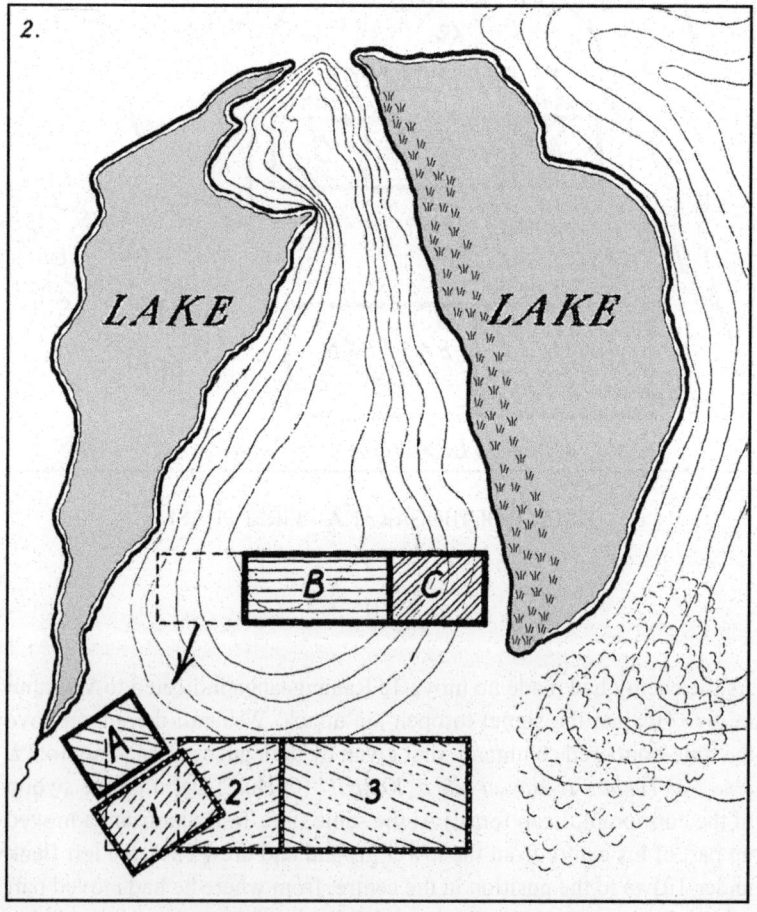

BATTLE OF HINGAKĀKĀ—SECOND PHASE

Tiriwa had by now disposed his force so as to form a prostrate letter L (└──), with the toe resting on the hill previously occupied by Huahua. The battle raged. Te Rauangaanga, Huahua, Tipi and other warriors, dealt relentless blows and a number of the enemy leaders fell. At the height of battle Pikauterangi, who had been vainly trying to reorganise his badly shattered forces, himself fell under a smashing blow from Te Rauangaanga.

The enemy's right flank, which was composed of a large section of the eastern force, had not been engaged up to this point. They had observed Tiriwa's move and, as the vacated ground had purposely been left devoid of *toroa* feathers, they assumed that this gap offered an opening for an outflanking move should Te Rauangaanga disengage his attacking force and retire to what the enemy thought was the main force in reserve—where the *toroa* feathers still waved in the breeze.

VIII

When the cry went up, "Pikau' has fallen! Pikau' has fallen!", the centre of Pikauterangi's grand army began to crumble and started to move toward the right. The eastern force on the right held firm. The centre thereupon commenced to fall back, but by this time Huahua and his men had moved around the rear of the enemy and the enemy's move in that direction only added to the confusion. A panic seized a section of the enemy's centre and they made a dash for the gap below Tiriwa's position. They were left unmolested and soon the vanguard had entered and were hidden in the scrub along the edge of the marshy land fringing the lake. An ambush awaited them at the northern end of the lake.

The defection of the centre forces exposed the eastern force on the right flank to the furious onslaught of the combined forces of Huahua on their rear and Te Rauangaanga bearing down on their left. They wavered and soon were moving off to join the fleeing remnants of the shattered left flank and the badly mauled centre. By this time the enemy's forces were sadly battered. A third of Pikauterangi's army lay thickly on the field of battle, maimed, mortally wounded and killed. But worse was yet to come.

With the enemy on the move in disorder, Wahanui signalled Tiriwa to move his force northward. At the same time Te Rauangaanga led his men back to the position they formerly occupied and which was now being evacuated by Tiriwa. Huahua, in the meantime, was keeping up a relentless attack on the enemy's rearguard. A selected body of men was

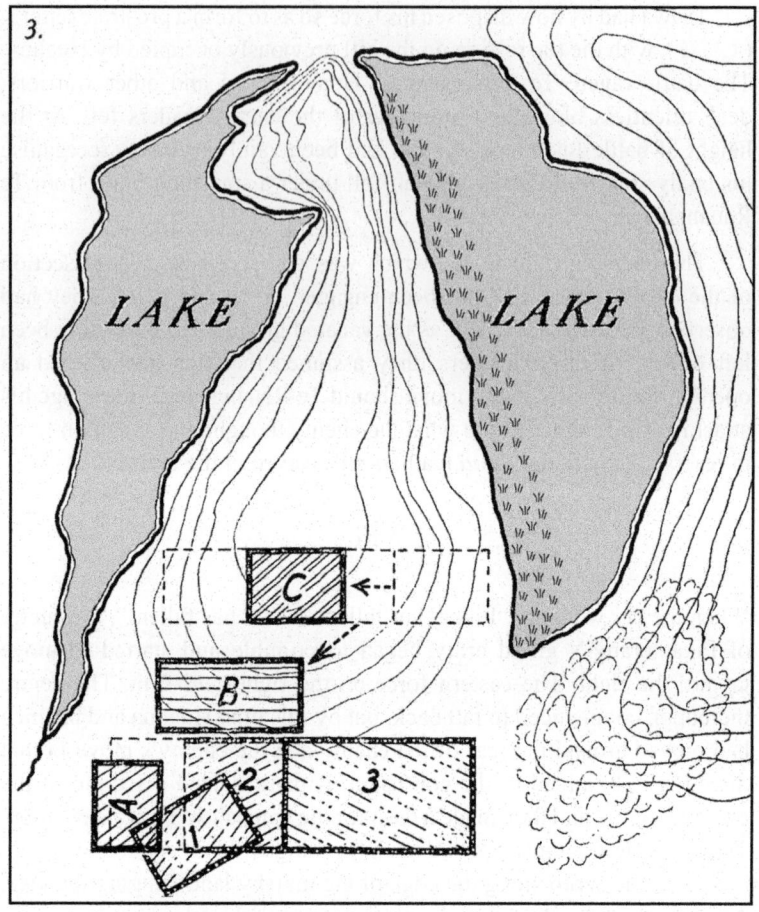

BATTLE OF HINGAKĀKĀ—THIRD PHASE

detailed by Te Rauangaanga to deal with isolated groups of the enemy who still held their positions on the battleground. The main body of the enemy had by now entered the "Gap."

IX

The next and the final phase of the battle soon developed. Tiriwa and his men quickly moved through the light fern on the high ground parallel to the enemy column, now sullenly and slowly moving through the scrub on the sedgy margin of the lake. At the northern end was a narrow exit between the two lakes and it was at this point where Tiriwa joined

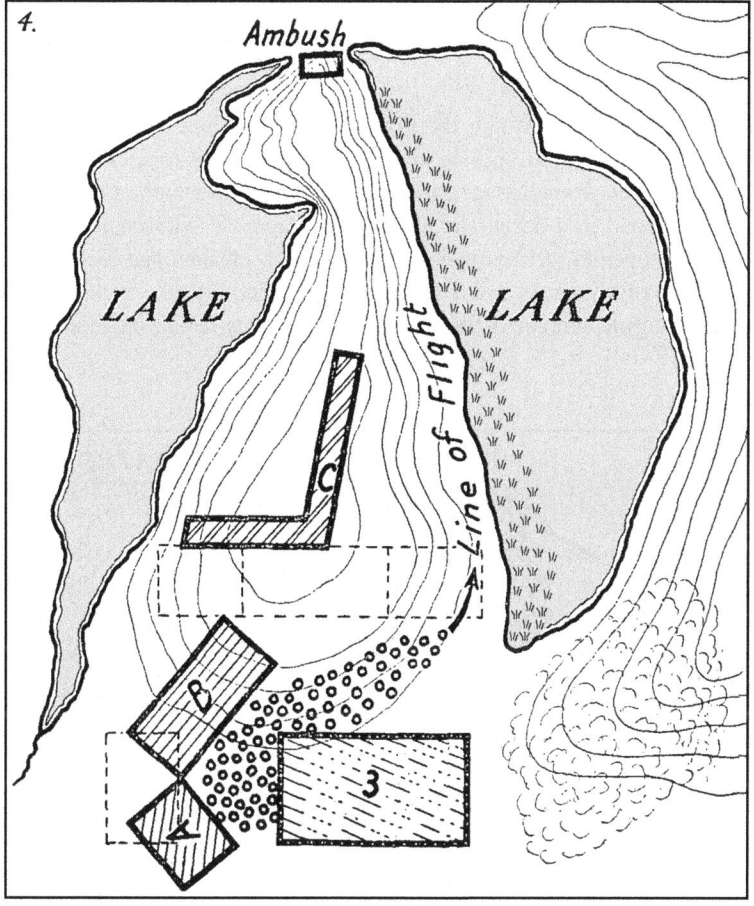

BATTLE OF HINGAKĀKĀ—FOURTH PHASE

the ambushing party. The first band of fugitives had already been disposed of, and with his men lined along the hill overlooking the lake and with a strong force to bar the way, Tiriwa waited for the main body of the enemy.

Shortly afterward the leading files of the defeated army appeared. Finding their way of escape cut off, they recoiled and fell back. Presently they began to mill about in the scrub-covered swampy land, which soon became a treacherous quagmire. This was Tiriwa's supreme moment. From the high ground 600 fresh and eager warriors of Ngāti Hikairo came down like a thunderbolt on the head of the moving mass of the enemy. And this was the prelude to the final annihilating blow. Te Rauangaanga and his men, now rested after their prodigious deeds earlier, arose as one and came thundering down all along the line while Huahua still kept a firm grip on the enemy's rear.

The impact came like the crack of doom. The enemy, dispirited, tired and helplessly struggling in the morass, were in a hopeless position. Beset on land, some essayed to struggle through the marsh to the clear water beyond in a desperate attempt to escape by swimming the lake. With the opening of the final attack, however, Huahua had disengaged a section of his forces and deployed them around the lake to the east to strengthen the screening force and to cut off this remaining avenue of

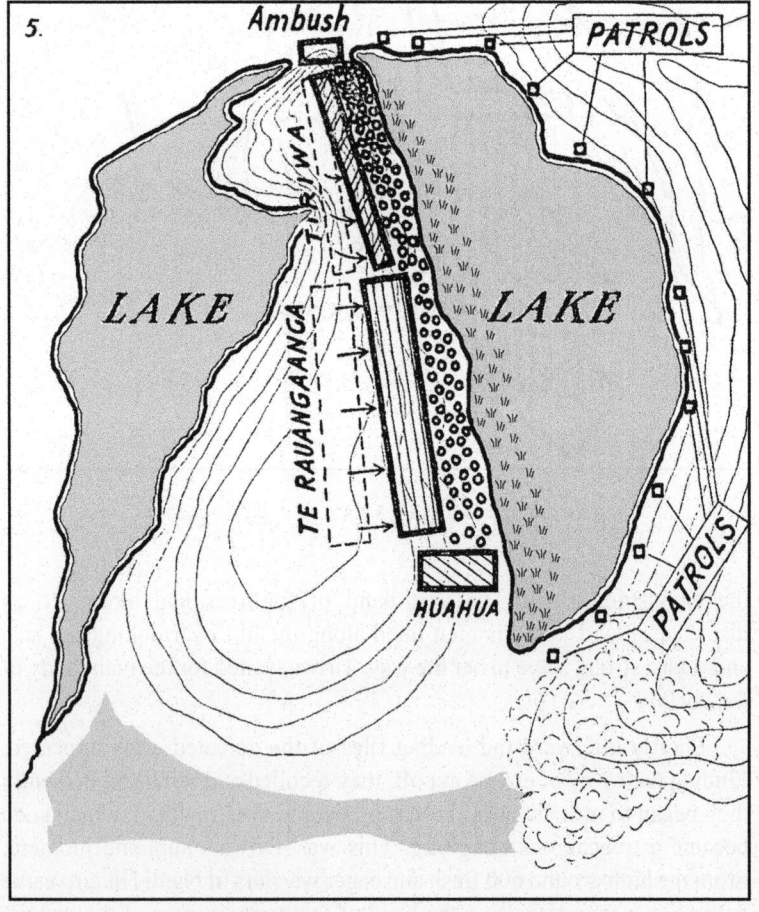

BATTLE OF HINGAKĀKĀ—FINAL PHASE

escape. A few did manage to cross to various points around the eastern shores of the lake, but they were promptly dispatched on landing. A large number, seeing the fate of those who had landed, swam round in the water until they collapsed and were drowned.

Those who attempted to fight it out where they stood soon fell to Te Rauangaanga, Tipi, Tiriwa and their exultant warriors. Even the ageing Wahanui joined in at this stage. The enemy's best fighting men, handicapped by the treacherous ground on which they fought, could do little better than the others. Te Rauangaanga was determined to make an example of Pikauterangi's invading army that would deter any further invasion of his ancestral lands, and the slaughter went on with no quarter given.

By late afternoon the battle was over and the enemy completely annihilated. Scores of high chiefs from distant tribes, distinguished by the fine parrot-feather cloaks they wore, lay on the battlefield. From their speech during the fighting Te Rauangaanga and his men were able to identify practically all the tribal dialects of the eastern and southern tribes of the North Island. As the sun sank slowly behind the Moerangi ranges and lighted up the cloud cap over the peak of Pirongia, Te Rauangaanga and his men walked slowly over the field of battle gathering the trophies of war. The search among the dead was discontinued in the gathering dusk, to be resumed on the morrow. The shades of evening came across the valley of the Waipā and over the rolling country along the course of the Waikato river to herald the approach of the night—the night that was to wrap in darkness the scene of strife and carnage on the epic battlefield of *Hingakākā*, "The Fall of the Bright-plumaged Parrots".

NOTES ON CHAPTER 1

Pikauterangi's Battle Song

The words and the explanations of the song were given to the author at Waahi, Huntly, on April 23, 1935, by Marae Erueti and Taui Wētere, elder chiefs of the Ngāti Hikairo tribe of Kāwhia.

(4-5) It comes from the front, it comes from behind: This is in reference to the wide area from which Pikauterangi had recruited his army.

(6) fetch my fish: There is a double meaning in this line. Firstly, there is a pointed reference to the fish harvest in which he was denied his share of the fat *kahawai* (*Arripis salar*, mullet). Secondly, fish in Māori warfare also means the slain in battle.

(7) the Great Sea of Kiwa: The Pacific Ocean. In particular, the sea that washes the shores of his ancestral lands in the Marokopa and Kāwhia districts.

(11) *kahika* 'bushes: Kahika' is an abbreviation for *kahikatea* (*Podocarpus dacrydioides*, white pine). The landscape around the Ōhaupō district is dotted here and there with *kahikatea* bushes, hence the reference in the song.

(14) cicada or *kihikihi*: Another figure of speech used by Pikauterangi for his army.

(16) mute greenstone: The Māori has many stories about the greenstone, in some of which it is related that any such object, when lost by its owner in foreign parts or if the owner is killed, will grieve for the home of its former owner and, sometimes, it has travelled by the waterways on its way back! In the song Pikauterangi likens himself to a greenstone on its return home.

Note 1

Wahanui: There were two chiefs of the Maniapoto tribe of this name, who were contemporaneous. This has often caused confusion. The Wahanui mentioned in this account was a son of Irohanga, and was a close relative of Te Rauangaanga, as the *whakapapa* will show:

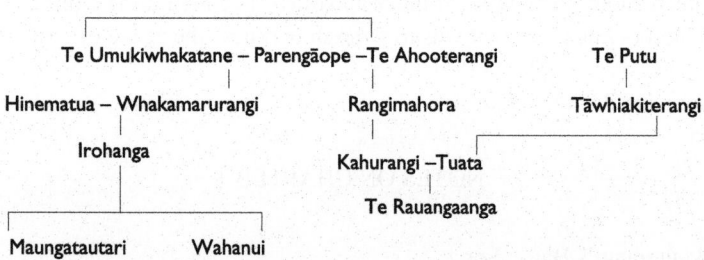

(Hinematua, the mother of Irohanga, was the elder sister of Te Putu, Te Rauangaanga's great-grandfather. Te Umukiwhakatane and Te Ahooterangi were brothers. The latter married his brother's widow, Parengāope.)

Maungatautari and his brother Wahanui led the first successful attack on Maungakiekie (now One Tree Hill, Auckland) the most formidable and extensively fortified *pā* or fort in Aotearoa. On another memorable occasion at the battle of Hurimoana, which was fought a few miles south of Kihikihi, Wahanui was wounded eight times, but still fought on. His elder brother on learning of this called out from the *pā*, "How fares it, O Waha'?" Wahanui replied, "*E waru ēnei; kia waru mai hoki!*" (I have eight, but there will have to be eight more!) Wahanui was a famous duellist and—reverting here to Pikauterangi's army— it is recounted that when Wahanui made contact with Pikauterangi's force near Ōtorohanga, the leading file recoiled immediately when he suddenly appeared above them, as they were about to cross a stream near the Waipā river. This *turaha* (to recoil in fright) was a bad omen for Pikauterangi and his army.

Note 2

toroa: *Diomedea exulans*, the albatross.

Note 3

Huahua: In later years, Huahua came to be recognised as the leading Tainui master in the use of all Māori weapons of war. Among others, he taught Te Heuheu Herea (Te Heuheu I) in the use of the *pou-whenua* (a sharp-pointed, round-shaped, unadorned, hard, smooth, and close-grained wooden weapon). It was with the *pou-whenua* that Te Heuheu overcame Te Wakaiti, his rival, for the overlordship of the tribes of Lake Taupō. Te Wakaiti was similarly armed, the *pou-whenua* being his favourite weapon.

Note 4

River or *Awa*: The reference is to the Waikato river.

Note 5

Kauri: The famous New Zealand forest tree (*Agathis australis*). In using the *kauri* as a figure of speech Te Rauangaanga conveyed two ideas; to the enemy, that his force was a large and powerful one and, to his own men, the inspiration of being likened to this mighty tree of the forest.

Note 6

pukatea: a soft-wood tree (*Laurelianovae zealandiae*). Te Rauangaanga here makes a disparaging reference to some of his own Waikato sub-tribes who had not come forward to join in the fight, by likening them to the *pukatea* tree.

Note 7

softened bones: There appears to be some allusion in this line to the secret river burial caves of the tribes living along the Waikato river. The idea referred to in the preceding note is also inherent in these lines. Even Ngāti Mahuta, Te Rauangaanga's own tribe, had put in a tardy appearance at Te Mangeo. This trait earned them the name of "Ngāti Mahuta-taka-roa" (Ngāti Mahuta slow-to-move). Other Waikato tribes also coined the saying about them: "He haringa anō tō te hoe, he haringa anō tō te whāriki." (First they take their paddles, then they return to fetch their sleeping-mats.) Once moved, however, the Ngāti Mahuta are dour, determined and resolute.

Note 8

dauntless ones are here: This line and the preceding one have been added by the author-translator in order to amplify Te Rauangaanga's Battle Song for European readers. The poetry of the Māori works by suggestion. It is full of contractions. The imagery and ideas that abound in the Māori language are intended to convey more than the words mean.

Note 9

kererū: (*Hemiphaga novaeseelandiae*) wood pigeon.

Note 10

kao: A preparation of the *kūmara* (*Ipomoea batatas*, sweet potato) grated, cooked and dried in the sun.

Note 11

rou: A long pole used to reach anything. Such a pole was used to loosen and beat down the *kiekie* (*Freycinetia banksii*, climbing plant) from which finely woven sleeping-mats were made. The fruit of the *kiekie* was also eaten.

Note 12

miti: A transitive verb, to lick up food etc. Before the coming of the European it was not considered bad form to eat with evident enjoyment and to make the appropriate accompanying noises. To *miti* one's food was the hall-mark of a chief. The host and hostess were made happy by these signs that the guest had enjoyed his meal. Only slaves and the low-born ate in silence.

"THE CANOES"
GENEALOGY OF KING PŌTATAU TE WHEROWHERO
(Table No. 1)

TE ARAWA	TAINUI	PANEIRAIRA	TOKOMARU

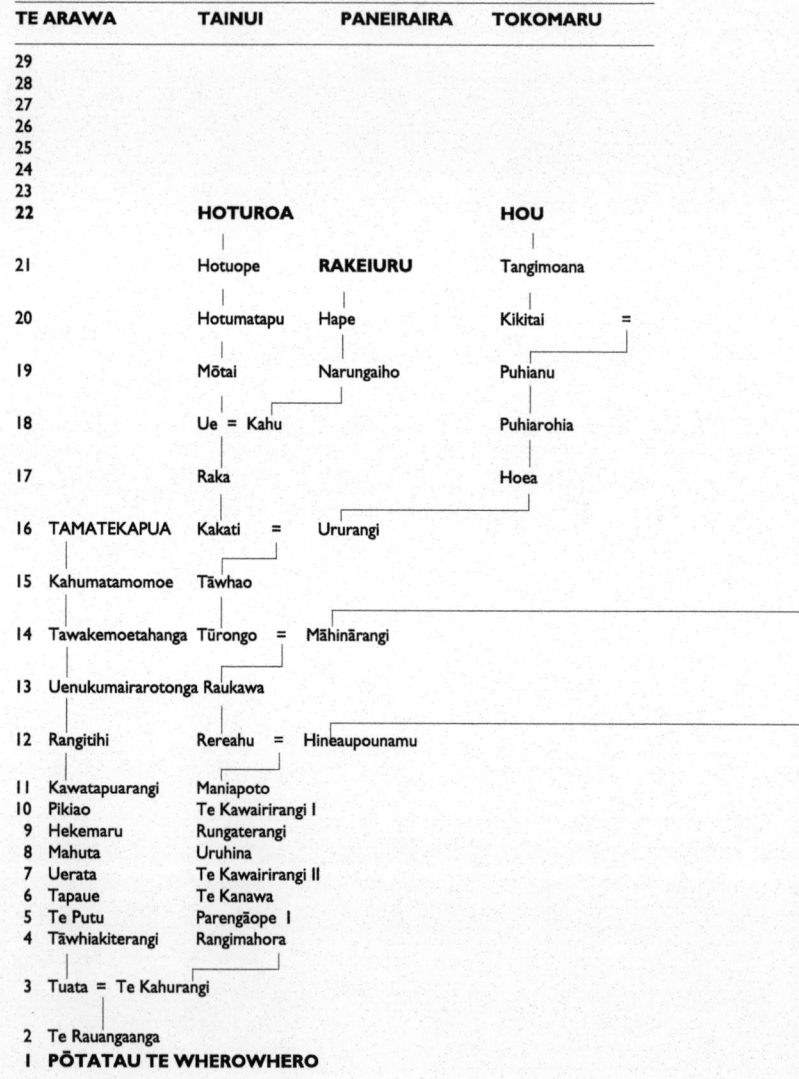

```
29
28
27
26
25
24
23
22              HOTUROA                         HOU

21              Hotuope      RAKEIURU           Tangimoana

20              Hotumatapu   Hape               Kikitai      =

19              Mōtai        Narungaiho         Puhianu

18              Ue  =  Kahu                     Puhiarohia

17              Raka                            Hoea

16 TAMATEKAPUA  Kakati    =  Ururangi

15 Kahumatamomoe Tāwhao

14 Tawakemoetahanga Tūrongo  =  Māhinārangi

13 Uenukumairarotonga Raukawa

12 Rangitihi     Rereahu   =  Hineaupounamu

11 Kawatapuarangi  Maniapoto
10 Pikiao          Te Kawairirangi I
 9 Hekemaru        Rungaterangi
 8 Mahuta          Uruhina
 7 Uerata          Te Kawairirangi II
 6 Tapaue          Te Kanawa
 5 Te Putu         Parengāope I
 4 Tāwhiakiterangi Rangimahora

 3 Tuata  =  Te Kahurangi

 2 Te Rauangaanga
 1 PŌTATAU TE WHEROWHERO
```

21

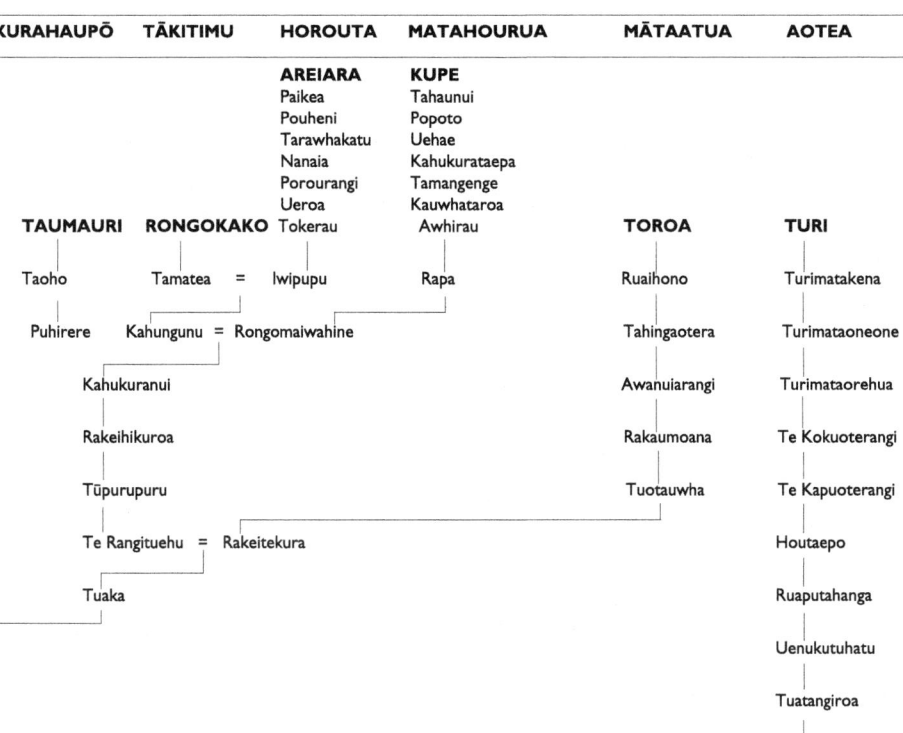

KURAHAUPŌ	TĀKITIMU	HOROUTA	MATAHOURUA	MĀTAATUA	AOTEA
		AREIARA Paikea Pouheni Tarawhakatu Nanaia Porourangi Ueroa	**KUPE** Tahaunui Popoto Uehae Kahukurataepa Tamangenge Kauwhataroa		
TAUMAURI	**RONGOKAKO**	Tokerau	Awhirau	**TOROA**	**TURI**
Taoho	Tamatea = Iwipupu		Rapa	Ruaihono	Turimatakena
Puhirere	Kahungunu = Rongomaiwahine			Tahingaotera	Turimataoneone
	Kahukuranui			Awanuiarangi	Turimataorehua
	Rakeihikuroa			Rakaumoana	Te Kokuoterangi
	Tūpurupuru			Tuotauwha	Te Kapuoterangi
	Te Rangituehu = Rakeitekura				Houtaepo
	Tuaka				Ruaputahanga
					Uenukutuhatu
					Tuatangiroa

THE "WAHANUI" WHAKAPAPA (Table No. 2)

HOTUROA ... ... — Commander and High Priest of the Tainui Canoe, which arrived in Aotearoa (New Zealand) in circa 1350 A.D.
Hotuope
Hotumatapu
Mōtai
Ue
Raka
Kakati
Tāwhao
Tūrongo
Raukawa
Rereahu
Maniapoto
Te Kawairirangi I
Rungaterangi
Uruhina
Te Kawairirangi II
Te Kanawa = Waikohika

```
    ┌──────────────────┴──────────────────┐
Parengāope                              Tiramanuhiri

Whakamarurangi      Rangimahora          Waiora
Irohanga            Te Kahurangi         Wahanui
                         │
                    TE RAUANGAANGA
    ┌────────┐
WAHANUI   Maungatautari
```

This is the Wahanui mentioned in the Battle of Hingakākā.

This Wahanui will be mentioned later in this account. — See Chapter 4, Para. xii, Book One.

THE PATHWAY OF TŪRONGO

My Pathway is that of Tūrongo,
Who proceeded to the Land of the Sunrise—
Where the tides ebb and flow,
And the crooning ripples from the sea,
Sing a symphony of Love
All the day long...

From Ngoki's Chant

CHAPTER 2

THE PATHWAY OF TŪRONGO

I

Te Rauangaanga was a robust and very powerful man and it is specially remembered he had a very hairy body. The story is told that when one chieftain's daughter, who had become enamoured by the tales of Te Rauangaanga's gallant exploits, was introduced to him, she was instantly repelled by his hairy chest and her infatuation then and there died within her. This fastidious young lady in her day-dreaming had expected the famous Te Rauangaanga to be lithe, handsome and smooth-skinned. The young chieftainess transferred her affections to one of Te Rauangaanga's companions and they were married. The man of her choice never amounted to much and in the tribal history even the young lady herself is only a nameless memory.

Parengāope, the beautiful and talented daughter of the priestly chieftain Tokohihi, later met Te Rauangaanga and these two were attracted to each other. They were married and in due time Parengāope presented her proud husband with two sons, Te Wherowhero and his younger brother Kati. No daughters were born to them. Te Rauangaanga. was a happy father. The battle of Hingakākā was followed by a time of peace and plenty. His wife was a cheerful and loving comrade. On her children she lavished a doting Polynesian mother's care and the two boys grew up keen-eyed and mettlesome. There was peace throughout the tribal lands and indeed, there was:

> The chortling of the *kererū*;
> The sound of *kao* a-scraping;
> And the beating of the *rou*:
> Ah! sweet, indeed, was the eating;
> The eating, the *miti* of the *kao*.

II

As his son and heir grew up to young manhood, Te Rauangaanga began to teach him the sacred lore of his forebears; the mythology of Polynesia; the tribal traditions of the Māori and the many *whakapapa* or genealogical lines of the Tainui peoples to whom he belonged. There was also the knowledge of the *hapū* or sub-tribal boundaries to be acquired, and forest lore, the fishing methods, the proper times for planting and harvesting, and all the *karakia* or ritual and invocations relating thereto. All these the young Te Wherowhero had to learn.

In his youthful activities Te Wherowhero never missed his daily morning swim on the broad bosom of the beloved Waikato river. He followed the fowlers to the bird-snaring forest trees in the Moerangi ranges, the trappers to the rat trails in the forest-clad hills of Hākarimata, and the fishermen to the eel-weirs at the outflowing waters of the tribal lakes of Waahi, Hakanoa, Waikare, Whangape and others. He learnt to net the *kahawai* (*Arripis salar* fish) at the outflow of Waikare lake. In the *inanga* or whitebait season there were exhilarating canoe races down to the fishing grounds at the broad expanse of the Waikato estuary above and below Tauranganui.

Te Wherowhero's high spirits were a constant spur to his companions with whom he wrestled, ran races, fought duels with imitation *taiaha*[1] and organised canoe races against the redoubtable canoemen of the Ngāti Whawhakia tribe, the northern neighbours of his own Ngāti Mahuta.

The decoying, netting and snaring of the wild bird-life on the rolling hills and on the marshy fringes of the lakes and on the banks and islands of the Waikato river were all part of the active and body-building life of the young Te Wherowhero.

III

In the long winter evenings Te Wherowhero delighted to hear his mother tell the folk tales of his people. Of his athletic warrior ancestor Hotumauea, her great-great-grandfather, the mother related how, in racing one rival overland from the mouth of the Marokopa river, they ran neck and neck along the winding course of the river and up on to the high hill at the top of the Marokopa waterfall. Here the other took to the river to swim it in the pool upstream from the fast-flowing waters above the falls. Hotumauea climbed to a high bush-clad bank overlooking the river and from there, with a prodigious leap, he landed on a sand-bank on the opposite side.[2] When his rival reached the flat ground above the river bank Hotumauea was disappearing over the far ridge.... Tuatangiroa, another ancestor, who ran from Mōkau to Kāwhia between the rising and the setting of the sun, was the only other ancestor to compare with Hotumauea.

Parengāope told her sons of the love life of their ancestor, Tāwhao; of his romance with the lovesick Marutehiakina. Marutehiakina was lovely and she was the cynosure of all eyes when she glided across the glistening sands of Heahea beach[3] below her father's *pā* at Horea.[4] Tāwhao, who was married to Marutehiakina's elder sister Puniatekore, lived at Te Whaanga on the shores of the lagoon at the foot of the forest-clad Karioi mountain. Tāwhao won Marutehiakina by his *ātahu*[5] and by the spell he had imparted to his *kuru tangiwai* or translucent ear-drop. On the water-worn boulders of the outer reef of the lagoon Tāwhao carried out his ritual and thus spiritually impregnated, he sent across a tiny raft with its precious cargo. The lazy summer swell was in league with him, for the little vessel sped across the Whāingaroa[6] harbour mouth and was soon seen off the beach at Heahea. Scores of the Horea maidens tried to capture the floating raft, but it always eluded them. Then Marutehiakina entered the water and, Io, a gentle zephyr seemed to lift the magic craft and it came floating into her arms. She recognised the ear-drop and presently she was hugging it against her throbbing breast. That same day she left Horea with a song in her heart and on the wings of love she made her way to Te Whaanga. There she joined her elder sister Puniatekore and became the junior wife (*wahine iti*, lesser wife) of the young chief Tāwhao.

There was also the story of the two sons of Tāwhao by his sister wives. Tūrongo was the first-born, by his junior wife; and Whatihua was the other son, by Puniatekore.[6A] The circumstances of the order of their birth and the respective status of their mothers contrived to bring about a life-long rivalry between the two brothers. This finally led to Tūrongo's odyssey to the Taranaki district and later to the Heretaunga (now Hawkes Bay). Tūrongo's life story with his brother Whatihua was a heart-breaking tale of woe. Then came his journey to Heretaunga where he won the hand of Māhinārangi, the glamorous daughter of the aristocratic Rangirangi. Māhinārangi was exquisite and the clinging fragrance of her *raukawa*[7] perfume was sheer sorcery to the love-torn heart of Tūrongo. The perfume which gave Māhinārangi her magic hour of love and ensnared Tūrongo in the toils of the sweet mystery and essence of romance, they were never to forget. When a son, their first child, was born they called him Raukawa.

The descendants of Raukawa became numerous in the land and they form an important tribal unit under the name of Ngāti Raukawa. The Ngāti Raukawa tribe had a romantic appeal for Te Wherowhero, for he was descended on many lines from that fruit of the love story of Tūrongo and Māhinārangi. On one occasion some of his fellow Waikato chiefs remonstrated with him because he had encouraged the marriage of many of the Waikato young women to Ngāti Raukawa chiefs. Te Wherowhero's reply was, "*E pai ana; waiho mā Ngāti Raukawa e moe, mā ngā ure atua.*" (It is well; let them be embraced by the demigods of Ngāti Raukawa.)

The romance of Tūrongo is one that will live on in the hearts of the Tainui people. It is woven into song and story with threads of poetry in the musical language of the Māori. Ngoki, the Kāwhia song mistress, when stung to the quick by a spiteful reference by a rival in an affair of love, composed a lively rejoinder in the form of a *pātere*[8] chant. It was sung in a lilting tempo and was accompanied by the *pūkana* dance with all its appropriate facial expressions, the haughty turn of the head and body, and the quivering hands. The blood of a Tainui fairly bubbles and his whole being tingles with pride and he loses himself in the exhilarating and romantic mind picture conjured up by the story of Tūrongo and Māhinārangi, which lives again with the singing of the haunting and captivating refrain of Ngoki:

THE PATHWAY OF TŪRONGO (A CHANT)

Taku ara rā, ko Tūrongo;
I wawaea ki te Tai-rāwhiti,
Ko Māhinārangi! I au ē!
Ko te rua rā i moe ai a Raukawa.
Nā Raukawa ko Rereahu;
Nā Rereahu ko Maniapoto:
He ara tau-tika mai ki ahau
E tū, e Hine!
Kia huri au ki aku ara
Ki te tai-tuauru:
Ko Tuhianga, ko Potitama, ko Haumia!
Nā Haumia ko Whatakai;
Nā Whatakai ko Wharerere;
Nā Wharerere ko Whaita:
He kāwei tau-toro nui ki te ao;

E kore rā e taea te whiriwhiri,
I te nui rā, i te tokomaha—
Ka whakatūria e au ko Huiao!
Ko Tuirirangi, ko Paiariki!
Me whakakotahi koutou e au
Ki a Kinohaku! i aha hā!

TRANSLATION

My Pathway is that of Tūrongo;
He proceeded to the Land of the Sunrise,
Where the tides ebb and flow,
And the creeping ripples from the sea
Sing a symphony of love
All the day long—
He sought for romance and found
None other than Māhinārangi!
And I applaud; *I au ē!*
For from that exquisite abode,
Came forth the great Raukawa!
Raukawa begat Rereahu;
Rereahu begat Maniapoto,
And here, I boast of this my noble line.
Stand thou there, O Lady!
The whilst I proudly trace
My lines of descent in the Land
Where the West Winds blow,
And where the Boisterous Seas
Thunder and crash below the Beetling Cliffs!
There, brave men have defied
The Tempestuous Sea of Kupe.
And here they are, Chieftains all!
Tuhianga, Poutama and Haumia!
Haumia begat Whatakai;
Whatakai begat Wharerere;
And Wharerere begat Whaita.
Their fame is great and known to all,
Beyond the power of speech to tell.
Let me now pronounce the name of Huiao!
He begat Tuirirangi and Paiariki:
And here I boast and say,
All ye that stand around

Do but trace to Kinohaku;
One only of my several lines!
There's my boast, and again
I applaud, *I aha hā!*

NOTES ON CHAPTER 2

Note 1

taiaha: A weapon of hard wood about a fathom in length, having one end—the *arero* or tongue—carved in the shape of a tongue with a face on each side, and adorned with a fillet of hair and feathers. The other end, about half a hand wide, is a flat smooth blade.

Note 2

Hotumauea's Leap: The Marokopa river, at this point, is over 40ft. across. At the risk of being castigated by his fellow tribesmen, the author suggests that Hotumauea had swung himself across on a vine which he had previously used for the same purpose when travelling alone.

Note 3

Heahea beach: A popular surf beach in olden times, famed in song and story, it is situated on the northern side of the entrance to Whāingaroa harbour (now Raglan harbour).

Note 4

Horea: Opposite what is now Raglan township.

Note 5

ātahu: A potent spell used to win the affections of someone.

Note 6

Whāingaroa: See note 3 above. The name means "The Long Pursuit" and was so given by Rakataura, one of the High Priests of the Tainui Canoe.

Note 6A

The author has conferred with the tribal genealogists concerned and the consensus of opinion is that the version given in the "*Mahinarangi*" booklet that Marutehiakina was the mother of Whatihua, and that Whatihua was the first-born son of Tāwhao, is incorrect. The "*Mahinarangi*" version was taken from the author's notes as dictated by the late Te Nguha Huirama. The genealogical records compiled by the author's grand-uncle (Te Hurinui Te Wano) are also at variance on this point with the account given by Te Nguha, and the Ngāti Māhanga elder Roore Erueti agrees with the version as set down by Te Hurinui Te Wano. It is, of course, possible that the author did not correctly set down Te Nguha's words.

Note 7

raukawa: A scent made from the leaves of an odoriferous plant, *Nothopanax edgerleyi*.

Note 8

pātere: An old-time action song with, usually, a topical theme.

THE PRIESTLY SCHOLAR

Ko te Kimihanga—
Ka kimi au ki whea?
Ka kimi au ki Tai;
Ka kimi au ki whea?
Ka kimi au ki Uta;
Ka kimi au ki whea?
Ka kimi au ki Raro;
Ka kimi au ki whea?
Ka kimi au ki Runga:
Ka kimi hoki au ki whea,
E kimi ai i a Io?

Nō te Tohi Whakauenuku.

Tis the Searching—
  Where shall I seek?
    I will search in the Flowing Tide;
  Where shall I seek?
    I will search o'er the Land;
  Where shall I seek?
    I will search in the After-World;
  Where shall I seek ?
    I will search in the Realms Above:
  Where else could I seek
    In this searching for Io?

Io: The Supreme Being

From the Raising-up Ritual of
the High Priesthood of the Tainui
Sacred House of Learning

CHAPTER 3

THE PRIESTLY SCHOLAR

I

When Te Wherowhero reached his teens his father decided it was time he was initiated into the lore of the *Whare Wānanga* or the Māori Sacred House of Learning.

Te Rauangaanga explained to his son that there were several branches of the sacred knowledge of the race brought to Aotearoa by the High Priests of the Tainui and Te Arawa canoes, and that it was necessary for the son of a chieftain to devote a good deal of his time to the study and memorising of the deeper and higher knowledge of the esoteric teachings of the *Whare Wānanga*.

The principal houses of learning of the Tainui peoples had been originally established, on the arrival of Hoturoa and the crew of the Tainui Canoe, on the Tāmaki isthmus, on the shores of the Waitematā and Manukau harbours; and southward, both inland and on the west coast. They were established in the following order:

1. Tāmaki, with Te Keteanataura as High Priest. This House of Learning became the centre of the cultural life of the district surrounding Waitematā, Manukau and the lower reaches of the Waikato river.

2. Ahurei, with Hoturoa himself as High Priest. Hoturoa was also the *Tohunga o te Tūāhuroa* (or Grand High Priest) of all the Tainui Houses of Learning. Hoturoa's son-in-law Rakataura acted as the *Kauhanganui* (Local High Priest) in the absence of his father-in-law, and when Hoturoa was in attendance Rakataura acted as his assistant and Examining High Priest or *Tohunga o te Tūāhu Tā-pātai*. The Ahurei *whare wānanga* was established at Kāwhia, close by the spot where the Tainui Canoe was hauled ashore to its last resting-place. Rising nearby is a hillock on which Hoturoa built and consecrated. his earth-formed *tūāhu*, or altar, which he named Ahurei.The Papatatau o Uenuku or the inscribed mystic stone emblems, and the Korotangi, or the image of the weeping dove, were deposited in the Ahurei House of Learning, together with other sacred stone emblems of the Tainui peoples.

3. Te Papa o Rotu, or "The Place of Rotu", was so named after the founder of the school, originally established at Waikarakia, but later moved inland and set up on the western bank of the Waipā river at Whatawhata. Rotu was also a High Priest of the Tainui Canoe. With Hiaroa and eight other priestly bearers of the sacred images, Rotu made up a party of ten of the crew of the Tainui who travelled overland on the watershed along the western side of the lower Waikato valley. This party left shortly after the Tainui Canoe was launched in the Manukau harbour and set off on its voyage down the west coast. Rotu and Hiaroa were recognised experts in the forest lore of the Tainui priesthood.

4. Kahuwera was established by Hiaroa, Rotu's companion, and the place chosen for the site of this school was on the south bank of the Mōkau river, near Piopio.

In Te Rauangaanga's time the Papa o Rotu school was the only *whare wānanga* of the Waikato section of the Tainui, and it was to Te Papa o Rotu that Te Wherowhero was sent. Te Rauangaanga himself was a high priest of the school.

The four sacred houses of learning mentioned above were the principal cultural centres of the Tainui peoples for some generations after their arrival in Aotearoa. In later times other schools were established: at Rangiātea, on the Mangarorongo stream, on the western side of Rangitoto mountain; at Hurakia, on the eastern watershed, near the tribal boundary with the Taupō or Ngāti Tūwharetoa tribe; at Miringa te kakara, at the headwaters of the Waipā river near the foot of Pureora mountain; and lastly, at Whenuatupu, at the junction of the Ōngarue and Waimiha rivers.

Of the last four mentioned *whare wānanga*, Rangiātea became the most important and the Ngāti Maniapoto and Ngāti Raukawa tribes made it their principal centre of learning. This house of learning was established by Tāwhao when his son Tūrongo settled there after he had brought Māhinārangi and his infant son Raukawa to the new home he had set up on the tribal lands of the Tainui. Several villages sprang up around Rangiātea. In later years Te Rongorito, the great-granddaughter of Tūrongo and the first-born of the priestly chieftain Rereahu by his high-born wife Hineaupounamu, set up her home a little to the south of Rangiātea. Te Rongorito named her home Te Marae o Hine (the courtyard of the daughter), and it was made the centre of a special area which was declared *tapu* or sacred, and over which war-parties were not allowed to pass. This reservation was strictly observed throughout the centuries.

In the course of time the esoteric teachings and ritual of the *whare wānanga* of Tainui had become standardised in most respects, with the important exception that only at Ahurei, Te Papa o Rotu and Rangiātea was the *tohi whaka-uenuku* or raising-up ritual of the high priesthood performed, and the meaning of the sacred inscribed stone emblems explained. Therefore in sending his son to Te Papa o Rotu, Te Rauangaanga gave Te Wherowhero the opportunity of absorbing all the highest branches of the extensive curriculum of the Tainui *whare wānanga*.

II

Much of what will now be recounted had already been told by Te Rauangaanga to his son before the latter left home for his first winter session at the Papa o Rotu school. When Te Wherowhero left his home at the foot of Taupiri mountain and across the Waikato river, he was about sixteen years of age.

A wide and very absorbing field of study is opened up when dealing with the course of studies at Te Papa o Rotu. As given by the priests, not in the order in which they were taught, but in chronological sequence from the higher to the lower branches of learning, the subjects ranged from the world's creator, Io, down through the cosmic creation to the mythical ancestors of the Māori, until the genealogical recitals linked up the ancestral lines of descent.

The actual order in which the curriculum was taught was in the reverse. That is to say, the studies commenced with the tribal genealogies and history; then came the hero stories of the ancestors, their inter-tribal wars; and then the inter-tribal relationships, such as that brought about by the union of Tūrongo and Māhinārangi. The next stage was the account of the coming of the Māori to Aotearoa from their former homeland in Hawaiki (Tahiti), in the traditional canoes Tainui, Te Arawa, Mātaatua, Kurahaupō, Tokomaru, Aotea, Tākitimu and Horouta. There were other important canoes, but the ones given here are those which are usually mentioned.

The next course of studies was the account of the origin and evolution of man. Higher still were the sacred recitals of the creation of the World of Stars, and by successive stages back to Te Kore, The Formless Void. The genealogical method was invariably used. It was the time-honoured Polynesian method of memorising and tabulating the chronological, sequence of events and order of birth. In the course of centuries the Polynesian genealogist had hit upon the device of the carved board and notched stick or rod as a visual aid to the memory. With the Tainui priestly hierarchy they came very close to a form of script in their *papa tatau*, or sacred inscribed stones.

III

The full story of these inscribed emblems belongs to the highest order of the Tainui priesthood. They are mentioned here because they link up important events in the history of the Tainui peoples, and also explain the attitude of Te Wherowhero toward the offer of the Māori Kingship, to be recounted later.

At the time Pikauterangi the rebel made the fateful decision which led to the battle of Hingakākā, his people of Ngāti Toarangatira (or Ngāti Toa for short) and the allied tribes of the Kāwhia district were the custodians of the sacred emblems of the Temple of Ahurei. Pikauterangi, being of the senior male line from Toarangatira, the eponymous ancestor, was a priest of the temple and he had access to the sacred emblems. During the turmoil following on Pikauterangi's war the temple at Ahurei was closed and at that time the rumour went throughout the lands of the Tainui peoples that the sacred emblems were missing. There was much conjecture as to what had become of them. At one time it was thought that perhaps Pikauterangi had taken them with him on his recruiting campaign. After the Battle of Hingakākā a thorough search was made among the slain, without result. Various theories were advanced, and in time Waikato suspicion fastened on Te Hurinui, son of Te Rawahirua, a cousin of Pikauterangi.

Te Hurinui was a high priest of Ahurei. On his male line of descent he belonged to an inland section of the Ngāti Maniapoto tribe. It was with this tribe that he lived, and he often officiated in the Rangiātea Temple. At frequent intervals Te Hurinui visited Kāwhia to attend at the sessions of Ahurei. It was on one of these visits that a Waikato chief named Te Uira endeavoured to persuade him to disclose the secret hiding-place of the sacred emblems. Failing in his design, Te Uira killed Te Hurinui in cold blood. This killing is recorded in tribal history as an unwarranted murder and it was one of the causes which led up to the outbreak of civil war between the Ngāti Toa of Kāwhia and the Waikato, Maniapoto and other Tainui tribes.

In the early decades of the nineteenth century several expeditions of Tainui war-parties, under various leaders, went to different parts of New Zealand. In the published accounts of those times no mention is made of one of the underlying Tainui motives for those warlike raids. Now it can be told that much of the blood that flowed was not for conquest or revenge, but was incidental to the intense search for the missing sacred emblems of the Sacred House of Learning of Ahurei.

The Tainui Priesthood believed that if they were to recover *te mea ngaro* (that which is lost, or is hidden) their prestige and general welfare would also be restored to them in full.

Before this chapter ends let us move along the years to the setting up of Te Wherowhero as the first Māori King in 1859. He was then a very old man. As a high priest of Tainui, he was steeped in the esoteric lore of the *wānanga*. And it is to be noted that at that time he was most anxious to preserve the peace and never countenanced the actions of some of the hot-headed leaders who sought to embroil his people in the Taranaki War. The philosophy of the priesthood had made so deep an impression on his mind that it governed most of his actions. Nevertheless, may it never be said that he lacked courage. Before the reader puts down this book it is hoped that he will have formed a correct opinion of Te Wherowhero as a noble character, and will subscribe to the claim put forward that, in the annals of Māori warfare, Te Wherowhero had no peer and that he was the foremost warrior of Aotearoa.

The evidence therefore indicates that the underlying motive behind Te Wherowhero's final acceptance of the Kingship was because it appealed to his priestly ego. The reason cannot be ascribed to the idea of a monarchial institution as understood by the European. The nature of *mana* or prestige as understood by the old-time Māori was not defined by the idea or title of a monarch. To the Māori, the setting up of the Kingship was an incident with a very deep spiritual significance. It is most unfortunate that the Pākehā, motivated by an insatiable land hunger, distorted the Māori King movement into something with a sinister aspect.

The true position as the Māori leaders of the time saw it was that the race was in need of a unifying institution characteristic of its Polynesian ancestry and traditions. Of Te Wherowhero it can be said that he had come to the conclusion that his acceptance of the *mana* of the Kingship from his fellow chieftains would be the means of recapturing the lost prestige of the Māori people—the loss of which he, in his priestly mind, forever associated with the loss of the sacred emblems. When he was raised to the position of high priest it was one of the big disappointments of his life that these sacred emblems were not used in the *tohi whaka-uenuku* or raising-up ritual.

IV

Let us return to Te Wherowhero's lusty young manhood. He had yet to reach the higher grades of the sacred house of learning. In the meantime, he was destined for a life of adventure and the *tohunga rangataua* or the high priest of war was to be his mentor for many dangerous years. The blood of his many warrior ancestors coursed through his veins and for more than two decades he carried his arms on to many a field of battle. Many a time he was to claim the *mātāngohi* or the first-slain in battle, which was considered a signal honour in Māori warfare.

Kei reira koe ka kite
I tāku mau rākau;
I te hāpai patu a ōku tūpuna!

There you will see my skill in arms; and the thrust and the parry of mine ancestors!

Having been initiated into the priesthood Te Wherowhero in accordance with the sacred and time-honoured custom of the Tainui and Arawa *whare wānanga*, eschewed cannibalism.

A GENEALOGICAL TABLE FOR CHAPTER 3

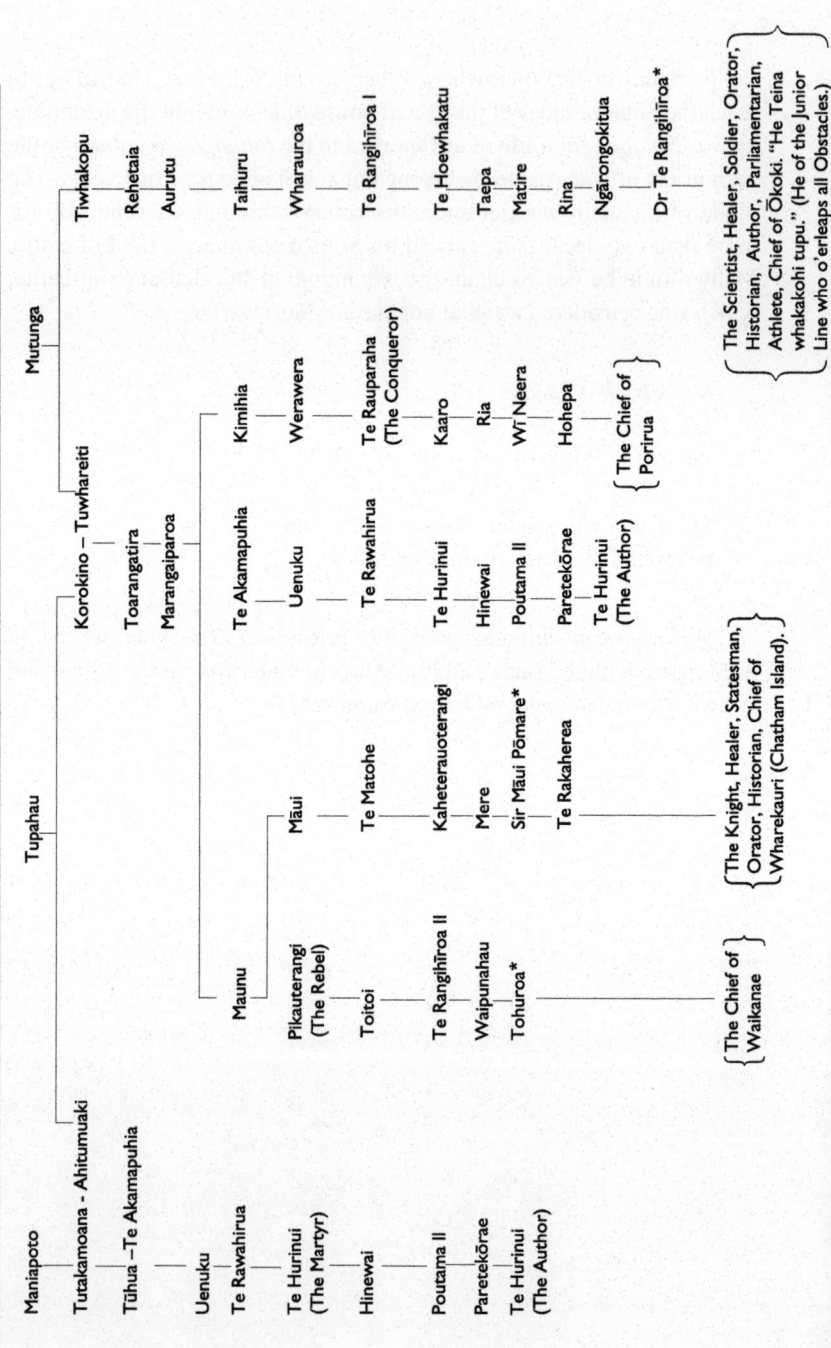

A GENEALOGICAL TABLE FOR CHAPTER 3 (Continued)

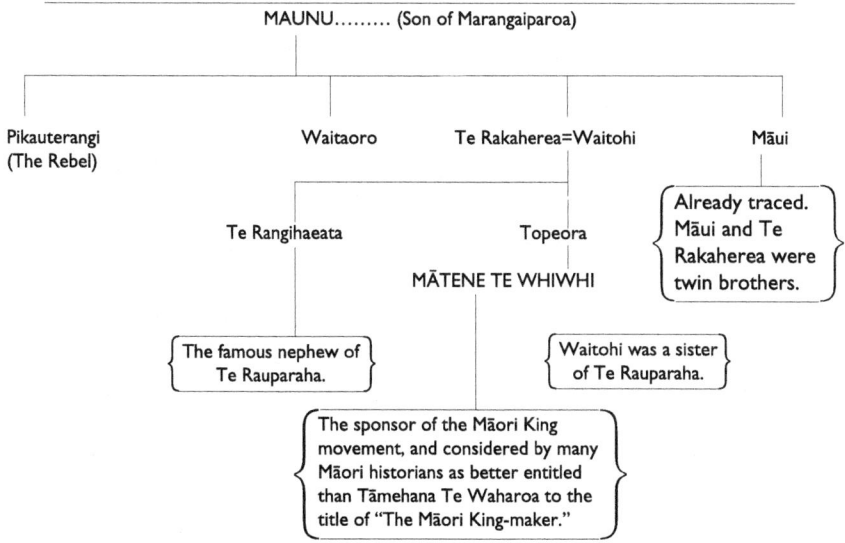

TE RAUPARAHA

Proceed you to the After-World
And there await tidings of my fame!

*Te Rauparaha to the dying Ngāti Raukawa
chief, Hape.*

CHAPTER 4

TE RAUPARAHA

I

The story of the life of the great Ngāti Toa leader Te Rauparaha, "The Conqueror of the South," is an interesting and colourful one. His father, Werawera, was of the Ngāti Toa tribe of Kāwhia and his mother, Parekōhatu, belonged to the Ngāti Raukawa tribe of the Maungatautari and Wharepuhunga district. When the Ngāti Raukawa high chief Hape lay dying and knew his end was near and asked who would take his place, none of his three sons answered him. Perhaps they were overcome by the solemnity of the occasion, or felt that it was not quite fitting to make any response. Te Rauparaha had no such scruples. Three times Hape asked and three times Te Rauparaha answered him, saying: "I will! I will!" On the third occasion Te Rauparaha added, "I, Te Rauparaha, will take your place! Proceed you to the After-World, and there await tidings of my fame!"

At that time the Aotea harbour district, immediately to the north of Kāwhia, the domain of the Ngāti Te Wehi tribe, was thinly populated on account of a movement inland of various sections of the tribe, who had trekked over into the lower Waikato valley to occupy the lands claimed by their ancestor Te Wehi after the overthrow of the tyrant Toangina. The vacated Aotea harbour lands were then occupied by colonies of Ngāti Toa and the allied tribe of Ngāti Koata. A section of the Ngāti Māhanga tribe, the inland neighbours of the Ngāti Te Wehi and who were closely related by numerous inter-marriages, objected to this occupation of the Aotea lands. It was at about this time, too, that Te Hurinui, son of Te Rawahirua, was murdered by Te Uira.

The Ngāti Toa were incensed as the result of this crime. A war-party was formed and proceeded to Makomako at the northwestern end of Aotea harbour, where they discovered Te Uira, the murderer, and killed him together with a Ngāti Te Wehi chief named Te Aomārama. Two other chiefs, Mohi and Tautara, were saved as the result of the intervention of a Ngāti Toa woman named Te Patu. Te Patu was a sister of Tahuriwakanui, who was related to both the Ngāti Koata and Ngāti Hikairo tribes. The latter tribe belonged to the Waipā, Pirongia and Ōpārau districts. Mohi was allowed to escape and his companion Tautara was conducted to the island *pā* Ngātokakairiri, where he was handed over to his Ngāti Hikairo kinsmen. The body of the murderer Te Uira was taken to the Ngāti Toa *pā* of Pouewe on the northern shore of Kāwhia harbour where it was cooked and eaten. (Subsequently, when the Ngāti Toa tribe was driven out of Kāwhia the land around Pouewe was given to the descendants of Te Uira).

II

As the result of the killing and eating of Te Uira a war-party of Waikato tribes was organised by his son, Te Hiakai to obtain *utu* or revenge. Te Hiakai's force was recruited from the following tribes: Ngāti Rehu and Ngāti Reko of the lower Waipā valley, Ngāti Māhanga of the Moerangi ranges, and Ngāti Mahuta of Taupiri. The invading force came over the northern shoulder of the Pirongia mountain and descended on the Ngāti Toa *pā* of Horoure at the southern end of Aotea harbour. The Waikato leaders were not particularly anxious about the outcome of Te Hiakai's expedition, as it was felt that the death of Te Uira was a just retribution for the murder of Te Hurinui. The object the Waikato leaders had in mind was to make a show of force to deter the Ngāti Toa from further aggression against their neighbours which might in time spread and involve the Tainui tribes in a general civil war. Consequently, after some desultory skirmishes, during which a Ngāti Māhanga woman named Rangipōtiki was killed, the Waikato forces withdrew. The young warrior Te Hiakai returned with his own tribe to his home at Whakairoiro, on the foothills of Pirongia mountain, breathing vengeance against the Ngāti Toa.

Shortly afterward a party of Ngāti Māhanga came over the ranges to occupy some of the vacated lands of the Ngāti Te Wehi, and finding two Ngāti Toa men settled at Aotea, they killed them. These two men were named Te Whata and Waitapu. At about the same time two women of rank (one a sister of Te Rangihaeata and the other a sister of Rangi Topeora) were killed by Ngāti Pou, Te Hiakai's people, at Whakairoiro. These two Ngāti Toa women had gone there to attend the *tangi* or wailing over the dead, for a relative. Te Hiakai was not present during the killing and he disclaimed any responsibility for their tragic death.

III

Incidents still followed on one another. Immediately after the events just related, Te Hiakai persuaded the veteran Ngāti Mahuta warrior Te Ahooterangi, son of Pukauae and Hourua, to organise a war-party for the invasion of Kāwhia. This force attacked the Ngāti Toa in one of their principal strongholds, Pouewe Pā. The leaders of Ngāti Toa in this engagement were Te Keunga and Tarahape. The Pouewe and Motungaio *pā* both fell to the Waikato invaders and among those who were captured was the sister of the young chief Te Wharepuhi. This young lady was a famous beauty. During her captivity she was subjected to abuse by the Waikato warriors. On the night following the fall of Motungaio Pā, Te Wharepuhi entered the Waikato encampment and, pretending to be one of the warriors, he filed in with them and made his way to his sister's couch. In a few hurried whispers he learnt from her the plans of the enemy for the morrow.

Early next morning Te Wharepuhi attacked with a specially selected band of young Ngāti Toa warriors. The Waikato were taken unawares. With their leading warriors enfeebled by the excesses of the preceding night, they were soon routed. Te Ahooterangi hastily reorganised his Ngāti Mahuta and set off on the trail for home, along the northern shore of Kāwhia harbour. Just at the point where the track to Aotea harbour branches off to the left, Te Ahooterangi and another Waikato leader broke away and endeavoured to reach the forest-clad hill to the west. As he crossed a mudflat of the long northern arm of Kāwhia harbour Te Ahooterangi was overtaken by the Ngāti Toa warriors. He was led on to the beach, and on a log which is still to be seen there, Te Ahooterangi was beheaded and his head carried back in triumph to Motungaio Pā. The remnants of the Waikato invaders fled in disorder, many being killed by the vengeful Ngāti Toa warriors. The name given to this engagement was Putakarekare, "the eagerness to escape."

IV

The scattered fires were now merging into a general conflagration. The death of his grandfather Te Ahooterangi now brought the great Te Rauangaanga into the Kāwhia troubles. He led an army of the Waikato tribes into Kāwhia with the avowed object of not only obtaining revenge, but also of driving the Ngāti Toa from the lands around the northern shores of Kāwhia harbour. After a series of savage engagements the Ngāti Toa evacuated the northern side of the harbour and retired to the hilly country on the south. Their main stronghold there was Te Tōtara Pā. Te Rauangaanga led his army across the harbour and attacked the Ngāti Toa in this *pā*. The attack was so resolute that the garrison was soon dislodged. Quickly reorganising their forces among the hills above

Taharoa lake the Ngāti Toa tribe returned and counter-attacked and inflicted a severe reverse on the surprised Waikato. Te Rauangaanga and another Waikato leader named Kiwi barely escaped with their lives, and only did so by making a desperate leap over a cliff and clambering down on to the beach where they rejoined the main body, who were hurriedly embarking in canoes along the beaches of Te Maika inlet. The Waikato retired to the northern side of the harbour for the night. Te Rauangaanga was not discouraged, and that same night he gave orders that they were to return to the attack at dawn next day.

The Ngāti Toa, in the meantime, had re-occupied their *pā* at Te Tōtara and had repaired the palisading and earthworks. A ruse was devised for the following day. All signs of life in the *pā* were carefully removed. The dried fish on the elevated frames were taken down, the dogs were taken elsewhere and all fires were extinguished. The garrison then took up strategic positions in the *pā*, and the main gateway was left wide open. Their preparations for the return of the Waikato being completed, the Ngāti Toa waited in silent vigilance.

At high water next morning the Waikato men paddled across from the northern side of the harbour to the Te Maika headland, opposite the headland on which Te Tōtara Pā was situated. The Waikato took particular notice of the seemingly abandoned *pā* and some of them were for an immediate landing on the beach below. But Te Rauangaanga, who suspected a ruse, directed the canoes on to the beach on the Te Maika side of the inlet. Two young Waikato warriors, however, in a spirit of rivalry paddled over toward Te Tōtara. One was in a small canoe and his companion on a raft. As they neared the *pā*, the youth in the canoe saw a greenstone *mere* or club slowly rise and disappear behind the high palisading. It was a silent warning from some relative who had recognised the youth as a kinsman. He called out to his companion on the raft to warn him and immediately turned about and paddled back across the inlet. The raftman still rowed on, perhaps thinking his companion was merely joking. Presently, the famous Ngāti Toa war-canoe Te Waruhanga rounded the headland and bore down on the tiny raft. The Waikato youth had no chance and he was quickly overtaken and killed.

The Ngāti Toa then slowly approached the Waikato men on Te Maika beach and, some distance off-shore, began to parley with the Waikato leader. Eventually peace was made and Te Rauangaanga and his army returned to the Waikato district.

V

The events so far described in this chapter indicate the general atmosphere in which Te Wherowhero and his famous rival, Te Rauparaha grew up into young manhood. There were brief periods of uneasy peace and it was during such a period when Te Rauparaha made his debut. Some time after the fighting and the peacemaking at Te Tōtara, Te Rauparaha conducted a party to the fishing grounds at Taumatawiwi, in the inner harbour of Kāwhia. Two Ngāti Maniapoto chiefs named Whakamaru and Te Rangituatea, on hearing of this trespass on their tribal fishing grounds, came over to remonstrate with Te Rauparaha. The two chiefs met Te Rauparaha near a place called Tūtaerere. With Te Rauparaha were two guests of his tribe named Haurora and Haupare. A heated argument took place during which Te Rauparaha came to blows with Whakamaru and killed him. Te Rauparaha then advanced on Te Rangituatea, brandishing his *taiaha*. Te Rangituatea, armed with a *mere*, stood his ground, a tree with wide overspreading branches behind his back. Te Rauparaha made a thrust at Te Rangituatea which the latter sidestepped and parried with his *mere*. Te Rauparaha then rushed at him to strike him down but his *taiaha* was caught in a limb of the tree and the blow deflected. Te Rangituatea had Ngāti Toa blood in him, and he reminded Te Rauparaha of this as he turned away and Te Rauparaha allowed him to leave unmolested.

The Ngāti Maniapoto tribe was not disposed to allow the Ngāti Toa to trespass on its fishing grounds with impunity and a war-party was organised. The Ngāti Maniapoto called on the Waikato tribes, and the Ngāti Pou, Ngāti Mahuta, Ngāti Hine and other tribes responded. A force of 1,600 assembled at Mangatoatoa on the Pūniu river, the headquarters of the great Ngāti Raukawa and Ngāti Maniapoto chief, Tūkōrehu. With Te Rauangaanga in command, the combined Waikato and Maniapoto army came over the ranges at Te Rauamoa by the Tirohanga-Kāwhia track. Te Rauparaha and his people took up their position in the Hikuparea Pā on the Tiritiri o matangi peninsula.

Some distance from the *pā* Te Rauangaanga's army halted and he announced his battle plans. He divided his force in two, and a party of 800 men was led up to the *pā*. The remaining 800 were disposed in advantageous positions so as to form an effective ambush. A sharp attack was launched against the *pā* and, when the garrison retaliated with some spirit, the attackers drew off, turned about and fled in feigned retreat. The greater part of Te Rauparaha's forces rushed out in hot pursuit, and were led directly into the ambush. Greatly outnumbered by the strong army of Te Rauangaanga, the men of the garrison were soon desperately fighting for their lives as they retired toward their *pā*, closely pressed by the Waikato and Maniapoto. The slaughter was heavy and continued right inside Hikuparea Pā, where several chiefs were killed, among them being Haunga, who was struck down by Mautara, a near relative of Taka, the father of Poakai the former Ngāti Pou chief of Hikuparea Pā and a close relative of Te Hiakai.

The invading army followed the Ngāti Toa who escaped from Hikuparea and laid siege to Te Tōtara Pā, where Te Rauparaha had led his tribesmen. After a time Te Rauparaha led the garrison in a desperate counter-attack and in fierce fighting outside the *pā* he lost some of the ablest leaders of the Ngāti Toa. Among others who lost their lives were Hikihiki, Kiharoa and Tarapeke. The last mentioned was killed in single combat by Te Wharengori, in full view of both war parties. According to tribal accounts this duel was a classic one, as both men were past masters in the use of the *taiaha*. After losing so many of his best warriors Te Rauparaha retired into the *pā* and called out to Te Rauangaanga to approach as he wished to make peace. Te Rauangaanga acceded to Te Rauparaha's overtures and he made a second peacemaking with the Ngāti Toa.

VI

Te Rauparaha for a time contemplated leaving Kāwhia to go and live with his mother's people of the Ngāti Raukawa tribe at Maungatautari. In the following winter he set out for Maungatautari to recruit an army for the overthrow of the Waikato and Maniapoto. The Ngāti Raukawa would have nothing to do with his plans, so he continued his journey to the Rotorua district. He could claim Arawa blood in his veins and he sought to appeal on this relationship for support. The Arawa were not impressed and not disposed to become embroiled with the Waikato. From Rotorua, Te Rauparaha went to the Taupō district. Before leaving the Rotorua territory, however, he and his companions persuaded a section of the Arawa to attack and kill a small travelling party of Ngāpuhi from the Whāngārei district, who were on their way home from the East Coast. The sequel to this incident was the invasion in force by the Ngāpuhi, under their famous war-leader Hongi Hika, of the lands of the Arawa and their severe defeat on their island stronghold of Mokoia. As Te Rauparaha was associated with the northern war leaders in several raids to the south, it is possible that he incited Hongi Hika to attack the Arawa in order to satisfy his disappointment and chagrin at being refused support. Te Rauparaha's companions returned home from Rotorua, and he went on alone to Taupō. Here he was again rebuffed. He was related to the Ngāti Tūwharetoa tribe of Taupō and he thought he might get them to change their minds if he taunted them. But this idea also went amiss and it was only through a timely warning from a member of the tribe that he was able to make his escape at night from the wrath of the Tūwharetoa.

Te Rauparaha fled from a village on the banks of the Tongariro river and taking a circuitous route he skirted around the shores of Rotoaira lake and found a refuge in the *pā* of the chief Te Wharerangi whose wife hid Te Rauparaha from his pursuers in a *kūmara* pit. It was to celebrate his deliverance that he composed his famous *haka* or war cry: "*Ka mate! Ka mate!*" in honour of the Rotoaira chief, Te Wharerangi. After this narrow escape Te Rauparaha left Motuopuhi, the Rotoaira home of Te Wharerangi, and reached Kāwhia without further incident.

VII

The Ngāti Toa brooded over their losses. Te Rauparaha on his return, finding his people in a mood to fight, organised a band of young warriors and with a number of their Ngāti Koata allies, he set off to reach harbour. There they caught Te Wharengori, the *taiaha* master who had killed the Ngāti Toa expert Tarapeke. With Te Wharengori were three other chiefs named Tutonga, Uehoka and Moanataiaha. Uehoka, who was partly related to Te Rauparaha, was invited to leave the *pā* before it was carried by storm and was offered safety. Uehoka replied in a derisive manner and, in consequence, when he was captured, he was killed and eaten.

Part of Te Rauparaha's force under Te Wharepuhi, already mentioned in connection with the fighting preceding the death of Te Ahooterangi, accompanied by Taiko as second-in-command, attacked the Ngāti Tamainupō tribe of the inner harbour of Whāingaroa, killing Totoia. At a place called Mangakōwhai they killed Pouha and Kāretu.

A punitive force of the Waikato tribes was immediately recruited from the ranks of Ngāti Mahuta, Ngāti Ngahia, Ngāti Reko, Ngāti Māhanga and Ngāti Tamainupō, and marched over into Kāwhia. At a place called Torea they found a section of Ngāti Toa who had just come over from Te Tōtara Pā. The Waikato attacked, killing the chiefs Te Wharepuhi, Taiko, Manukitawhiti, Te Hahana and Poukura. The Ngāti Toa and their allies suffered heavy casualties in this engagement.

Te Wharengori and the three chiefs who were killed with him belonged to the Ngāti Pou who felt the Ngāti Toa and their allies should suffer further punishment for their deaths. This tribe, with other sections of the Waikato people, accordingly mobilised a force and in seven canoes set off from the Waikato heads for Kāwhia. The names of these canoes and the tribes who manned them were:

1. Kauteuri: Ngāti Tipa of Waikato heads.
2. Taikiharau: Ngāti Pou of Tuakau
3. Rākaumangamanga: Ngāti Mahuta of Waahi
4. Maukuwai: Ngāti Mahuta of Waahi
5. Tautearahi: Ngāti Mahuta of Waahi
6. Te Ahahiaroa: Ngāti Te Ata of Waiuku
7. Te Wahakaikuri: Ngāti Pāoa of west Hauraki gulf

During the voyage the Rākaumangamanga canoe ran aground a short distance south of Whāingaroa. It was refloated and later the whole invading force landed near Otiki Pā. The combined force was under the leadership of Karewaho. The Ngāti Toa immediately attacked, but were driven off, losing three leading warriors named Te Weu, Pātea and Te Ingoa. The Ngāti Toa retreated to Ōhāua where they were closely pressed by the Waikato. At this place Waitohi, a sister of Te Rauparaha, recognised four relatives among the Ngāti Te Ata named Awarua, Rahurahu, Te Tuhi and Te Kauae and to these four kinsmen Waitohi made an impassioned appeal, pointing out that the killing of the four Ngāti Pou chiefs was justified on account of the loss of so many of the Ngāti Toa warriors and the unwarranted and unrequited killing of Te Whata, Waitapu and the two women who had gone to wail over the dead at Whakairoiro.

VIII

An uneasy peace followed the truce made by Waitohi, during which a Ngāti Māhanga chief named Te Unuatahu went on a visit to the Ngāti Tama tribe in their *pā* of Te Kawau, south of Mōkau. Te Unuatahu had a sister who had married a man of Ngāti Tama and the purpose of his journey was to see her. While he was there, some Ngāti Raukawa guests of the Ngāti Tama chief Raparapa suggested to him that they should pay off old scores against the Waikato by killing Te Unuatahu. This suggestion was overheard by Te Unuatahu's brother-in-law and he was warned. Te Unuatahu thereupon hurriedly left for home, followed by Raparapa. Te Unuatahu soon reached Kāwhia harbour, found a small canoe, and paddled across to Ngātokakairiri Pā at the northeastern end of the harbour. The Ngāti Hikairo people of Ngātokakairiri urged Te Unuatahu to move on. His reply was, "Who am I, Te Unuatahu, that they should pursue me thus far?" Te Unuatahu was tired and stayed. The Ngāti Tama pursuer, Raparapa, found him there that night and killed him.

We have now reached the year 1819 and during this time Te Rauparaha accompanied a northern expedition of the Ngāpuhi tribe to the southern end of the North Island. In his absence his first wife went to Waikato to attend the *tangi* of a relative and while she was there Te Kanawa and Te Ikatu, two Waikato chiefs, persuaded a lesser chief named, Te Rangimoewaka to kill her. On his return Te Rauparaha grieved over the death of his wife and vowed that a chief would have to die "as a relish" for his revenge, and he picked on Te Moerua, a Ngāti Maniapoto chief, whose death he instigated. Te Moerua had two wives who could not agree to live together. One lived at Totorewa Pā, near Ōtorohanga, and the other at Arapae, near Piopio, in the Mōkau valley. Te Moerua was on his way from Totorewa to Arapae to visit one of his wives when he was waylaid and killed on a "peace track." There were three "peace tracks" by which the Ngāti Maniapoto travelled to and from the coast, and the killing of Te Moerua on one of them was the very first occasion the rule of immunity had been transgressed by any of the Tainui tribes. The name of one of these tracks, which ran from Ōparure to Marokopa, was Mangahaua.

Te Rauparaha had now become the most audacious fighting chief among the Tainui peoples, and with all the Ngāti Toa and Ngāti Koata leading warriors killed in the several engagements already recounted, Te Rauparaha had also assumed virtual overlordship of the tribes on the seaboard between Kāwhia and Mōkau. Following on the death of Te Moerua, his body was preserved and portions of it were shared out by Te Rauparaha to various chiefs. Among others who shared was a Marokopa chief named Te Mahutu who, as he ate, kept his head down as if deep in thought. Te Rauparaha noticed this and said to him, "Lift up your head! Know you that the food you eat is the body of Te Moerua, and in the eating of a chief one does not bow the head."

IX

Shortly afterward Te Rauparaha learnt that a chief named Ngātapa had a grievance against the Raukawa-Maniapoto chief Tūkōrehu. Te Rauparaha was much interested in this news, so he called on Ngātapa and urged him to accompany him in an attack on Tūkōrehu's *pā*, Mangatoatoa. Tūkōrehu was warned of the impending attack on his stronghold and he gathered his three tribes of Ngāti Ngāwaero, Ngāti Kahu and Ngāti Uru into Mangatoatoa.

Te Rauparaha and Ngātapa went over the ranges with their warparty and on arriving before Mangatoatoa they laid siege to it. Early in the siege Te Rauparaha endeavoured to lure Tūkōrehu out of the *pā*. Advancing boldly up to the main gateway Te Rauparaha made as if he was about to scale the palisading. Tūkōrehu came up to the gateway and threw it open. The two looked into each other's eyes and neither spoke a word. It was a test of will power. One of the inmates of the *pā*, unable to bear the suspense any longer, called out to Tūkōrehu, "*Whakahokia!*" (Send him back!) The spell was broken. Te Rauparaha leaped away, then turned round and addressing the speaker he said, "*Māu anō mā tēnā rore weka ahau e kī mai kia hoki!*" (Indeed, you who art but a captive weka should call out that I be sent back!)

The siege continued. Te Rauparaha found that his force was not large enough to carry the *pā* by storm and, furthermore, there was very little food to be had as Tūkōrehu had applied a "scorched earth" policy, and all unharvested crops had been destroyed. Te Rauparaha then bethought himself of the strategy previously employed against him by Te Rauangaanga at Hikuparea and he disengaged his forces, lifted the siege and moved off in the direction of Kāwhia. But Tūkōrehu was not to be caught by such a manoeuvre. As Te Rauparaha's force disappeared behind a ridge, Tūkōrehu moved out of the *pā* in the opposite direction. Tūkōrehu and his men moved slowly, for he knew Te Rauparaha's scouts were on the watch. However, as soon as they reached a sunken track, they moved fast by an outflanking route. They followed tracks well-known to them and soon were astride the Kāwhia main trail and, unobserved, took up a position behind a hill.

Te Rauparaha thought he would lure Tūkōrehu well away from the *pā* and, although he knew they had moved off in the opposite direction, he expected they would later turn about and follow him along the Kāwhia track. Te Rauparaha and his men moved steadily along the track and presently were abreast of Tūkōrehu's position. In a savage and sharp attack the Kāwhia force was routed and the survivors were soon fleeing homeward. Te Rauparaha himself was very nearly captured by a Ngāti Maniapoto warrior and only escaped by slipping his cloak off as it was caught in the hands of his pursuer. That was Te Rauparaha's last incursion into that part of Ngāti Maniapoto and Raukawa territory.

The Ngāti Maniapoto now entered into the Kāwhia troubles in earnest. A war-party made a quick raid into Marokopa and killed Mahutu for his part in the Te Moerua episode. Te Rauparaha retaliated by making his way to the upper Mōkau river and, at Arapae Pā, he took captive two Ngāti Maniapoto women named Niho and Te Arataua. Niho, who was partly of Ngāti Toa, was set free. Her companion Te Arataua, a highborn woman of Mōkau, was killed. A Maniapoto band of warriors with Te Whāinga in command was immediately formed and set off in pursuit of Te Rauparaha and his Ngāti Toa. At Te Raupō the Ngāti Toa made a stand, but after losing twenty of their number they turned and fled. They were hotly pursued and were again overtaken at Mangaohae. At this place Te Whāinga killed Te Pekapeka, one of the last of the seasoned warriors of Ngāti Toa, and a well-known fighter.

X

Te Rauparaha had now embroiled himself in a sea of troubles and was encircled by a ring of inveterate foes. From Mōkau in the south and inland along the dividing ranges on the east were the warlike Ngāti Maniapoto, and to the northeast and the north were the powerful confederation of Waikato tribes. The Ngāti Raukawa of Maungatautari and Wharepuhunga, who might have been helpful, were cut off by the intervening Maniapoto and Waikato territories.

We are now approaching the time in the eventful life of Te Wherowhero when he first came in contact with Te Rauparaha. Te Rauparaha had received warning of the impending invasion of Kāwhia by a large combined army under Te Wherowhero, preparations for which were well advanced. Te Rauparaha rushed down to the Ngāti Tama country south of the Mōkau river and prevailed on Tūpoki, the warrior chieftain of that tribe, to make a diversionary raid into the upper Mōkau valley.

Tūpoki came up the Awakino valley and over by the Taumatamaire track and at Rangikohua Pā which was ungarrisoned, they discovered the chieftainess Parerahui and killed her. The Ngāti Tama force continued on to the falls at Wairere on the Mōkau river, near Piopio, and here they camped for the night. Early next morning they were attacked by a force of Ngāti Maniapoto under Whaaro and were compelled to beat a hasty retreat. Whaaro followed close on their heels down the Mangaotake river, a tributary of the Mōkau river. The second-in-command of Tūpoki's forces was a chief named Te Ngaehe, who was partly of Ngāti Maniapoto blood. During the retreat Te Ngaehe took charge as he had a better knowledge of the country through which they were passing. At the river crossing on the Mangaotake river (about half a mile below the present highway bridge) Te Ngaehe was the first to reach the high ground above the steep rise from the river. Whaaro recognised him across the gorge and called out to him not to wait for Tūpoki, otherwise he would share his fate. Te Ngaehe took this advice and continued on his way. This incident is commemorated in a song.

Just beyond the river crossing Tūpoki and his party were benighted and they camped at a place called Pararewa. This spot is situated on the northern bank of the Mōkau river near Mahoenui. It was at this place, the next morning, that a fierce battle occurred. During the fighting one of the few guns the Maniapoto possessed was loaded and given to Hauāuru, a young lad at that time. Hauāuru's grandfather Maungatautari was killed by the Ngāti Tama at Poutama and the Maniapoto leaders had decided that it was for Hauāuru to obtain *utu* or revenge by shooting Tūpoki, after the manner in which Maungatautari had been killed. The Ngāti Tama were completely encircled and at the critical stage of the fighting Tūpoki was cut off from his main force. Hauāuru was about to shoot him when a Ngāpuhi man who had been with the Ngāti Maniapoto for some time stepped forward with a gun and was about to take aim when a Ngāti Maniapoto chief pushed him aside saying, "This is not your quarrel." Hauāuru then took aim, fired, and killed the great Ngāti Tama chief Tūpoki. The Ngāti Tama force was completely routed.

During the pursuit the Maniapoto had noticed that the beautiful daughter of Tūpoki, named Te Waero, was with the party and Wahanui, the veteran Mōkau warrior chieftain, son of Waiora, had made it known that Te Waero was not to be killed as he desired her to be his wife. Pikirangi, a young kinsman of Wahanui, who was rapidly making a name for himself as a coming fighting leader, had ideas of his own. When Tūpoki realised that he and his party were doomed he had directed Te Waero to flee in the direction of home. She was, however, caught by Pikirangi. He took her to a secluded place and there shamefully and cruelly treated her. After assaulting the unfortunate young woman Pikirangi killed her. It was at this juncture that Wahanui came upon the scene. The veteran advanced threateningly toward Pikirangi muttering, *"Ā Pikirangi! Pikirangi!"* Pikirangi took up an equally hostile attitude and retorted, *"E Wahanui!*

Wahanui!" If the other chiefs had not happened upon the scene at this stage the two Maniapoto warriors would have engaged in a life and death struggle over the dead body of the beautiful Ngāti Tama chieftainess. Wahanui uttered a curse upon the young chief Pikirangi and it is said that it was from that day that the decline began in the fortunes of the Pikirangi clan. Wahanui then carefully removed some of the hair of the dead Te Waero, and the strands he subsequently used to decorate his favourite *kōauau*, a carved bone nose-flute.

XI

Events were now moving rapidly to a climax. The dark clouds of war loomed threateningly along the whole of the hinterland of the Ngāti Toa country. The killing of Te Unuatahu of Ngāti Māhanga, of Te Moerua of Ngāti Maniapoto, and of Te Arataua the high-born Mōkau lady, were all episodes that were destined to raise overwhelming forces against Te Rauparaha and his people. The account of Te Rauparaha's visit to Rotorua and later to Taupō had by now been fully reported to the Waikato and Maniapoto leaders. Pikauterangi's war was recalled and a parallel was drawn from that critical incident in the fortunes of the Tainui peoples which pointed to Te Rauparaha as being a very dangerous man who should be speedily eliminated. Te Wherowhero sent out word to hurry on the mobilisation of the Waikato forces and simultaneously the Maniapoto, under Tūkōrehu and Te Rangituatea, were also mobilised. Punatoto of Ngāti Māhanga, a close relative of Te Unuatahu, the man whom Raparapa the Ngāti Tama chief had pursued and killed, recruited a formidable force from the coastal tribes inhabiting the land between the Waikato heads and Aotea harbour.

The Maniapoto were divided into two armies, the southern section being placed under the command of Tūkōrehu, and the other under Te Rangituatea. This latter force was to link up with the main army under the supreme command of Te Wherowhero. The force under Te Rangituatea was composed of particularly active men, used to hilly country, and the special task assigned them was to sweep around the southern hill fortifications of the Ngāti Toa position at Taharoa. There were many notable leaders under Te Wherowhero. Among them was Pikia of Ngāti Hikairo who was to make a drive around the northern shores of Kāwhia harbour and then link up with Kiwi, another Waikato leader, in charge of a force from the Waikato heads, who were to be transported by sea to the scene of battle. The main force under the direct control of Te Wherowhero was to deliver the hammer strokes that would open the way to the final blow in the heart of the Ngāti Toa stronghold at Te Taharoa.

There were some notable absentees among the Maniapoto leaders, who elected because of blood ties with the Ngāti Toa tribe to remain neutral. When the large forces that were to make up Te Wherowhero's invasion army were mobilised, the following tribes under their chiefs were accounted for:

1. Southern Force of Ngāti Maniapoto tribes, under Tūkōrehu, comprising 1,000 men.

2. Main Force of the Maniapoto under Te Rangituatea, and the Waikato inland tribes, 2,000 men, under the direct control of the commander-in-chief, Te Wherowhero. The various groups in this force comprised:

    (a) *First group*: Ngāti Mahuta, Ngāti Māhanga, Ngāti Te Wehi, Ngāti Reko and Ngāti Patupō under Punatoto, Te Tihirahi, Te Paewaka and Te Ake, numbering 1,000 men.

    (b) *Second group*: Ngāti Hikairo under Pikia, of 500 men.

    (c) *Third group*: Ngāti Maniapoto under Te Rangituatea, of 500 men.

3. The Seaborne Force of the tribes of Tainui of Whāingaroa, Ngāti Tamainupō also of Whāingaroa, the Ngāti Hourua and Ngāti Pou, under Kiwi, Te Kanawa, Te Hiakai and Te Awaitaia, and numbering 1,000 men.

The battle plans of Te Wherowhero and his Waikato and Maniapoto war-chiefs were to be on a grand scale. The southern force and the seaborne force were to apply the pincers and the main body was to strike at the heart of the land of the Ngāti Toa.

Tūkōrehu, the Maniapoto leader of the southern force, had shortly before passed through the Ngāti Toa lands by way of Waikawau Pā, on his return from a foray into Ngāti Tama lands. He had not fared too well and was hurrying back home when he passed along the beach below Waikawau. The Ngāti Rārua garrison of the *pā* made ribald remarks at Tūkōrehu from the security of their strong fortification and called out, "*Tēnā hoki tō māhunga hina ka mamaoa haere!*" (Indeed your grey head is steaming!) This remark about his head, which was sacred, stung Tūkōrehu to the quick. This was the main reason why Tūkōrehu had specially elected to lead the southern force. The insulting taunt by Ngāti Rārua had to be wiped out in blood.

The invasion plan having been settled, the armies awaited the orders of Te Wherowhero. This assault on Kāwhia was to spell the approaching doom of Te Rauparaha's people.

XII

Te Rauparaha had by no means been idle. His tribes of Ngāti Toa, Ngāti Koata, Ngāti Te Akamapuhia and Ngāti Rārua were strengthened by a contingent of the fighting tribe of Ngāti Tama of the south Mōkau district. The Ngāti Tama were under the renowned warrior Raparapa, Tūpoki's brother-in-law. Te Rauparaha had as war leaders Raparapa, Te Rangihaeata who was Te Rauparaha's nephew, Te Peehi Kupe, Te Pokaitara and Te Pūoho.

In the south the defences of Waikawau Pā were strengthened by its Ngāti Rārua garrison and in the north the Ngāti Koata took up their positions in their famous *pā* of Pouewe and Motungaio. (These two *pā* were sited on the two hills that now dominate the quiet little seaside township of Kāwhia.) Te Rauparaha's main forces were concentrated at Te Tōtara Pā on the south side of the harbour and near the Taumatakanae stream, at the outflowing waters of Te Taharoa lake, in the two *pā* of Te Kawau and Te Roto. Strong outposts were established to the east near the Kinohaku gap and also to the south at Harihari on the coast, and a string of forts was manned to connect these two points along the crest of the Taharoa hills.

Having completed these preparations, Te Rauparaha then attended to the renovation of his own place of refuge. This was on a cliff face at Tīrua point. It was inaccessible except by a rope ladder which was drawn up when the cave was occupied by the Ngāti Toa leader. It had served as a retreat in times of personal danger. It had been made very comfortable—the walls were lined with woven panels on a wooden framework and the floor was covered with finely woven sleepingmats. A plentiful supply of preserved food was stored and water was collected. It was in this impregnable retreat that the great Ngāti Toa leader planned and schemed. Te Rauparaha called this eyrie by two descriptive names, Te Titimatarua and Te Urungaparaoa, "the vigilant-eyed opening" and "the whalebone club-pillow".

THE BATTLE OF KĀWHIA

Haramai ana te rongo o te riri!
I mua;
I muri;
I a Muriwhenua,
I a Te Maha i ara!

Nō te Ngeri a Te Rauparaha

Ha! 'tis tidings of war that come!
It comes from afore;
It comes from aft;
It comes from the Muriwhenua Clan!
It comes from The Many!

From Te Rauparaha's War Chant

CHAPTER 5

THE BATTLE OF KĀWHIA

I

In the summer, early in the year 1820, the invasion army was on the move. The first blow was struck by the Maniapoto southern force, under Tūkōrehu. With the famous Arapae Pā as its rallying point, this force was quickly mobilised and soon moved off down the Awakino river, and thence swung northwestward over the Taumatamaire hill to strike at the Waikawau Pā of Ngāti Rārua.

Just before reaching his objective Tūkōrehu was joined by a flying column of Ngāti Hikairo under the chief Te Au. This small force had been specially detailed by the Ngāti Hikairo leader Pikia to make a quick reconnaissance along the Tapirimoko track. After dispatching a messenger to report on the result of his observations as to the disposition of the Ngāti Akamapuhia forces, Te Au could not resist the attraction of joining the Ngāti Maniapoto in striking the first blow at the southern allies of Ngāti Toa, the Ngāti Rārua of Waikawau.

The attack on Waikawau was undertaken after a matter of three or four days, as Tūkōrehu first made certain that all avenues of escape were cut off. The canoes in the Waikawau river, just below the ramparts on the precipitous southern side of the *pā*, perched up on the plateau above, were removed to a safe place by Tūkōrehu. His main camp was established on the sandspit on the southern side of the mouth of the Waikawau river. Te Au and his men kept watch on the north side of the high ground overlooking the long sandy beach leading to Tīrua point.

The attack was made from the landward side along the narrow ridge connecting the mainland with the sea-girt plateau on which the *pā* was situated. In a resolute rush Tūkōrehu and his men surmounted the defensive earthworks across the ridge. Some of the garrison had, in the meantime, been beguiled to the western end of the *pā* by a party of men who had for the previous three or four days been visiting the reef at that point. This reef was a favourite fishing place and it annoyed the people of the *pā* to see the enemy enjoying the fishing while they were cooped up and, to vent their anger, they indulged in throwing stones at the fishermen as they passed along the beach to and from the reef.

Once the breach was made in the defences the defenders, who had all their women and children in the *pā* with them, were soon thrown into utter confusion. Terrible slaughter followed, many of the occupants of Waikawau being killed by being hurled over the cliff edge on to the rocks below. Only those who had Maniapoto blood and had relatives in the attacking force were saved. The rest were ruthlessly slain under the orders of Tūkōrehu to wipe out that taunting reference to his "grey steaming head."

II

Simultaneously with the storming of Waikawau, the northern arm of the pincer was brought into play under the leadership of Kiwi. This force of 1,000 men foregathered at Whāingaroa, and embarking in canoes, had sailed for Aotea and the Kāwhia harbour. A decade earlier such a proceeding would not have been safe as the Ngāti Toa and their allies, with the northern shores of Kāwhia as their starting point, often raided the Whāingaroa country. Indeed, colonies of the Ngāti Koata tribe at one time settled on the slopes of Karioi mountain, on the south side of the entrance to the harbour.

Kiwi's invasion fleet on approaching Kāwhia divided into two. The first section entered Aotea and made a landing at the southern end of the harbour. The remaining canoes continued slowly to the entrance of Kāwhia harbour. The first section, after an unopposed landing in the Aotea joined up with Pikia's force of Ngāti Hikairo at Mōkaikainga, on the narrow land barrier between the two harbours. The combined force, now numbering 1,000 men, moved off toward Motungaio and Pouewe *pā*. It was found that with the exception of these two strongholds the whole of the northern shores of the Kāwhia harbour had been evacuated by the Ngāti Toa and allies. The two *pā* were manned by garrisons of Ngāti Koata. By the time the invaders had surrounded Motungaio and Pouewe, the second section of the seaborne force had entered the harbour and landed at Mātaatua point about a mile away. This force numbered 500 men.

After a short conference the war leaders decided to leave the two *pā* of Motungaio and Pouewe to be dealt with by Pikia and his Ngāti Hikairo men and an extra 250 men under Te Hiakai, making in all 750 men. That left 750 men under the command of Kiwi, whose force was destined for the assault on Te Maika and Te Tōtara *pā*. With Kiwi was the seasoned warrior chieftain Te Kanawa (sometimes called Haututu).

III

Te Wherowhero's overland force came by the Te Rauamoa saddle and along the famous Tirohanga-Kāwhia track. On reaching the Ōpārau river near its mouth, Te Wherowhero detailed Pikia and his Ngāti Hikairo force of 500 men to proceed along the northern stretch of Kāwhia harbour by way of Puti to Mōkaikainga where the junction was to be made with Kiwi.

The remaining force of 1,500 men with Te Wherowhero himself in command turned southward and proceeded on its way. They were unchallenged until the Kinohaku gap was reached. Here a further division was made and Te Rangituatea and his force of 500 of the Ngāti Maniapoto tribe swung southwestward around to the south of the Taharoa hills, the southern bastion of the centre of the Ngāti Toa lands around Taharoa lake. Te Rangituatea's task was to attack in detail the chain of fortified outposts along the Taharoa hills and to probe a way into the inner defences of Taharoa.

IV

On word being received that Te Wherowhero had reached Kinohaku, Kiwi sent a small force under Te Kanawa across the harbour in canoes. This force landed at night on Te Maika point just inside the entrance to Kāwhia harbour.

Te Maika point was only lightly held by Ngāti Toa. They had a much larger force in reserve across the inlet in the famous Te Tōtara Pā. Ngāti Toa scouts reported the landing and before dawn next morning a detachment from Te Tōtara garrison had joined the force on outpost duty at Te Maika. In the meantime, Te Kanawa had sent word back to Kiwi of the success of his landing.

With the first streaks of dawn lighting up the summer mists over Pirongia mountain, Te Kanawa set off up the ridge which forms the backbone of Te Maika peninsula. He had proceeded about half a mile along the ridge when he was confronted by a party of Ngāti Toa warriors. On turning to go back, he found he had been cut off. He gave a warning cry and made a dash down the eastern slope of the hill. Jumping and leaping he was soon down on the beach, only to find himself cut off by another party of Ngāti Toa warriors who barred his way back to his encampment at the point.

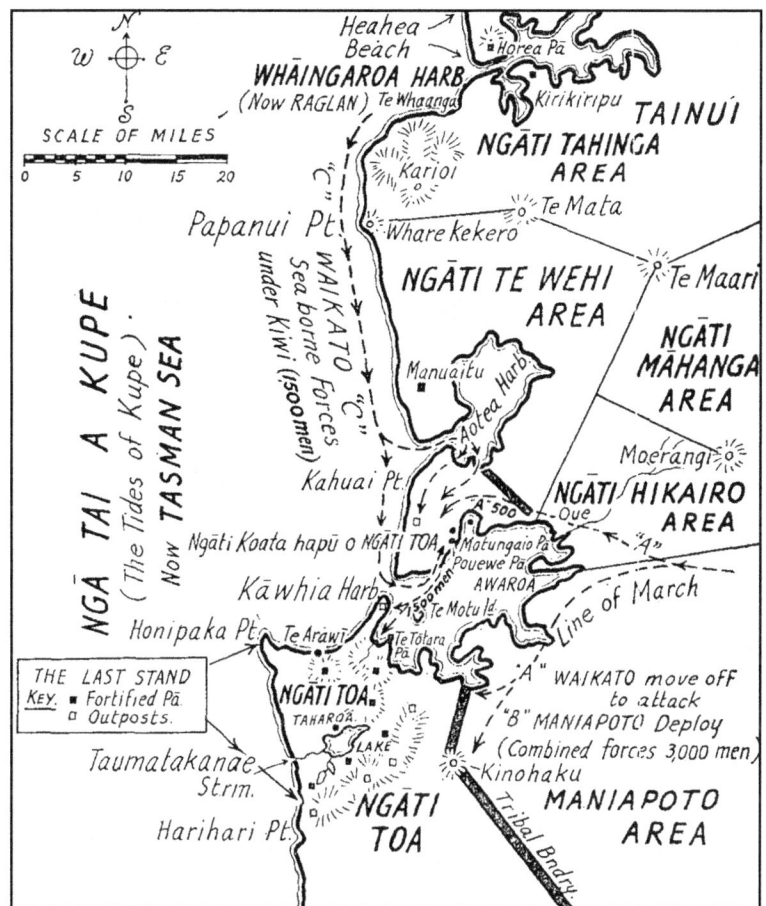

THE APPROACHING DOOM OF NGĀTI TOA

Meanwhile, a party of Te Kanawa's men had rushed up the hill from where his call had been heard and they had driven off the Ngāti Toa. By this time Te Kanawa had retreated along the beach to a point under an almost perpendicular cliff. Beyond that point was a treacherous mudflat. Te Kanawa made a quick appraisal of his position. Above him a *pōhutukawa*[1] tree grew out of the cliff face. The four Ngāti Toa men who had barred his way had advanced slowly upon him as he moved along to where he now stood at bay. The position where they had him closed in was flanked by heaps of broken rock. Te Kanawa's men on the hill above were unaware of their leader's predicament.

The four Ngāti Toa were young and untried fighting men and one of them had recognised in Te Kanawa one of the redoubtable warriors of Waikato. At a safe distance the young warriors stopped. They were overwhelmed by the great reputation of their quarry and for the moment were quite undecided as to how they were to deal with him. At last the one who had recognised Te Kanawa called out. "Hā! ka okaoka he ara mō te tama a Rahuruake!" (Ha! the son of Rahuruake will have to bore his way out now!) A nervous laugh from his companions, which Te Kanawa particularly noticed, greeted this sally.

This was the psychological moment, thought Te Kanawa, and the next instant, using his *taiaha* to pole vault, he leaped to one side and upward toward the *pōhutukawa* tree above. Before the Ngāti Toa men realised what he was doing Te Kanawa had drawn himself out of their reach and was looking down on them several feet above from where he had leaped and on the top side of the tree. In his leap Te Kanawa had grazed his shins against the sharp edge of a projecting rock, and as he stood above on the cliff face, the blood from his wound dripped down on to the stones below.

From his present position Te Kanawa found that a fairly easy way led to the cliff top. After resting a while he set off, and as he did so the spokesman for the Ngāti Toa came up to the foot of the cliff and stooping down began to lick up the blood. Every now and again he would look up at Te Kanawa with a look of evident enjoyment on his face and would ejaculate, "*Ā hā, hā!*" and return to licking up Te Kanawa's blood. High up on the cliff face Te Kanawa paused and looking down at the young man he called out, "*Koi nā anake māu. Tukua ake nei, ko koe, pakapaka ana i tāku hāngi!*" (That is all you will have. And as for you, you will shortly be roasted to a turn in my earth-oven!)

Te Kanawa rejoined his men on the hilltop and was greeted with the news that the first lot of the main force under Kiwi had already landed and the rest were on their way across from the northern side of the harbour. He also learnt that the Ngāti Toa had begun to evacuate Te Maika. Before midday the main force had already been landed at Te Maika and Kiwi and his war chiefs had foregathered on the beach to discuss the plans for the battle of Te Taharoa.

V

With the occupation of Te Maika by the Waikato, Te Rauparaha decided to move a particularly strong force to the foothills near the extremity of the inlet which separates Te Maika from Te Tōtara peninsula, to bar the way to Te Tōtara Pā.

But danger threatened from another quarter, for by this time Te Wherowhero had speedily broken through the Kinohaku gap to the east and had closed in on the forts guarding the eastern approaches to Te Taharoa lake. A strong detachment had also been moved up to seal off the garrison in Te Tōtara Pā. The rest of Te Wherowhero's forces had fanned out to link up with the Ngāti Maniapoto to the south.

These tactics of the Waikato leader proved successful and Te Rauparaha had to make a rapid reorganisation of his defences. The Ngāti Toa garrison in Te Tōtara Pā was evacuated before the position could be bypassed or isolated. By this time, too, the Maniapoto under Tūkōrehu had joined up with Te Rangituatea, and they had sealed off the Ngāti Akamapuhia forces at Harihari on the coast. The systematic reduction of the outposts along the Taharoa hills was also well advanced.

The following days were hectic and trying ones for Te Rauparaha. At this critical stage in the fortunes of his people fate seemed to mock the great Ngāti Toa leader, for he became ill and had to retire to his impregnable *pā* at Te Arawī and the command of the Ngāti Toa and their allies was handed over to his nephew, Te Rangihaeata.

VI

The unrelenting pressure of Te Wherowhero's invading army broke through the outer crust of the Ngāti Toa defences and the Waikato forces under Kiwi moved steadily over the high hills between the harbour of Kāwhia and Taharoa lake. Te Wherowhero attacked and reduced the series of fortified positions along the southern shores of the lake. While these hammer blows were being delivered the Maniapoto were loosening the coastal hinge of the Taharoa defences after having eliminated the outer defences between Kinohaku and the sea. In a final assault from three points, the south, north and east, the invasion army finally broke through on to the sandhills at the western end of the lake and the Ngāti Toa were driven back into the two *pā* of Te Kawau and Te Roto at the western end of the lake where the Taumatakanae stream flows to the western sea.

VII

Te Wherowhero and his army encamped on the banks of the Taumatakanae and he called a conference of his war chiefs. That night they discussed the problem of whether they should attack the two Ngāti Toa *pā* in force, or whether they should be besieged and the garrisons starved out. But as events turned out this problem was to be solved for them by the Ngāti Toa. During the night a large number of them made contact with some of their Ngāti Maniapoto kinsmen and, as opportunity offered, these people were conducted safely through the lines of the invasion army and allowed to escape southward. These refugees formed the vanguard of the flight from Kāwhia.

That night Te Rauparaha rose from his sick couch and painfully made his way over the intervening hills to Te Kawau Pā. His body was covered in boils and he ached in every limb. A council of war was held and Te Rangihaeata urged that they should break up into small groups and scatter to various points among the surrounding ranges from where they could carry on a guerrilla war. Pokaitara was for a break-through in one body to the south of Mōkau into Ngāti Tama territory, there to regroup their forces and recruit a large army for the re-conquest of their ancestral lands. Te Pūoho, who possessed a gun, was for fighting it out and deciding the issue on the banks of Taumatakanae. Te Pūoho and Ranginumia had come from the south with Raparapa and they had come to fight they said. Raparapa, the famous Ngāti Tama warrior, was particularly anxious to test his skill as a *taiaha* man against the best the Waikato had to offer. At the end of a lively discussion Te Rauparaha made his decision. They would fight it out on the field of Te Kakara, the flat land at the western end of the lake, above the place where generations of their people had harvested the succulent silver-bellied eels on their annual migrations out to sea.

The next day came with a blood-red dawn and with clouds strung out along the eastern ranges. Some days before the Ngāti Toa had fired the scrub on the Te Kakara flat, and in the early morning light the Waikato sentries reported that a large force from Te Kawau and Te Roto *pā* had assembled at the far side of the cleared ground. The two forces took up their positions face to face and for a time there was silence. Both armies were recumbent. The only sound came from the breaking surf of Ngā Tai a Kupe, "the tides of Kupe"— the Western Sea.

The Ngāti Toa formed up into ranks and were addressed by Te Rauparaha. He exhorted them to fight as they had never fought before.

In an impassioned peroration, he conjured up pictures of the past, of Kāwhia harbour and the tree-covered island gem of Te Motu (now only a bare sandbank, devoid of vegetation). He called to mind their illustrious dead lying in their last long sleep in the subterranean burial cave of Muriwhenua—their ancestral sepulchre outside Te Maika point, the entrance to which was by an underwater opening among the rocks.[2] The great Ngāti Toa then led his people in his famous *haka*:

TE NGERI A TE RAUPARAHA

Whiti Tuatahi

Haramai ana te rongo o te riri!
I mua;
I muri;
I a Muriwhenua,
I a Te Maha i ara!
E hara teke pakupaku, e Kui!
E hara teke pakupaku, e Koro!
E kei te Uru?
E kei te Tonga!
E kei te rākau pakeke ki au,ē!

Whiti Tuarua

Kīkiki!
Kokoko!
Kei waniwania taku hika;
Kei tara-wāhia!
Kei te rua i te Karokaro
He pounga rāhui!
He uira ki te Rangi!
Ketekete mai hoki tō poro kai-riri;
"Māu au, e Koro ē?
I a, ka wehi au, ka mataku!"
Ko wai te tangata kia rere ure?
Tirohanga ngā rua rerarera
Hei a kurī ka kamukamu!

Whiti Mutunga

Ka mate! Ka mate!
Ka ora! Ka ora!
Tēnei te tangata pūhuruhuru,
Nāna nei i tiki mai
I whakawhiti te rā!
Upane! Upane!
Upane! Ka upane!
Whiti te rā!

TE RAUPARAHA'S WAR CHANT [3]

FIRST STANZA

Solo   Ha! 'tis tidings of war that come!
      It comes from afore;
      It comes from aft!
Chorus It comes from the Muriwhenua Clan!
5   It comes from The Many!
      It cometh not from a small cavity, O Lady!
      It cometh not from a small cavity, O Sire;
Solo   Does it come from the West?
Chorus Nay, it comes from the South!
10 Solo Ah! Then it comes with evil intent
      For me and mine!

SECOND STANZA

Solo   Let your valour arise!
      Let your temper rage!
Chorus We'll ward off the desecrating touch;
15   We'll ward off the impious hand;
      We'll ne'er let the foe
      Outrage our cherished ones!
      We'll guard our women and our maidens;
      And be thou, O Leader, our boundary Pillar!
20 Solo For ye all, I'll defy the lightning of the Heavens!
Chorus The foe, he will stand frustrated;
      In his mad and impotent rage!
Solo   Mine ears will then be spared

>   The maidens' despairing cry
> 25 "Will ye, O Sir, possess me?
>   The thought it makes me quail!"
> Chorus Who, in his manhood will stand affrighted;
>   Or in his terror, flee?
>   For he will surely perish
> 30 And in the refuse pit will lie
>   As food for dogs to gnaw with relish!

FINALE

>   Avaunt, O Death! Avaunt, O Death!
>   Ah, 'tis Life! 'Tis Life!
>   Behold! There stands the hairy man
> 35 Who will cause the sun to shine!
>   One upward step! Another upward step!
>   One last upward step;
>   Then step forth! Into the Sun—
>   The Sun that shines!

By the time the Ngāti Toa leader had finished his *haka* his warriors were fully roused. But he, the great Te Rauparaha, was a mass of running sores and was on the verge of collapse. At this moment an incident occurred which disturbed Te Rauparaha and which he interpreted as a foreboding of evil. A dog with almost golden hair, a *kurī kura*, which the Waikato looked upon as a mascot, rushed out and ran through the ranks of Ngāti Toa and returned unharmed. Te Rauparaha slowly moved off and in great agony of mind and body retired to the Te Kawau Pā, where he was carried up on to the look-out tower. From this vantage point he watched the progress of the battle of Te Kakara for a time. He then asked to be rowed out in a canoe on the lake. Some distance offshore with the field of Te Kakara in view, Te Rauparaha ordered the boy who took him out in the canoe to stop paddling. The lad lay down at the bow, and with his head cupped in his hands, he gazed wide-eyed toward Te Kakara. At the stern Te Rauparaha sat bolt upright, with all his senses on the alert, and followed the battle with eye and ear. Now and again he would turn slowly around, his eyes sweeping the whole panorama spread out around him. He knew every nook and corner; on the shores of Taharoa he had played about as a boy; he had swum on its kindly bosom and he knew its every mood; he had trudged over every ridge; he had snared the bird life on the forest-clad ranges. Along the many trails he had come and

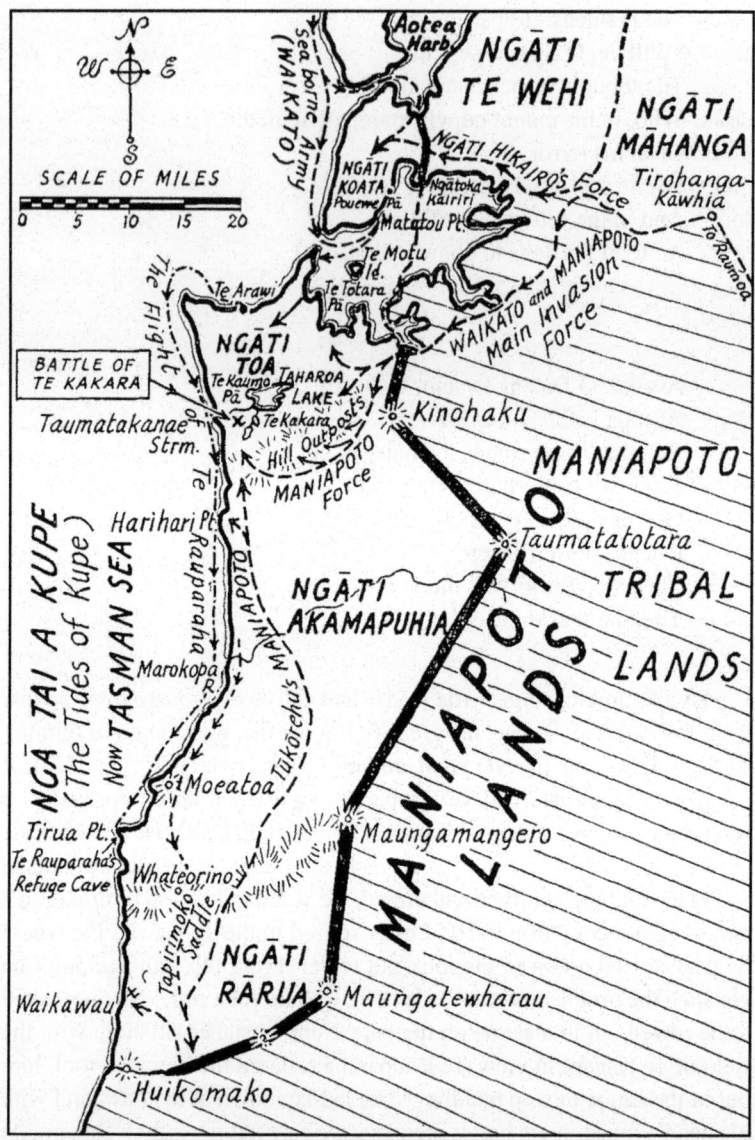

THE BATTLE OF KĀWHIA

gone, sometimes with a song in his heart and sometimes with sorrow and anxiety dogging his every step. Generally life in Te Taharoa was quiet and peaceful and he loved this ancestral home of his people with his whole being. As he gazed around him his heart ached within him. Here let us leave Te Rauparaha with his poignant thoughts, a lonely figure silhouetted against the waters of Taharoa as he drifted in that forlorn canoe—sometimes sharply etched against the gleaming waters, and often almost lost in the shadows as the lake changed its mood with the passing clouds.

We now return to the scene of combat to recount the opening of the battle of Te Kakara. The aged Te Rauangaanga who had accompanied the invading army in the role of high priest and as mentor to his son Te Wherowhero, after the Ngāti Toa had finished their war chant, arose from the ranks of the Waikato and with the old fire in his voice he chanted his battle song. The memory of the epic field of Hingakākā was vividly brought to mind. Several Waikato warriors were transported, and in their excitement they grasped their *taiaha* and *mere*. They pranced to and fro, they leaped and made passes and sweeping strokes with their *taiaha*. They grimaced and slowly made their way across the field toward the Ngāti Toa.

The latter watched in tense silence as the Waikato steadily approached, every now and again pausing to pose in the challenging stance of the *marangai areare*.[4] Suddenly there was a loud report and one of the Waikato fell writhing in the ash-strewn ground and among the fire-blackened clumps of *tutu* (Coriaria ruscifolia). Te Pūoho had claimed the first slain in battle or the *mātāngohi* with his gun. The remaining warriors paused momentarily and then again advanced. Te Pūoho reloaded and fired. Another Waikato fell heavily to the ground. The Waikato warriors still advanced and Te Pūoho still fired with deadly effect.

With the fall of some of their leading warriors the Waikato ranks were agitated and a number who were related to those who had fallen now began to move forward. Te Pūoho's gun still claimed its toll. At last, as the ranks of the advancing Waikato were thinned, the remaining warriors began to fall back. At this point Te Pūoho was about to fire again when Raparapa, his comrade the great Ngāti Tama leader and *taiaha* expert, moved up to him and pushed his gun aside, at the same time exclaiming, "*Kāti rā mā tō pū, kei kore hoki mā taku ringa!*" (That is enough for your gun, or there will be none for this weaponed hand of mine!)

Now it was Te Pūoho who had prevailed on Raparapa to come through for the Kāwhia fighting. Raparapa's wife, Te Maropounamu the sister of the Ngāti Tama chieftain Tūpoki and a noted poetess, had a premonition of evil and had strenuously objected to her husband accompanying Te Pūoho. She had hidden her husband's heavily woven body-covering which he always wore in battle, and which had been named Matarua, "the dual-eyed one", because he could rely on this protective covering against thrusts and blows he failed to parry, as it was so heavily woven that it was impervious to the Māori weapons of war. But Raparapa had decided to go and his wife's action in hiding Matarua did not stop him. He came to Taharoa without it.

With the cessation of firing, some of the Waikato warriors stopped in midfield and looked back toward the Ngāti Toa ranks. Some were half-minded to continue the advance against the foe. At this juncture Raparapa was getting ready to make a dash, his *taiaha* firmly grasped in his muscular right hand and his *pātītī* (hatchet) in his belt. As he was about to rush forward to engage the foe, Te Ākau, one of Te Rauparaha's wives who was moving through the ranks of the Ngāti Toa to encourage them and who overheard what Raparapa had said to Te Pūoho, called out to Raparapa, "O Rapa! Let the gun settle!" To this Raparapa disdainfully replied, "Who said I should be taught by a woman!"

The next moment Raparapa had moved off toward the Waikato warriors who still stood their ground in the centre of the field. Several Ngāti Toa warriors followed him. Advancing boldly, Raparapa appeared to overawe the waiting Waikato men and several of them fell under his swift blows. With the fall of the first, Raparapa called out, "I claim the *mātāngohi*!" He thus conveyed his contempt for Te Pūoho's gun, the plebeian weapon of the European which killed at a distance but did not give one renown; nor did it require the skill and courage to use and face the weapons of the Māori. Several Waikato warriors fell under the lightning blows of Raparapa and he still moved forward. At this stage Raparapa had discarded his *taiaha* and had pulled out his *pātītī*. The next Waikato warrior was able to keep Raparapa at a distance for a time and they fought on. At last, however, Raparapa stepped inside his guard and struck him down. In delivering the deathblow Raparapa buried his *pātītī* so deeply into the body of the Waikato that he could not immediately pull it free. This victim was some chief of note and before the Waikato warriors realised what was happening Raparapa had slung the inert body across his shoulders and started back across the battlefield with his trophy. The Ngāti Māhanga and Whāingaroa leader Te Awaitaia was the first to react to the audacious action of the Ngāti Tama warrior. Te Awaitaia rose from the ranks of the main body and set out in pursuit. Raparapa kept steadily on. Halfway across the field Te Awaitaia was very rapidly overtaking Raparapa when the latter tripped over a burnt clump of *tutu*. Some accounts say Raparapa was felled by Te Awaitaia which, of course, would add more lustre to the fame of the Ngāti Māhanga leader, but this story is not generally accepted by the tribes other than by the Ngāti Māhanga.

There was a violent struggle on the ash-covered ground. Here again accounts differ. Some say Te Awaitaia stood by while Raparapa struggled with a powerful Waikato wrestler named Te Rangiwhakaia and only stepped forward to strike the deathblow after Raparapa had weakened. Another account has it that Te Awaitaia did not kill Raparapa when he struck him and that it was another warrior named Rota who delivered the deathblow.

When Raparapa at last lay dead Te Awaitaia arose and called out, "I have killed Raparapa!" No one disputed Te Awaitaia's claim. In any case, at that time the Waikato, after seeing the fall of Raparapa, were surging across the battlefield toward the ranks of the Ngāti Toa.

Te Pūoho, after his rebuff at the hands of Raparapa, was so insulted that he left the field of battle, and we hear little more of him until some years later when he led an expedition down the west coast of the South Island and across the Southern Alps, to meet his death in the fighting with one of the tribes of the region.

To return to the battle of Te Kakara: The fall of Raparapa had been the signal for a grand assault by Te Wherowhero's army, for it was at that moment that he had given the order to advance to the attack. A merciless struggle took place, with the now thoroughly roused Waikato pressing forward relentlessly. The Ngāti Toa were gradually forced back and finally split in two. One section fled southward and after coming up with Te Pūoho, who had watched the battle from a high hill, they selected him as their leader and continued their way to the land of the Ngāti Tama in the south Mōkau district. The remaining half of the Ngāti Toa and their allies retired into Te Kawau Pā. By the late afternoon the battle of Te Kakara was ended with Te Wherowhero's army victorious.

Te Kawau and Te Roto *pā* were besieged, and this lasted for some days during which time large numbers of the garrison were allowed to evacuate in small parties and to make their way southward to the Ngāti Tama land. Te Kawau and Te Roto, with their garrisons much depleted, shortly afterward fell. Te Rauparaha, with a small number of his tribesmen—mostly his close relatives—had made their way to Te Arawī Pā on the day of the defeat at Te Kakara.

In the meantime the early refugees from Te Taharoa had reached Te Kawau Pā, south of Mōkau in Ngāti Tama territory, where Te Maropounamu anxiously awaited news of her husband Raparapa. The news of his death was a severe blow to the Ngāti Tama, following as it did so soon after the fall of Tūpoki, his brother-in-law, and the brother of Te Maropounamu, at Pararewa. For Te Awaitaia it was a signal honour and in song and story his name has been commemorated in connection with the fall of Raparapa. Te Maropounamu was distracted with grief. In her pain and sorrow she composed and sang this lament:

TE TANGI MŌ RAPARAPA

E Rangi, i raro rā, whakarongo mai rā!
Ka whiwhi 'nō au i ngā paura nei?
Nāu, e Te Pūoho, i tioka haere;
Tuku ana mai te ia o Taumatakanae!
I haere kahu-kore te kiri o te makau!
Tēnei Matarua nāku i kaiapo:
Kei te titi-poutia te manu a Titapu,
Hei urupare mōhou tana uru-māwhatu!
Ki konei tonu au whakamau atu ai,
Ō-kuku ai ō pae-tārewa.
Tō mata whakatangi ki te uhi a Tonga;
Ka tau 'nō, ē!

Ako noa au ō tītahatanga,
Ō hau-miringa i ako ai rā nge au!
E tika koutou nā runga o Kāwhia;
Mō Waitangi, ē, mō Te Unuatahu
E takoto i raro rā
Tēnei kei roto, e rau a Pare'!
Tohitū te haere ki roto o Waikato;
Kia whakaputa koe ki mua ki te upoko!
Nāu i kaiapo i te riri māhau!
Hare rawa tō rongo Te Rerenga Wairua!
Kia ruku atu koe ngā Ngaru a Kupe!
Kia kumea mai ko te pū kei Oropi
Ka huri atu ki tua te moana i hoea:
Kia kai atu au i te wai takataka:
Nā Ngāti Māhanga e haere i raro rā!

LAMENT FOR RAPARAPA[5]

O *Rangi*, in the north, hearken unto me!
May I not become possessed of some powder?
It was you, O *Te Pūoho*, who lured him away,
And o'erwhelmed he was by the current of *Taumatakanae*!
5 Alas, unclad was the body of my beloved when he went his way!
For here, behold, is *Matarua*, which I selfishly withheld.
And here, in readiness, O Beloved, is your Plume of the Heron!
In mute inquiry it awaits your wavy locks:
Here also am I patiently waiting,
10 To smooth away the lines from your furrowed brow,
And from your face, scored o'er with poetic lines of *Tonga*:
Alas, I sink down with grief, Ah me!

Too well, I learnt to enjoy your embrace,
And your fond caresses too I now long for in vain!
15 Proceed you by way of Kāwhia
Where ye o'ercame *Waitangi* and *Te Unuatahu*
They do now repose in here below—
Indeed, here, within they do lie,
O ye hundreds of *Pare'*!

20 Undeviating, proceed ye into Waikato;
So that ye may be seen in the forefront!
Thou didst selfishly take more than your share of battle!
Your fame had already reached The Leaping Place of Spirits!
Plunge thou then into the Waves of *Kupe*!
25 And bring back the gun from *Oropi*.
O'er, yonder are the navigable waters
Where I could partake of the brains
Of that *Ngāti Māhanga* who travels about in the North!

NOTES ON CHAPTER 5

Note 1

    pōhutukawa: (*Metrosideros tomentosa*), the Christmas tree of New Zealand.

Note 2

    Muriwhenua burial cave: The Ngāti Toa, when depositing their honoured dead in this subterranean cave, swam out to a sea-girt rock called Te Kawau, which marked the opening to the cave. Here they dived down to the opening and into the cave where they left the bodies.

Note 3

    Te Rauparaha's War Chant.

(4) Muriwhenua clan: Many Waikato warriors were descendants of a noted warrior ancestor of this name.

(9) Nay, it comes from the South: This is a reference to the Maniapoto force under the leader Tūkōrehu, which had come from the south after the fall of Waikawau Pā.

(14) We'll ward off the desecrating touch: There was a pointed reference in this and succeeding lines to the sister of Te Wharepuhi who was outraged and shamefully treated by the Waikato some years before. (See page 53)

    General comment: As is usual with chants of this nature the topical allusions are generally altered to suit the circumstances and the personalities concerned at the time the performance is given.

Note 4

    Marangai areare: As stated, this is a challenging stance. The *taiaha* or spear is carried aloft and the point is turned toward the enemy. At the same time the warrior makes grimaces at the foe.

Note 5

    Lament for Raparapa

(1) O Rangi: A term of endearment much used in Māori poetry, with the literal meaning, "O thou heavenly being." In the present instance the reference is to Raparapa.

(2) some powder: Powder for the new weapon of the European was a much sought after commodity. In this instance the poetess, nursing

feelings of revenge, is hoping that powder will be obtained to enable her people to assuage the pain of sorrow.

(3) Te Pūoho: The reference to Te Pūoho in this lament is explained in the account of the battle of Taharoa (page 64)

(4) Taumatakanae: "The Pathway of the Mullet," is the name of the stream that flows out of Taharoa lake.

(6) Matarua: This body protector was worn like a waistcoat. It was woven from specially prepared flax fibre and was of a double thickness. The name Matarua might also be interpreted descriptively as "the double surface."

(11) lines of Tonga: This refers to the intricate, and specially distinctive tattooing on Raparapa's face. An untattooed face was termed *mōwai*, or plain, and a man with a good tattooed face was often referred to as having a *mata ora*, "a living countenance".

(16) Waitangi and Unuatahu: Two Waikato men whom Raparapa had killed in previous fighting. The latter is mentioned in Chapter 4. The poetess boasts that she had partaken of the flesh of these two men when she says "...here, within they do lie." These references to cannibalism are often only used as taunts. The actual eating may have been by other members of the tribe.

(19) Pare': The name in full is Paretekōrae who was also a poetess, but more famous because she accompanied the Tainui war-parties in their expeditions and acted as a priestess in the lifting of the hauhauaitu (said of a warrior who was demoralised, felt listless and unequal to the strain of fighting). In the ritual, the warrior, at the end, was required to pass under the thighs of the young chieftainess or priestess.

(24) Waves of Kupe (Ngā Ngaru a Kupe): A name applied to the sea along the west coast of the North Island of New Zealand. It was also called *Ngā Tai a Kupe*, "the tides of Kupe." Kupe was the name of the Polynesian discoverer of Aotearoa.

(25) Oropi: Māori version of Europe.

(26) Navigable waters: Refers to Whāingaroa (now Raglan harbour), the ancestral homeland of Te Awaitaia, the Ngāti Māhanga chieftain who had killed Raparapa. Te Awaitaia also belonged to the Tainui tribe of Whāingaroa, and other tribes of the Waikato. The poetess, with the thought of revenge in her mind,' conjures up a picture

of a war-party armed with "the gun from Europe", marching into Whāingaroa and killing Te Awaitaia.

(28) that Ngāti Māhanga: Refers to Te Awaitaia.

APPENDIX TO CHAPTER 5

TE AWAITAIA

A narrative by Roore Erueti of the Ngāti Māhanga-Hourua tribes.

Te Awaitaia, the Ngāti Māhanga warrior, was the outstanding *toa* on the Te Kakara field of battle. He had to be restrained by Te Wherowhero when Raparapa was advancing through the ranks of the Waikato warriors, so anxious was he to engage Raparapa, the Ngāti Tama *toa*. At one stage Te Punatoto, the Ngāti Māhanga leader, ordered his company to retire so as to leave the Taumatakanae stream between them and the enemy. Te Awaitaia on hearing the order called out from the ranks, *"E kawea ana te riri a te tama a Rawharangi ki whea?"* (To what place is the son of Rawharangi taking his fight?) Rawharangi was the mother of Punatoto. This question by Te Awaitaia caused Punatoto to stop. It also drew the attention of Raparapa to Te Awaitaia, and the Ngāti Tama fighter moved across and issued a challenge to the Ngāti Māhanga *toa*.

Te Awaitaia immediately responded and soon they were engaged in a fierce duel. Both men were tall, Te Awaitaia being slimly built, while Raparapa was of a heavier type and very powerful. Te Awaitaia was armed with a *tewhatewha* (a wooden weapon about 5ft. long with an axe-shaped head). Te Awaitaia was supple and was very skilful in avoiding blows and thrusts. The duel continued for some time without either man gaining the advantage. Then Te Awaitaia quickly stepped aside and held his *tewhatewha* in a *kōrapa* (awkward) stance. Raparapa immediately stepped forward to deliver a powerful blow. As he did so Te Awaitaia brought the blade end of his *tewhatewha* up with a quick jerk catching the back of the blade of Raparapa's weapon which was sent flying through the air to be caught in flight by Tireke, a Waikato warrior. Thus disarmed, Raparapa turned and fled toward the ranks of the Ngāti Toa with Te Awaitaia in pursuit.

In his flight Raparapa circled a high clump of *tutu*. As he moved around this obstruction he was struck by Te Awaitaia with his *mere* which the latter had aimed and thrown at his adversary, at the same time leaping over the *tutu* clump to land on Raparapa and bear him down. A desperate struggle took place on the ash-strewn ground. Te Rangihokaia at this stage rushed up and jumped on one of the struggling men whom he thought was Raparapa. Rangihokaia was an uncle of Te Awaitaia and after a while he recognised the *rape* (thigh tattoo) of Te Awaitaia. Realising his mistake he called out, "*Auē, e tama āku ē!*" (Alas, O son of mine!) and immediately turned toward Raparapa. The latter had now recovered his breath and he immediately caught hold of Rangihokaia and, throwing him over his shoulder, began to carry him off the field. Another Waikato warrior named Pikimaunga now ran in front of Raparapa and, calling out to Rangihokaia, "*Tareratia tō poho!*" (Draw in your belly!), he thrust his spear into Raparapa's body and killed him there and then.

TE ARAWĪ

AND THE

FLIGHT FROM KĀWHIA

(Te Arawī— "The Slender and Dangerous Pathway")

Tērā ia ngā Tai o Honipaka,
Ka wehe koe i au, ē,
He whakamaunga atu nāku
Te au ka tākawe
Nā runga ana mai o Te Motu,
E tū noa mai rā koe ki au ē.

Nō te Waiata Poroporoaki a Te Rauparaha ki Kāwhia

O'er yonder, flow the Tides of Honipaka,
Now parted from me for ever:
In spirit still to thee I cling
And my heart oppressed
Grieves o'er that world apart
That lies outspread above Te Motu,
My woeful fate unheeding...

From Te Rauparaha's Farewell Song to Kāwhia

CHAPTER 6

TE ARAWĪ AND THE FLIGHT FROM KĀWHIA

I

We now come to the last phase in the battle of Kāwhia. Te Rauparaha with a small remnant of his Ngāti Toa were now in Te Arawī Pā. Te Arawī is a cliff-faced tableland jutting out into the bay outside the entrance to Kāwhia harbour. It lies to the north of Taharoa Lake and is connected to the mainland on the south by a short and narrow neck of land. The *pā* is inaccessible except by this narrow strip, wide enough for only one man to pass at a time. As it could not be carried by storm the invasion army laid siege to it with the intention of starving out its garrison.

Among the Ngāti Toa leaders who made a belated attempt to reach Te Arawī were Te Arawaka and Te Whakataupotiki. The former was engaged in single combat by Te Whakaete and killed. Te Whakataupotiki was killed by Takiwaru, or Kati, Te Wherowhero's younger brother, also in single combat. An incident concerning Te Kanawa is related of the time when he was nearly overtaken by Te Rangihaeata, Te Rauparaha's nephew, and escaped only by leaping over a cliff. In another account the incident is transferred back to Te Maika beach and Te Rangihaeata is named as the young warrior who licked up Te Kanawa's blood.

That night the *pā* was completely sealed off. Two strong parties stood guard and patrolled the beaches on each side of Te Arawī and the main investing force took up its position at the entrance and on the hill overlooking the *pā*.

During the first night of the siege there was a lot of trafficking between the beleaguered forces and various leaders of the invaders. Many in the opposing forces were related and several of the besieged either made overtures through their relatives among the invaders, or were invited to leave Te Arawī. All of these were allowed to escape by means of ropes let down the cliff face to the beaches below. Two high-born women of Ngāti Toa who were captured outside the *pā* were allowed to join Te Rauparaha in Te Arawī. This was done at the request of the commander-in-chief (Te Wherowhero) himself. It will have been noted that Te Wherowhero has not been specially mentioned in connection with the actual fighting. The conduct of the war had occupied most of his time and he had been particularly busy in this respect. There are also indications that he had a sneaking regard for his adversary, and that he admired Te Rauparaha for his unquenchable spirit.

The parley between the two leaders over the fate of the two women was concluded by Te Rauparaha who called out to Te Wherowhero, "*Ki a koe te wāhi nui o te marae o Pāwera, ki au te wāhi iti.*" (You are taking unto yourself the greater part of the courtyard of the apprehensive mind; mine is now but a small part.) Among those who were captured before they could reach the safety of the *pā* were Taungawai, the younger brother of Te Rauparaha, and their aged father, Werawera. (Some say this Werawera was also a brother of Te Rauparaha.) Taungawai was killed by a Waikato warrior and Werawera met his death at the hands of a Ngāti Hikairo chief.

The siege of Te Arawī lasted for some weeks, different sections of the invading army taking it in turns to maintain it. Finally it came the turn of Ngāti Maniapoto under their chief Te Rangituatea who was related to Te Rauparaha (Chap. 4). Te Rangituatea had no wish to see things carried to the bitter end so far as Te Rauparaha personally was concerned.

When the opportunity offered, and the Waikato tribes were away foraging for food, Te Rangituatea approached the entrance to the *pā* and addressing the sentries from high ground overlooking the spot, asked them to fetch Te Rauparaha as he wished to speak to him. Te Rauparaha came and Te Rangituatea said, "Withdraw from here and go before it is too late. Go all that can and leave those who are unable to travel as cinders for your dying fires. Go to Taranaki, to Āti Awa (tribe) and to safety!" The Āti Awa tribe lived to the south of Ngāti Tama and Te Rauparaha—and Te Rangituatea too—could claim relationship to these people. Te Rangituatea knew then that the Waikato leaders were already talking about attacking the Ngāti Tama tribe, hence Te Rangituatea's advice to Te Rauparaha to go further south to the Āti Awa country. Te Rauparaha suggested that he might flee to his Ngāti Raukawa kinsmen of Maungatautari and Wharepuhunga. To this suggestion Te Rangituatea at once said, "You cannot pass that way. Your *pā ngaio* (ngaio a tree; stronghold or haven of refuge) lies there!" and pointed in the direction of Taranaki. Then Te Rangituatea added, "If you persist in going to the Ngāti Raukawa (tribe) the upper jaw (Waikato tribes) will close down on the lower jaw (Maniapoto tribes)."

Te Rangituatea arranged for canoes that same night and he also persuaded Te Hiakai to assist with the procuring of canoes. The latter was invited by Te Rauparaha into Te Arawī to confer with him, and Te Hiakai went. As they parted at the entrance to the *pā* Te Rauparaha called out to Te Hiakai, "Let this be your land!" To this Te Hiakai stretched out his hand behind his back, opening it and closing it in silent acquiescence.

II

Most of the garrison was allowed to escape by land. Canoes were provided for Te Rauparaha, Te Rangihaeata and Te Kākākura, the three remaining Ngāti Toa leaders in Te Arawī. In the dead of night Te Rauparaha and his people embarked and after rounding Honipaka point they set a course south for Tīrua point where Te Rauparaha had his refuge cave at Te Titimatarua and Te Urungaparaoa.

We will here make brief mention of the siege of Motungaio and Pouewe *pā*, which were besieged by the forces under Pikia. The Ngāti Koata garrisons of these *pā* were related in varying degrees to both the Ngāti Toa and Ngāti Te Wehi tribes and this circumstance soon led to an armistice being declared during which the Ngāti Koata party divided into two sections, one throwing in their lot with the Ngāti Te Wehi, the other deciding to follow the Ngāti Toa. This arrangement was completed before Te Rauparaha left Te Arawī and explains the appearance of Te Hiakai there just before Te Rauparaha sailed.

After reaching Tīrua Point Te Rangihaeata and Te Kākākura did not remain there for any length of time. These two left Te Rauparaha in his cliff refuge and turned back north to Kiritehere on the northern side of their ancestral mountain of Moeatoa, the place that had previously been selected as a rendezvous. At Kiritehere, Te Rangihaeata and Te Kākākura found a large number of the refugees from Kāwhia and Te Taharoa.

The remnants of the Ngāti Toa, Ngāti Koata, Ngāti Akamapuhia and Ngāti Rārua tribes were gathered by their leaders Te Rangihaeata, Te Peehi Kupe, Tungia, Te Rangihīroa and others. In all they numbered about 1,500 men, women and children. Before leaving Moeatoa on their southward trek Te Rauparaha was brought from Tīrua and plans were discussed. It was decided that they should proceed in separate parties and travel as rapidly as possible before any attempt was made to intercept them at the Mōkau river. Te Rauparaha would stay on until he was fully recovered from his illness, together with a number of the wives of some of the other chiefs, and his own wives and family, and a number of children of his fellow tribesmen. In Te Rauparaha's cliff refuge they would be quite safe.

Before the tribes moved off Te Rauparaha addressed them. It was a moving spectacle and a sad occasion as Te Rauparaha recalled the past and referred to the loss of all their ancestral lands. His people listened with bowed head. Here and there some of the women wept silently. Addressing the tribal leaders he fired their imagination by telling them he had decided to lead them to fertile lands and to the conquest of southern tribes. He then again paid a tribute to the land of his ancestors. He mentioned its vales, and hills, the forest ranges, the lakes and rivers, and the burial places of their honoured dead. Cries of lamentation accompanied his oration. At last, with tears streaming down his bold, tattooed face, he looked toward Kāwhia and sang his song of farewell:

TE WAIATA POROPOROAKI A TE RAUPARAHA KI KĀWHIA.

Tērā ia ngā Tai o Honipaka,
Ka wehe koe i au, ē,
He whakamaunga atu nāku
Te ao ka tākawe
Nā runga mai o Te Motu....
E tū noa mai rā koe ki au, ē.
Ka mihi mamao au, ē,
Ki te iwi rā, ē,
Moe noa mai i te moenga roa.
Ka piki, e te tai;
Piki tū, piki rere;
Piki takina mai rā!
Te Kawau i Muriwhenua
E kawea e te tere!
Tēnā tāku manu,
He manu ka onga noa;
Rūnā ki te whare
Te hau o Matariki:
Mā te Whare pōrutu
Mā te Whare Āti Awa,
E kau-tere mai rā,
Whaka-urupā taku aroha
  Nā, ī

TE RAUPARAHA'S FAREWELL TO KĀWHIA [1]

O'er yonder flow the Tides of Honipaka,
Now parted from me for ever.
In spirit, still to thee I cling.
And my heart, sore oppress'd.
5 Grieves o'er that world apart
That lies outspread above Te Motu....
My woeful fate unheeding.
O all ye tribes that sleep—
In the last long sleep—
10 A far-off tribute now I give.
The tides will still ebb and flow...
Flowing strongly, rising and leaping;
Until, o'erleaping Te Kawau at Muriwhenua
I'll see the waves rushing by!
15 See there to my cherished bird,
'Tis with grief distracted;
And betimes, within the House of Mourning,
'Twill be hidden from mine eyes.
This gentle breeze of Summer
20 Brings hither the sound of wailing:
O thou House of Mourning!
O thou House of Āti Awa!
Lament and let tears of sorrow flow,
Ye shall indeed be a sepulchre
25 For this, my song of sorrow....
    Alas, ah me!

III

The southward march of the Ngāti Toa now commenced in earnest. Te Rauparaha himself returned to Tīrua point. Te Rangituatea, who had come overland, shortly afterward visited him there. Te Rangituatea had come alone and had been hauled up into Te Rauparaha's cave. This was the first time Te Rauparaha and Te Rangituatea had been at close quarters since their encounter at Tūtaerere some years before (para. vi Chap. 4). After saluting each other in the *hongi* (touching of noses) the two chieftains sat in silence. It is Māori etiquette in such circumstances not to be too forward in making known the purpose of one's visit, or for the host to evince too much curiosity as to the other's objective. The womenfolk set about preparing a meal for the visitor. The Maniapoto chief had brought a full calabash of preserved pigeons for the Ngāti Toa leader. It might be mentioned here that Te Rangituatea had also surreptitiously supplied the Te Arawī garrison with ample provisions during the siege.

After an appropriate interval Te Rauparaha arose and briefly welcomed his visitor. During his speech he hinted that perhaps Te Rangituatea had come to gloat over his misfortunes. The speech of the Ngāti Toa chief was calculated to give an opening to Te Rangituatea to make known the reason for his visit. Te Rauparaha throughout his life was noted for the firm grip he always tried to hold on himself and those susceptible to his dominating influence. He always preferred to be master of any situation that arose. On this occasion he wound up his speech by making mocking references to Te Rangituatea and his people. He even hinted that Te Rangituatea would not leave Te Titimatarua alive!

Te Rangituatea sat unmoved. Having finished his speech with a veiled threat Te Rauparaha retired to the far end of the cave for a time. Knowing the history of Te Rauparaha it can be said that the threat was only uttered for effect. The womenfolk, however, who had been listening intently to his speech, were much perturbed and one of them, Tiaia by name, the wife of Peehi Kupe, went up to Te Rauparaha and earnestly begged him not to carry out his threat. Like the consummate actor he was Te Rauparaha demurred for a time and then graciously acceded to the pleadings of his brother chief's wife, much to the relief of the womenfolk who were fearful of the fate that would await them at the hands of the vengeful Ngāti Maniapoto.

Te Rangituatea patiently waited until Te Rauparaha had returned and had quietly said that the meal would presently be ready. When Te Rauparaha resumed his seat Te Rangituatea rose to speak. He quickly traversed the events that had led up to Te Rauparaha's present predicament. He quoted their genealogical lines of descent and made feeling reference to former times when there was peace throughout the land. Te Rangituatea then went on to speak of the real purpose of his visit. He assured Te Rauparaha that it was out of regard for their blood ties that he had come to assist Te Rauparaha in making good his escape from the wrath of his enemies. He then informed Te Rauparaha that the Ngāti Maniapoto men were preparing to cut off all avenues of escape and he urged Te Rauparaha not to delay any longer otherwise he would be doomed.

After the meal the two chieftains discussed plans long into the night. Te Rangituatea described the route Te Rauparaha and his party should follow and he gave an undertaking to distract the Maniapoto warriors until he, his wives and children and the womenfolk with him, were free from all danger of pursuit. Early next morning Te Rangituatea left. And on the day arranged Te Rauparaha and his party of women and children set off.

The arrangements worked out as was planned and, although a party of Ngāti Maniapoto scouts was close at hand after they had crossed the Mōkau river, the pursuers were deterred from following them across by Te Rangituatea's account that there was a large force under Te Rauparaha. Te Rauparaha and his party had come by difficult tracks over the ranges and they were very tired. On a high hill on the southern bank of the river they prepared to camp for the night. As the womenfolk and children made the necessary preparations Te Rauparaha kept a watchful eye on the Maniapoto warriors on the opposite bank, who were standing about in groups arguing and discussing different plans. Finally the Maniapoto retired to camp for the night. They had been convinced by Te Rangituatea's story and had decided to await further reinforcements for which fleet-footed messengers had been sent. To aid in the deception that night Te Rauparaha's party lit several fires around which they draped their cloaks on the scrub nearby. From the Maniapoto encampment it indeed appeared that there was a large force sitting around Te Rauparaha's camp fires. At intervals Te Rauparaha went from one fire to another to harangue his imaginary warriors and some of the women would punctuate his orations by leaping to their feet and acting in the manner of warriors keen for battle.

The ruse was a complete success. In later times the deception was commemorated by giving a name to Te Rauparaha's trek from Tīrua point and the name chosen was Te Heketahutahuahi, "the refugees who lit fires." During the night Te Rangituatea, satisfied that his plan had not miscarried, gathered his relatives around him and sang his song of farewell to Te Rauparaha, his Ngāti Toa kinsman. Interspersed in the song were special lines which, as part of their plan, conveyed a hidden meaning to Te Rauparaha and which also reassured him as to their safety for the night and warned him as to where danger might threaten on his southward journey to the lands of the Āti Awa people.

TE WAIATA POROPOROAKI KI A TE RAUPARAHA

Nā Te Rangituatea o Ngāti Maniapoto

Karanga pā mai!
Tēnā ka mene kei waho,
Kei tai e kokoti kino ana;
I te ngaru tua-manomano!

Tai ki Karewa!
Ko te paenga i waho o Maketū;
Ko te one tiatia ki te tau mata-rau
Te tōnga puaroa.
Ka rimua ō iwi ki runga o Tauwhara
E taka mai rāwhiti,
E mau ana te toa nā.
Whakahaerea rā nā runga i ō hau tapere
Ka tuhera kau mai te Rua o Kaiwhare!
Tau-pua kau ana te toka i a Te Whata
I te pae tirohanga nei hoki.

Wherawherahia rā, ē, te kapu o tō ringa;
Kīia Hou-taketake:
Tō ringa parapara i haukeria ai
Te mano o te whenua!
Kokopa mai nei ki ōna pāpā;
Ka heua nei hoki;
Me koko ā-tao, ē,
I te tūranga whakawareware

Whakawarea ana koe rā,
Ki te ngaki ngā mate ki a Tamamutu;
Ngawaki tonu atu, ē, i te ara whekowheko
Runga o Tarawera, he tuki upoko roro
Ka iri mārō;
Te hiakai tangata ki a Whakaue-Kōpako!

THE FAREWELL SONG TO TE RAUPARAHA[2]

By Te Rangituatea of the Maniapoto Tribe

From afar your voice is now heard
And in dangerous flight thou art;
For along the strand are many dangers
From the engulfing waves that crash:
5   Like the wave that rushed past *Karewa*
And o'erwhelmed ye at *Maketū*
Where the shore did bristle with a thousand spears!
Thou wert always prone to be wayward
And thus exposed thy people to many dangers,

10 Whilst you travelled to *Tauwhara* in the East,
Thou didst heedlessly embroil thyself in warlike exploits.
And now the Cavern of *Kaiwhare* is opened wide!
Te Whata' now stands like a lonely rock pinnacle,
On that look-out summit!

15 Why didst thou not open wide thy purposeful hand
And repeat the *Hou-taketake*
With thy strong arms that did smite
The many in the land?
Now thou didst close but an empty hand,
20 In silent salute to thine elders,
Whom you now leave behind thee:
You that did cause a myriad spears
To come and send the many down to oblivion!

Ye did also stay away to no purpose
25 In the seeking of revenge for *Tamamutu*
Afar off ye went along the misty pathway.
To *Tarawera* where many heads were crushed,
And that gave the great offence
That hath made a foe of *Whakaue-Kōpako*
30 With whom we have no quarrel.

By next morning, following the events described in the song, Te Rauparaha and his party of women and children were miles away and by midday met a well-armed force of his own people who had come to meet him and conduct his party to the Ngāti Tama stronghold of Te Kawau.

NOTES ON CHAPTER 6

Note 1. Te Rauparaha's farewell to Kāwhia

The song was composed by one Wharetiki sometime before Te Rauparaha. Wharetiki was taken prisoner by an inland raiding party and before he was executed (near Tirohanga-Kāwhia summit overlooking Kāwhia harbour) he asked his captors to allow him to sing his song of farewell to his ancestral home, Kāwhia. The song was overheard and memorised by his father, who had followed closely behind the raiders in the vain hope of rescuing his son. The only change in the song as sung by Te Rauparaha was the substitution of "Honipaka" for "Kāwhia" in the opening line.

Honipaka is the name of the place now called Albatross point, lying to the northwest of Taharoa lake and almost due west of the entrance to Kāwhia harbour.

(6) Te Motu: A small low-lying island in Kāwhia harbour. It is now completely devoid of vegetation, but at one time it is said that it was tree-covered and a popular playground of the Kāwhia people.

(13) Te Kawau: A sea-girt rock offshore from Te Maika peninsula at the entrance to Kāwhia harbour. It marked the spot where the entrance was to the subterranean sepulchre of the honoured dead, of the Kāwhia people.

Muriwhenua: The under-sea burial cave already referred to. Tradition also has it that Hoturoa, the leader of the Tainui migration and commander of the Tainui Canoe (*circa* 1350 a.d.), was the first to be buried in Muriwhenua.

(15) my cherished bird: This is in reference to a Māori belief that in some cases the souls of the departed linger near the habitations of their loved ones and for the time being abide in the *pīrairaka* (*Rhipidura flabellifera* and *R. fuliginosa*, the fantail) which may be distinguished from others of its kind when it persists in flying in and out of the home of the bereaved family.

(22) Āti Awa: The tribal name of the people living in and around the Waitara district.

Note 2. The Farewell Song to Te Rauparaha

(5) wave... Karewa: Karewa is a small island off the coast of Kāwhia. "Wave" is in reference to the seaborne force under Kiwi which formed part of Te Wherowhero's invasion army.

(6) Maketū: The name of the little village alongside the spot where the Tainui Canoe was hauled ashore in Kāwhia harbour.

(10) Tauwhara: More often spelt Tauhara, is the mountain at the northern end of Lake Taupō. Reference to the mountain is made in this song because Te Rauparaha had paid two visits to Taupō. On one visit he went with a section of the Ngāti Raukawa tribe to assist the Ngāti Tūwharetoa against the Tūhoe tribe of the Urewera district, who had inflicted a severe defeat on the Ngāti Tamamutu sub-tribe of the Ngāti Tūwharetoa, tribe of Taupō, at a place called Ōrona.

(12) Kaiwhare: A traditional *taniwha* or dragon of the Waikato river, and the reference here is to the Waikato tribes who had overrun the ancestral lands of Te Rauparaha and his people.

(13) Te Whata': Te Whatakaraka, to give him his full name, was a well-known Kāwhia warrior who, like Te Rauparaha, had a warlike spirit. Now that Te Rauparaha had left Kāwhia Te Whata' was like "a lonely rock pinnacle."

(14) look-out summit: A reference to the summit near Te Rauamoa of the famous Tirohanga-Kāwhia ("the view of Kāwhia") track, which the present main road from Kāwhia follows.

(16) The Hou-taketake: There is a long story here. In the time of the ancestor Maniapoto a migratory tribe from the east under their chief Hou-taketake came and settled on the Pukenui hills above Te Kūiti. He and his people had been driven from their ancestral lands in Heretaunga (now Hawkes Bay) during some inter-tribal fighting. He built an earth *pā* which he called Pā-oneone (the earth-formed). For a time they were afraid to disturb the peace by trespassing in the forest to obtain timber. After they had harvested their first crop of *kūmara*, however, they procured some logs to strengthen their *kūmara* pits. When questioned by the people of Maniapoto they facetiously remarked, "Anybody would think these trees were the ribs of Rereahu." (Rereahu was Maniapoto's father.) There was trouble immediately. Finally Hou-taketake persuaded his people that they could defeat Maniapoto and his people and dispossess them of their land. He descended from his *pā* and advanced against Maniapoto's village on the banks of the Mangaokewa stream. Maniapoto had then just taken unto himself a young wife and he was enjoying her company when the alarm was given. He did not leave his quarters immediately and his people were much put out over the delay. It was not until Hou-taketake was halfway across the *marae* (courtyard) that Maniapoto decided to come out. Taking up a crouching position Maniapoto awaited Hou'. The latter came forward uttering threats and making violent passes with his *taiaha*. When he was only a few paces away Maniapoto arose, at the same time scooping up some sand and dirt in his hands and, uttering a blood-curdling war cry, he threw the sand and dirt into the glaring eyes of his adversary. He then calmly picked up his weapon and with one fell swoop killed Hou-taketake. His people were then attacked and were completely annihilated.

In the farewell song to Te Rauparaha the question is asked of Te Rauparaha why had not he thought of some similar strategy against the invaders of his ancestral lands.

(25) Tamamutu: See reference to Tauwhare.

(27) Tarawera: This is a reference to Te Rauparaha's journey to enlist the help of the Te Arawa tribes of Rotorua. (See para. 7, Chapter 4). It was at Rotokākahi lake near Tarawera where Te Rauparaha instigated the killing of the Ngāpuhi, which led up to the invasion of Rotorua by Hongi Hika.

(29) Whakaue-Kōpako: This hyphenated name combines the names of two tribes of the Arawa conferation, namely Ngāti Whakaue and Ngāti Uenuku-Kōpako. These are two very closely related Arawa tribes and they were the principal sufferers as the result of the Hongi Hika raid.

AN EPIC DUEL

Ko Te Wherowhero, ko te ana o te tangata!

'Tis Te Wherowhero, the Sepulchre of Man!

CHAPTER 7

AN EPIC DUEL

I

Closely following the events related in the last chapter an army of 800 adventurous warriors from various Waikato and Maniapoto tribes marched toward Waitara from the south under the command of Tūkōrehu who had led the Maniapoto at Waikawau. This army had set out with the avowed purpose of inflicting punishment on various North Island tribes who were represented in Pikauterangi's ill-fated army (Chap.1). The search for the missing sacred inscribed emblems of the Tainui sacred house of learning was also involved.

This army comprised some of the finest fighters and most daring spirits of the time. A passing reference might here be made to a notable encounter which took place while Tūkōrehu's army was passing through the territory of that warlike people, the Tūhoe or "the children of the mist" as the late Elsdon Best has called them. At Te Whāiti, Tūkōrehu skirted the formidable *pā* of Te Purewa the Tūhoe chieftain-warrior. Te Purewa challenged Tūkōrehu to single combat and the latter eagerly accepted. With the entrenched Tūhoe and the 800 Tainui tribesmen lining the adjoining hill as interested spectators the two leaders fought their duel on the small flat-topped ridge connecting the *pā* to the adjacent hills. Te Purewa at last began to show signs of extreme fatigue—neither had up to this stage been able to penetrate the other's guard. Both were tired, but the Tūhoe was the first to drop his guard momentarily and Tūkōrehu stepped inside it to deal the deathblow with his *mere*. As the Tainui grasped at the handle of his *mere* the Tūhoe gave a heave to loosen the one-hand hold of his adversary and Tūkōrehu fumbled his grip on the weapon. At this point, as if it had been previously arranged, the two leaders embraced each other and in this attitude they swore their undying friendship. They exchanged *mere* and Tūkōrehu departed with his army from the lands of the Tūhoe never to return. This peacemaking had far-reaching effects, for in later years it was the reason for the Tūhoe people coming to assist the people of Tūkōrehu and also Rewi Maniapoto in his memorable stand at Ōrākau against General Cameron's 3000 men and all his artillery.

After battling through the East Coast and the Wairarapa Tūkōrehu crossed over to the West Coast and continued his remarkable expedition into Taranaki after a brief rest at Whanganui. From Pātea northward to Waitara his army dealt out death and wide destruction in their forward march. Near Waitara, however, they were surrounded by an overwhelming force of the Taranaki tribes and were besieged in Ngāpuketūrua Pā a few miles south of Waitara. Tūkōrehu's army was sorely pressed. But at this juncture—as often happened in Māori warfare—help was forthcoming from a Taranaki tribe (Ngāti Rungaterangi) who were also partly of Tainui blood, and the besieged army was safely conducted to the spacious and strongly fortified *pā* of Pukerangiora on the south bank of Waitara river.

Pukerangiora Pā was also strongly besieged, but with the help of the Ngāti Rungaterangi the beleaguered forces never ran short of provisions. Some of the Taranaki leaders facetiously referred to this fact by saying that in any case it was not wise to starve *raihe poaka* (penned-up pigs); and actually the Taranaki besiegers thereupon proceeded to erect another line of earthworks and palisading around the *pā* to make doubly certain the "pigs" would not escape.

Tūkōrehu was not disposed to endure the deadlock and the indignities forced upon him without making a bid for freedom and he called for volunteers to run the gauntlet and carry a message back home to the Waikato and Maniapoto districts to inform the tribes of his plight. He sent a special message for his son-in-law Te Wherowhero. Two young men, fleet of foot, volunteered.

On a dark, stormy night these messengers carefully picked their way through the earthworks and palisading and made a dash for the open rolling country northward to the coast. One of them was unlucky and was struck down by a Taranaki party which was on its way to join the besieging forces. The other young man, known to history as Manukorihi (a name he subsequently took from the *pā* of that name on the north bank of the Waitara river, now the site of the Māori village of the same name), who belonged to the Ngāti Kahutōtara sub-tribe of the Maniapoto, broke through the enemy cordon unscathed. Manukorihi travelled with such speed that he reached Kāwhia the following afternoon. His journey thus far had not by any means been uneventful. Many of the people of the land he had passed through belonged to or were allied to the Ngāti Toa, Te Rauparaha's tribe. Manukorihi narrowly escaped capture and death several times. Passing through Marokopa he was closely pursued by two men and it became a race for life along the sandy beach. Near the end of the sands one of the pursuers gave up the chase. A short distance further on Manukorihi allowed the remaining pursuer to gain on him and, after rounding a projecting headland, he stopped dead in his tracks. As his enemy dashed by he struck with such speed and skill that he decapitated the Marokopa warrior. (The pursuer was probably a Taranaki man who had followed Manukorihi all the way from Pukerangiora.)

After Manukorihi reached Kāwhia swift runners were sent to the inland tribes and the message quickly flew from village to village. Manukorihi himself continued on his way and eventually reached Te Wherowhero's *pā* at Kaitotehe, situated across the Waikato river from Taupiri mountain.

II

Te Rauparaha at this time had thrown in his lot with the northern Taranaki tribes and was living with the Ngāti Mutunga of the Urenui district. On learning that Manukorihi had managed to get through to his redoubtable adversary Te Wherowhero, the Ngāti Toa leader advised the Ngāti Mutunga, to whom he was related, to prepare for the coming of the Waikato. The Ngāti Toa, Ngāti Mutunga and Ngāti Tama, with some help from other northern tribes, set to and repaired the earthworks and palisading of their great *pā* at Ōkoki.

The news of the impending invasion spread like wildfire and all the famous warriors of the Taranaki tribes made their way to Ōkoki. A specially selected and strong force was left to conduct the siege of Pukerangiora. All was now ready for the coming of Te Wherowhero and his army of the Waikato and Ngāti Maniapoto tribes.

III

Te Wherowhero, in the prime of life, had now assumed undisputable war leadership of the Waikato tribes. His aged father Te Rauangaanga was looked up to as a priestly patriarch of the Tainui tribes and in that capacity he decided to accompany the army. No doubt he also felt that he should be near at hand to give advice to his son as to the conduct of the war.

Te Wherowhero quickly mobilised a considerable force of the Waikato river and West Coast tribes and, with additional warriors from the Maniapoto and other allied tribes joining him en route, he found himself with an army of more than 1,000 by the time he left Kāwhia on his march to Taranaki.

He crossed the Mōkau river at its mouth and proposed to his war chiefs that they should rest there until the next day, but his impatient lieutenants, Te Hiakai and others, urged him to go on. "We came to fight, not to sit down," they said, and Te Wherowhero yielded most reluctantly. He sensed that Te Hiakai in particular was in a very highly-strung state of mind and not in a fit state to fight against a resolute foe. He communicated his fears to his father and Te Rauangaanga agreed with him.

IV

The astute and resourceful Te Rauparaha had his scouts reporting to him at frequent intervals and being thus fully informed of the approaching danger he developed a plan of defence which proved to be characteristic of his future military genius. Te Rauparaha selected a party of his swiftest runners and instructed them as to how they were to lure Te Wherowhero's army to its doom in a cunningly and skilfully laid ambush.

Some distance from Ōkoki, and in full view of the *pā*, Te Wherowhero again called a halt and gave orders for bivouacs to be erected for their camp. With a *kō* (wooden digging implement) Te Wherowhero himself set an example to his men by setting to and beginning to cut and heap up rushes for his own shelter. In truth he was rather troubled in mind because of the excited behaviour of Te Hiakai, who was complaining against the decision to defer action until the following day—a decision Te Wherowhero reached after conferring with Te Rauangaanga. The time was then midday. Te Rauangaanga at last made an appeal and addressing Te Hiakai and a crowd who had gathered around him, he said, "*E pā mā, kaua e hīkaka ki te riri; āta noho koa kia mutu ngā karakia.*" (O Sirs, do not be over-eager for battle; wait and remain until the incantations are ended.) And with those words he turned and moved off and climbed a nearby hillock where he proposed to perform his priestly rites to ensure a successful outcome to the coming battle. Te Wherowhero, leaning on his *kō*, watched his father in silence, every now and again glancing about at the group surrounding the bellicose Te Hiakai. After reaching the summit of the hillock Te Rauangaanga sat down and gazed out to sea. The priestly patriarch, silhouetted against the sky, his grey locks ruffled by the breeze, was a striking and noble figure as he sat there like a graven image.

V

Te Rauparaha's plan was to prove successful. While Te Wherowhero and part of his army were busy with their camp preparations, Te Hiakai and Mama, two of his outstanding fighting chiefs, with a large following, began to move off for Ōkoki. They had proceeded a short distance when Te Wherowhero caught up with them and was later joined by his father. In vain father and son argued and tried to dissuade Te Hiakai and Mama from their purpose. At last Te Rauangaanga said, "You must wait. The work of the camp is not done. And my *karakia* (incantation) has not yet begun." This had no more effect on Te Hiakai and his companions than the arguments already used. Te Hiakai moved off and motioned the others to follow him. As he went he called back laughingly, "*Mahia ngā mahi, karakiatia ngā karakia.*" (Proceed with the work, and chant the incantations.)

Moving steadily along the dry bed of a stream in the direction of Ōkoki, Te Hiakai with about 600 followers presently came upon Te Rauparaha's selected band of warriors. The Ōkoki men appeared surprised and hurriedly rose to their feet and turned toward their *pā*. Te Hiakai and Mama excitedly gathered their men around them and in high spirits they immediately gave chase as the seemingly startled band of Taranaki warriors sped toward Ōkoki. Te Hiakai, Mama, Nuku and other braves were elated. Here was their chance to beat the great Te Wherowhero for the much coveted *mātāngohi* (the first enemy slain in battle). The fleeing band was but an insignificant body of men and there were some swift runners among the Waikato and Maniapoto warriors. With Te Hiakai, Mama, Nuku and other leaders in the van, the Waikato and Maniapoto in hot pursuit were led directly into the ambush so skilfully laid in the valley leading up to Ōkoki Pā. Te Hiakai, well in advance of the others, was allowed to go on right up to the *pā* before the attack was opened.

Beset on all sides, the Waikato and Maniapoto were soon in a most perilous position. The attack was fierce and the sadly disillusioned Tainui warriors had literally to fight every yard of their way out of that valley of death. Despite their extreme danger Te Hiakai and Mama, with a number of other keen warriors, still fought their way toward the *pā*. Te Hiakai actually scaled the outer palisading and after stunning a Taranaki chief with his *mere* he proceeded to carry him out of the *pā*. As he climbed the palisading, with the body over his shoulder, a shot rang out from the *pā* and Te Hiakai fell back with his burden. Te Hiakai was seriously wounded and as he lay on the ground Te Rauparaha passed by and, stooping down, said, "Did I not tell you to stay in Kāwhia?" Te Hiakai weakly nodded his head. Te Rauparaha was about to speak, again when a Taranaki relative of the chief whom Te Hiakai had attempted to carry off, and who had been killed outright by the shot that had wounded Te Hiakai, came up and before Te Rauparaha could do anything about it shot Te Hiakai and killed him on the spot. The fact that Te Hiakai might have proved a useful hostage may have been in Te Rauparaha's mind as he remonstrated with the Taranaki chief. The body of Te Hiakai was later hung up on a tree in Ōkoki Pā.

VI

With the fall of Te Hiakai the Waikato men wavered. They never really recovered from the first onslaught. Summoning all their remaining fighting strength they finally broke through the encircling foe. Their retreat from Ōkoki back to where they had come from would have developed into full-scale rout had it not been for the coolness of their leader Te Wherowhero and his father Te Rauangaanga. The defeated forces rushed back on the encampment with such haste that before order could be restored the whole army was on the move. As the men rushed by Te Rauangaanga kept on calling out, "*Kia ū! Kia ū!*" (Be firm! Be firm!)

Te Wherowhero stayed on to make sure that his father was well guarded and had joined the retreating army before he slung his *kō* over his shoulder and followed. Seeing their leader in the rear some of his men called out to Te Wherowhero, "Come with us!" "My elders are in Pukerangiora, and we die together!" was Te Wherowhero's reply. With Te Wherowhero, as he followed in the wake of his army, was the diminutive and faithful warrior Manukorihi.

At one point, as they travelled along the beach track, a Taranaki warrior recognising the redoubtable Te Wherowhero some distance in the rear of his fleeing men thought he had a god-given opportunity of earning undying fame. He thought he would steal up on Manukorihi, whom he took to be an immature youth, kill him and then deal with the great Te Wherowhero himself. Out of the corner of his eye the ever-alert Manukorihi saw the Taranaki man manoeuvring to get to close quarters. Behind a huge boulder Manukorihi awaited the pursuer. Te Wherowhero proceeded on his way. He was for the moment ill in body and depressed in spirit over the loss of many of his leading warriors. His fortunes were indeed at a low ebb.

The Taranaki warrior cautiously rounded the rock and seeing Te Wherowhero a few paces off he raised his *taiaha* in a position to strike and was about to rush forward upon the Waikato leader when the agile Manukorihi quickly stepped up and with an unerring stroke he knocked the Taranaki man spinning to the ground, dead.

A little further on the track left the beach and Te Wherowhero and Manukorihi mounted to the level ground above. It was here that they came upon Mama who had been wounded earlier by a shot from one of the garrison in Ōkoki Pā. He had lost a lot of blood and it was plain that he had only a short while to live. Mama, who was a man of herculean stature, was the leading Maniapoto warrior of his time and he had been the hero of many a hotly contested duel. Manukorihi was very closely related to the dying warrior and he wept unrestrainedly. As Mama breathed his last Te Wherowhero settled down by his side and lifted his head on to his lap. Putting aside his *kō* and turning his face to his birthplace in the north he pronounced a dirge to his departed comrade. Manukorihi sat motionless by his side.

VII

It was on this pathetic group that the flushed Taranaki gazed as they came over the ridge. "*Ko Te Wherowhero, ko te ana o te tangata!*" ('Tis Te Wherowhero, the sepulchre of man!), a Taranaki musketeer cried as he threw himself on the ground and prepared to shoot. He was determined to rid his people of a much-feared and hated foe. It was a tense moment.

Te Wherowhero reverently laid Mama's head down and quietly took up his *kō*, which was the only weapon he had at hand other than Manukorihi's *taiaha* which he had declined when it was offered. The *kō* was fashioned from the close-grained *maire* wood (*Olea cunninghamii*; a species of olive) and as a fighting weapon it had often figured in the history of Te Wherowhero's forebears. Te Wherowhero and Manukorihi were prepared to sell their lives dearly.

"No! A Waikato chief and my kinsman shall not be killed like a dog! Let a chief die the death of a chief! *Me tau-mātahi te riri, hei te rangatira anake!*" (Let it be by single combat, and between chiefs only!) This unexpected speech had broken the silence, and the speaker was Te Rauparaha. As he spoke he went up to the prone marksman and kicked the gun aside to emphasise his remarkable order.

The motive behind Te Rauparaha's command to the Taranaki warrior chiefs has since been the subject of much debate. Some will have it that it was designed to impress his Taranaki allies with the sanctity of the life of a Tainui chief—he himself being one. To allow a great Waikato chief to be shot out of hand "like a dog" might endanger his own life among the tribes with whom he had but recently joined forces. Others contend that Te Rauparaha relied upon the marvellous skill of Te Wherowhero to rid him of some unruly Taranaki warriors who were beginning to question his motives and who resented his attempts to exercise his authority over them. Those of this opinion go on to say that this was the method he had used in his rise to the leadership of the Ngāti Toa, but that in that case he had overdone the elimination of his rivals and exposed the tribe to the fury of its enemies. Each side is entitled to its opinion, but the majority will probably say it was an act of chivalry, which is a Māori characteristic in the conduct of war. Whatever the verdict might be Te Rauparaha's noble speech on that occasion, uttered in unmistakable terms and in a commanding voice, became an order with all the force of law. Trial by single combat was to settle the issue.

VIII

When Te Rauparaha concluded his dramatic intervention he took up his stand to one side of the crouching Taranaki warriors. Among these warriors were Te Tupeotu and Te Hautehoro, two of the outstanding Taranaki warriors of that time. Te Wherowhero rose to his feet, his *kō* in the *pae ā-ruru* (the watchful owl) stance, ready to parry or to attack. He had silently accepted the challenge and awaited the onslaught with the recumbent Mama at his feet. The watchful Manukorihi crouched behind Te Wherowhero.

Te Wherowhero knew every thrust and parry and he had an unerring eye. His strength and stamina were prodigious and his courage was high. A typical Ngāti Mahuta of the Waikato, he kept a firm grip on himself and was cool and collected. A warrior rushed forward and Te Wherowhero met the challenge instantly. Faster than the eye could follow and with a swift blow from his *kō*, he sent him quivering to the earth. As each warrior rushed down the slope toward him his keen eye watched every move. With some he would step forward, feint, and in a flash drive the *kō* home with a sickening thud to some vital part of his adversary's body. He appeared to vary his methods for each attack and in some cases he allowed his opponent to make the first thrust or stroke. The blow would be parried and in the next instant the attacker slain.

One by one the flower of Taranaki valour flung themselves in quick succession against that mighty warrior. And each fell dead, mortally wounded, or severely incapacitated. Some were maimed for life. Among those who suffered severe head wounds were Te Tupeotu and Te Hautehoro. The single-handed duel against the many went on until fully 50 men—some accounts say more—lay prone on that historic testing ground.

The story of this epic fight has no equal in the annals of Māori warfare. Years later, when the Taranaki and Waikato tribes fought side by side in a gallant attempt to preserve their ancestral lands against the well-armed European soldiers, there were then living many Taranaki warriors who were able to point with pride to honoured head scars which they were not ashamed to testify had been received on that memorable day from the hand of Te Wherowhero.

By this time the retreating army had been halted by the repeated exhortations of Te Rauangaanga. Then the question went through the ranks, "Where is Te Wherowhero? Where is Te Wherowhero?" Finding he was not with them, the disordered ranks rapidly reformed and the army again moved toward Ōkoki and at last came upon the scene of strife, where they found their leader engaged in a life and death struggle. Drawn up in battle array, with every man occupying a vantage point, they watched the fight with tense excitement and wonder. As a Taranaki aspirant for imperishable glory rushed forward and was felled by Aotearoa's mighty *toa* (warrior) there were shouts of uncontrollable joy and admiration.

At last, as the sun hung low out to sea, there was no further movement from the ranks of the Taranaki warriors. A party of Maniapoto rushed forward at a gesture from Te Wherowhero and removed the body of their fallen chieftain Mama. Manukorihi still knelt, statue-like, with a look of silent determination and admiration in the direction of the foe and their great leader. The heroic figure of Te Wherowhero stood forth cool, defiant and unbowed. The last dare-devil lay dead at his feet on the plain. The best that Taranaki could produce had been flung into the arena and each had fallen. These warriors had flung themselves unhesitatingly into the fray. To have overcome Te Wherowhero would have clothed the fortunate man with undying fame. As the body of Mama—the inanimate trophy of this epic struggle was borne away Te Wherowhero spoke for the first time. (His was a family of few words.) *"Kua mau i ahau te hiku o te riri!"* (I have retained the issue of battle!) "And Taranaki is mine!" was Te Wherowhero's. brief summing up of the day and there was no one there to dispute him.

IX

Both armies moved off in opposite directions with their dead and dying, the Waikato and Maniapoto to camp for the night, and the Taranaki force to Ōkoki Pā. Te Rauparaha lingered for a time and called out to Te Wherowhero, "*Ka pari te tai-moana, ka timu te tai-tangata!*" (As the ocean tide comes in, the human tide will ebb!) Te Wherowhero's reply was to the point. In a confident and ringing voice he said, "*Mō te ata!*" (Let the morning decide!) As he was about to turn away Te Rauparaha recognised Te Rangituatea among a group of warriors and to him he addressed these words, "*Kia tūpato kei ngau te kauae runga te kauae raro!*" (Beware lest the upper jaw closes down on the lower jaw!) Te Rangituatea, who had been involved in the fighting at Ōkoki earlier in the day and was still badly shaken, on the spur of the moment called out, "O Raha'! What regard have you for us two?" (Te Rangituatea had included Te Wherowhero in this appeal.) To this Te Rauparaha replied, "If you return north by the way you have come the upper jaw will open and close on the lower jaw! But if you proceed to Pukerangiora you will be saved!" It was learnt later that a very large force of Ngāti Tama had marched by forest tracks and was at that time preparing an ambush at the Mōkau river crossing. It was this force that Te Rauparaha referred to as the "upper jaw." By continuing on to Pukerangiora the Waikato and Maniapoto would not only release their compatriots, but also would then be strengthened by the addition of 800 seasoned warriors.[2]

Within Ōkoki Pā that night the Taranaki war lords discussed the events of the day and the prospects of the morrow. "Te Hiakai, Mama, Nuku and many other leading Waikato and Maniapoto warriors have fallen. Waikato is beaten!" declared a Taranaki leader, at the same time looking at Te Rauparaha for some sign of confirmation. That astute general had been sitting silently summing up the events of the day and the next day's chances. He was also reviewing the position of himself and his people as not altogether welcome guests of some of the Taranaki people. He had no illusions as to the indomitable spirit of Te Wherowhero and the great fighting qualities of the Waikato and Maniapoto. He was convinced that nothing would deter Te Wherowhero from attempting to raise the seige of Pukerangiora and, having done that, set about the destruction of the Taranaki. At last, after considering every possibility, Te Rauparaha spoke. In carefully chosen words he said, "If you see the dust rising northward Waikato is beaten; if you see the dust moving southward Waikato is firm and is unbeaten!"

X

Next morning the garrison of Ōkoki Pā looked out with anxious eyes on the route to Pukerangiora. They were not left in doubt for long. Above the low-lying morning mists they saw the great army of Te Wherowhero moving along the ridge tracks on its way in the direction of Pukerangiora Pā. Te Rauparaha knew that Ōkoki itself would be the next objective and advised the Taranaki to evacuate and to follow him on the southward trek, a course which he had been urging on his Ngāti Mutunga kinsmen for some time and which they had been putting off on one pretext or another. They could travel by inland forest tracks, said Te Rauparaha. The story of Te Rauparaha's march from Taranaki belongs to the history of the Ngāti Toa leader, so we shall leave him in Ōkoki to follow Te Wherowhero and his men.

On their way to Pukerangiora they were opposed at intervals by bodies of Taranaki fighting men and there was much hard fighting before they reached Pukerangiora. A fierce battle was fought around that historic stronghold before the siege was finally raised. It was the combined onslaughts from within the *pā* and from without which finally brought victory and Tūkōrehu and his 800 men or what was left of them, still a formidable force, were at last saved after a siege that had lasted for several months.

Pukerangiora was beseiged and taken on two subsequent occasions by the Waikato and Maniapoto, with Te Wherowhero as leader on each of these raids into Taranaki. These later raids of Te Wherowhero dealt many grievous blows to the people of the Taranaki district and many large areas were depopulated—some of the tribes fleeing to the south to join Te Rauparaha, others going across to Chatham Islands (Wharekauri). At the advent of Governor Fitzroy there was no outstanding Taranaki leader with whom he could negotiate for the purchase of land for European settlement, and when Te Wherowhero with his brother Takiwaru or Kati put forward the claim that "Taranaki is mine," the claim was accepted. A deed of sale was drawn up for all the land between Tongapōrutu river in the north and the Waitōtara river in the south (now embracing some of the richest dairying lands in the country) which was signed by Te Wherowhero and Kati in consideration of the payment of "£150 in money, 2 horses, 2 saddles, 2 bridles and 100 blankets!"

NOTES ON CHAPTER 7

Note 1

Hiku o te riri (the issue of battle): According to Roore Erueti, the first Waikato to fall before the *pā* of Ōkoki (this clash is usually referred to as the fight of Motunui) was a man named Taungawai. A desperate contest for possession of his body took place, several warriors from each side losing their lives in the attempt. Finally the Waikato recovered the body and bore it off the field of battle. Roore states that it was in reference to the recovery of the body of Taungawai that Te Wherowhero used the expression, "*Kua mau i ahau te hiku o te riri!*" (I have retained the issue of battle). The "issue" or *hiku* was the dead body of Taungawai.

Note 2

Te Rauparaha and Te Rangituatea: There is an interesting sequel to this Ōkoki meeting between Te Rauparaha and Te Rangituatea, and as a preface to it, the author thinks that it would be helpful to have a synopsis of the several meetings between these two men.

1. First Kāwhia meeting: Encounter near Maniapoto fishing grounds at Tūtaerere; Te Rauparaha allowed Te Rangituatea to depart unmolested after his *taiaha* had been deflected by an overhanging branch of a tree. Te Rauparaha, in his version of this affair, said that he had purposely struck at the branch as he did not wish to harm his own kinsman Te Rangituatea, but only to give him a fright.

2. Second Kāwhia meeting: Te Rauparaha while besieged in Te Arawī Pā was assisted to escape by Te Rangituatea. There is also an account that as chief of many Maniapoto tribes Te Rangituatea was supplied by his people with a plentiful hoard of preserved forest birds, eels and sea-foods, and these he had surreptitiously shared with Te Rauparaha during the siege.

3. Third meeting at Tīrua Point: After Te Rauparaha had fled from Kāwhia he was visited by Te Rangituatea who brought with him an offering of preserved pigeons. Before Te Rauparaha and his band of women and children left his cliff refuge cave of "the whalebone club-pillow," Te Rangituatea had arranged for food depots at various points on the line of march over the hills to the Mōkau river.

4. Fourth meeting, Mōkau: Te Rangituatea here misled his Maniapoto kinsmen as to the composition and strength of Te Rauparaha's party. Te Rangituatea and his people sang their song of farewell to Te Rauparaha.

5. Fifth meeting at Ōkoki: As described in Chapter 7.

The sequel: The time was some years after Ōkoki. Te Rangituatea had struck up a friendship with the European captain of a trading vessel, and he had been prevailed on to go as supercargo on a southern voyage to Kapiti island. The ship in due course anchored off Kapiti and the ship's officers went ashore to trade with Te Rauparaha's people who, as conquerors, were now occupying the lands between Rangitikei river and Whanganui-a-Tara (now Wellington harbour) and parts of the northern end of Waipounamu (South Island). While ashore the officers had mentioned that there was a Maniapoto chief on board named Te Rangituatea. Immediately the fiery Te Rangihaeata (Te Rauparaha's nephew) heard this he was all agog and at once went down to the canoe landing-place. Te Rauparaha followed him and together they went across by canoe to the ship. Te Rangituatea was seated on the raised poop at the stern of the vessel when Te Rauparaha and his nephew boarded the ship. As soon as Te Rangihaeata saw Te Rangituatea he worked himself up to a high state of fury. He posed with his *taiaha*, he grimaced and made threatening gestures. The Maniapoto sat unmoved. Then Te Rangihaeata paused in his wild display of *taiaha* play, glared at Te Rangituatea, and in a menacing voice said:

Koia anō kei tō pāpā—pātiki!
Me hī koe ki te matika,
Ka hurihia ki runga ki te waka;
Ka tīraha tō poho,
Ka motu koe!

Ah, your father must have been a flounder
Ye can be fished up with the sharpened hook,
And turned belly upward on the canoe,
Thou art now ready for carving up!

Te Rauparaha throughout had been looking keenly into the face of the Maniapoto chief and what he saw there must have impressed him. As soon as Te Rangihaeata finished his speech Te Rangituatea threw off his shoulder mat and rose to his full height. Te Rauparaha motioned to his nephew to subside. With his *taiaha* in his right hand Te Rangituatea spoke up manfully and addressing himself to Te Rauparaha he said:

> *Mahi mai tērā iwi māku te kai;*
> *Mahi mai tērā iwi māku te kai;*
> *Nāku te kai—*
> *I tū ai te tikitikiki tō rae,*
> *I horo ai te rapa i tō upoko;*
> *Nāku te kai!*

Those people gathered food for me;
Those people gathered food for me;
It was my food
That sustained you who now wear a head-plume;
Indeed, it healed the festering sore on your head;
It was my food!

The noble bearing of Te Rangituatea and the justice of the reproof he had uttered in his rejoinder to Te Rangihaeata's wild speech were not lost on Te Rauparaha. It is also possible that like the far-seeing leader he was, Te Rauparaha already foresaw the time when his Taranaki allies would because of their superior numbers and the ease with which they could call up further reinforcements, dispute the conquered lands with him, and in such circumstances he would have need of assistance from the Maniapoto and other Tainui peoples.

Up to this stage Te Rauparaha had remained silent. He pondered over Te Rangituatea's speech for a moment or two. (It was couched in the derogatory language befitting the occasion and it was appropriate as coming from one chief to another—the three actors in this interlude fully appreciated that in ignoring Te Rangihaeata and addressing his remarks to Te Rauparaha, a high compliment was being paid.) At last Te Rauparaha looked up and motioned Te Rangihaeata to follow him as he prepared to leave the ship. As Te Rauparaha moved off he put out his hand—-opening and cupping it—in silent salutation toward Te Rangituatea then, turning to his nephew he said, "*Ka haere tāua!*" (Let us go). And they went.

APPENDIX TO CHAPTER 7

COPY FROM "MAORI DEEDS" VOL II, page 1

Deed No.1

Waikato Interests in Taranaki Lands.

Kia mohio nga tangata ki tenei pukapuka ko maua ko nga rangatira o Waikato ka tuku ka hoko atu i enei kaainga o matou ki a Hori Karaka te Kaitiaki o nga tangata Maori mo Wikitoria te Kuini o Ingarangi mo ona uri mo tetahi Tangata Wahine ranei e waiho ai e Ingarangi hei Rangatira mona te wenua me nga aha noa iho i runga i raro o taua wenua ka tukua kia Hori Karaka te Kaitiaki o nga tangata Maori hei kainga mo te Kuini me ona uri iho mo tetahi tangata wahine ranei e waiho ai e Ingarangi hei rangatira mona ake tonu atu.	1842 31st January New Plymouth District.
Ko te rohe hauraro ka timata ki Tongaporutu ki te rohe hauauru ka haere i Tongaporutu ka haere i tatahi a—Te Waitotara ko te rohe ki te tonga ka timata i te Waitotara ka haere ki uta a tae rawa atu ki Piraunui.	Tongaporutu to Waitotara Waikato Claims Boundaries
Ka tangohia nei e maua enei mea mo ta Waikato wahi i roto i te Kainga nei koia enei. Kotahi rau e rima tekau pauna moni rua hoiho e rua nohoanga hoihoi e rua paraire kotahi rau paraikete.	Consideration £150 2 horses 2 saddles 2 bridles 100 blankets
Tirohia a matou ingoa me o matou tohu ka tuhituhia nei ki Akarana i tenei ra te toru tekau ma tahi o Hanuere i tenei tau o to tatou Ariki Kotahi mano e waru rau e wa tekau ma rua.	

(Signed) KATI TE WEROWERO

Kaititiro: J. COATES
        GEORGE CLARKE, S.P.A.

Kua riro mai i a matou nga pauna moni kotahi rau e rima tekau me nga paraikete kotahi rau he utu mo Taranaki.	Receipt for £150 & etc.

(Signed) KATI TE WEROWERO

Witness:

(Signed) EDWARD SHORTLAND
H. D. SMART

TRANSLATION

KNOW ALL MEN by this book we chiefs of Waikato do let go and sell these lands of ours to George Clarke the Protector of Natives for H.M. Victoria Queen of England her heirs, and successors whether male or female the land and all things that are on or under this land we sell to George Clarke the Protector of Natives for an estate for the Queen her heirs and successors whether male or female for ever.	1842 31st January
The beginning of the Northern boundary is at Tongaporutu the Western boundary is along the sea shore between Tongaporutu and Waitotara and on the South beginning from Waitotara and going inland to Piraunui.	Tongaporutu to Waitotara Boundaries
We receive these payments on behalf of our tribes of Waikato for their interest in the said land — One hundred and fifty pounds, two horses two saddles and two bridles one hundred blankets.	Consideration
Witness our names and signs written in Auckland on this thirtyfirst of January, in this year of our Lord One thousand eight hundred and fortytwo.	

(Signed) KATI TE WEROWERO

Witness: (Sd) J. COATES
    GEORGE CLARKE Sub-Pror.

True translation

   (Sd). THOMAS S. FORSAITH

Received by us the sum of One hundred and fifty pounds sterling (£150) and one hundred .blankets as payment for Taranaki.²	Receipt for £150 & etc.

(Signed) KATI TE WEROWERO

Witness:

(Signed) EDWARD SUTHERLAND
        H. D. SMART

A true Copy of Original Deed and Translation

    Wellington, August, 20th. 1875

    H. HANSON TURTON.

    (Maori Deeds of Land Purchases, 1878, Vol. II, Deed I.)

1. Receipt: It is supposed that the vendors received the "2 horses, 2 saddles and 2 bridles" later.—Author.

A SEVERE DEFEAT

(Mātakitaki – May 1822)

Te Wherowhero: *Tērā rānei ahau e maru i a koe?*
Can you shelter me?

Te Otapeehi: *Āe, ka maru koe i taku pūreke:*
He kahu pītongatonga, whakatari-hauhunga,
Ka maru koe!
Yes, my cloak will shelter you:
It is closely woven and made for wintry weather,
It will indeed shelter you!

CHAPTER 8

A SEVERE DEFEAT

I

Hongi Hika, the famous northern fighter and leader, was on the warpath. He had come into the land of the Waikato at the head of 3,000 of his Ngāpuhi warriors, fully armed with the new weapon of the European, the *pū*, or the gun. In northern missionary records the date is given as May 1822. The gun was a rarity in the war experience of most of the Waikato people up to that time. Their leaders who had some knowledge of it despised it as the weapon of a plebeian.

Hauling his canoes overland into Manukau harbour and again from that waterway into the Waikato river, Hongi Hika and his army in due course reached Mātakitaki Pā at the foot of Pirongia mountain and on the east bank of the Waipā river. The threat of the Ngāpuhi had driven the Waikato—men, women and children—up the river into the great Mātakitaki Pā. When the northern army reached the Waikato stronghold it was packed with thousands of Waikato people under the leadership of Te Wherowhero.

II

This was the first time Te Wherowhero had been forced to fight a defensive battle. He fretted and was impatient at the enforced inactivity. In the meantime he kept a watchful eye on the dispositions of Hongi's forces. Presently Te Wherowhero observed that a section of Ngāpuhi, numbering about 200 men, all armed with guns, had taken up a position on the flat land to the east of the *pā*. Te Wherowhero thereupon called for his most seasoned warriors to follow him in a sortie on this section of the enemy. Between 70 arid 80 men immediately responded. In a short time they quietly moved out of the *pā* at various points and from their knowledge of the country they were able to foregather, unknown to the enemy, at a rallying point to the rear of the Ngāpuhi force, as arranged by their leader.

At a given signal Te Wherowhero's men bore swiftly down on the unsuspecting foe, some of whom were preoccupied in building rough shelters for the night. Those on guard were intent on keeping a watchful eye on Mātakitaki Pā. Any noise Te Wherowhero and his warriors may have made in their advance was drowned in the roar of the gunfire of the main body of Ngāpuhi on the opposite bank of Mangapiko stream, which flows into the Waipā river a short distance below the northwestern corner of the *pā*.

The Ngāpuhi outpost was taken completely by surprise, but the encounter, because of the superior Ngāpuhi numbers, developed into a desperate struggle. The Waikato were not to be denied, however, and eventually the Ngāpuhi men fled from their position in a dash to rejoin their main force across the Mangapiko. They had lost a considerable number and were thrown into disorder. The move to rejoin the main body had been foreseen by Te Wherowhero and he had already detailed a section of his men to cut off this line of retreat.

Finding their way disputed and with many more of their men falling to the Waikato, the Ngāpuhi doubled back on their tracks. Badly winded, they were now no match for Te Wherowhero's resolute men. Caught between two bodies of the pick of Waikato fighting men the Ngāpuhi were in a sorry plight. Small bands of the enemy made desperate dashes, some in the direction of the Waipā river, and others back again toward the Mangapiko.

The enemy suffered in maimed and killed about 150 men. Te Wherowhero and his men were in their element in the hand-to-hand fighting. Once the clash had started, and under the relentless blows of the swift-moving Waikato men, the majority of the Ngāpuhi could not make use of their guns. After their first hurried volleys they were given no time to reload.

Te Wherowhero himself performed deeds of characteristic valour in this clash with Ngāpuhi—a new enemy of his people. It was afterward related that in that hectic encounter the leader of the Waikato alone accounted for upward of 80 of the enemy killed and wounded. Complete masters of the situation, the Waikato picked up some of the firearms of the fallen Ngāpuhi and set off back to the *pā*, laden with 90 guns. These were the first guns the Waikato possessed and sometime later they were used by their new owners with disastrous results against the Ngāpuhi themselves.

III

During the course of the fighting a section of the Ngāpuhi main force had deployed on the northern bank of the Mangapiko, from where they delivered a furious fusillade across the stream into Mātakitaki Pā. But as their ground was practically on the same level as the *pā*, the Waikato were fairly safe within the entrenched positions in the earthworks. Most of the Waikato were having their first experience of the musket.

It is recorded that when Hongi Hika arrived before Mātakitaki, he called out to Te Wherowhero to surrender. The Waikato warriors whose battle experience had been with Māori weapons only, laughed derisively when Hongi said that they could not possibly hope to stand before his Ngāpuhi men and the *pā*. *Pū* also happens to be the name of a Māori trumpet and it was on this account that the inexperienced Waikato warriors laughed when Hongi threatened them with it.

Some of the garrison of the *pā* had been interested and excited spectators of the fighting and of the inspiring spectacle of the great Te Wherowhero in action. At the sight of the Ngāpuhi being put to flight some of the spectators ran to the northern end of Mātakitaki Pā and there poured out the latest news of the fighting to those who were manning that part of the fortifications. This news so excited some of the garrison that a number clambered up to the parapets and shouted defiance at the Ngāpuhi. The distance across the stream was too great a range for accurate shooting by the Ngāpuhi. A specially selected party of marksmen was therefore moved down to the low ground below the *pā* just above the junction of the Mangapiko and the Waipā. It is recounted, however, that one Waikato warrior was unlucky enough to receive a mortal wound at this extreme range and he fell back into the trench with blood pouring from his mouth. Those who attended him had never heard that this new weapon killed at a distance. Some put forward the opinion that the fallen warrior must have eaten the poisonous berry of the *tutu* (a shrub, the berry stalks of which are poisonous).

By this time many more had mounted the parapets and began a *haka*. The Ngāpuhi marksmen had in the meantime moved up close to the *pā*, and presently were within short range of the excited performers on the parapets. Some of the women joined the *haka* party and they were thoroughly enjoying themselves. A number of them every now and again would hurl defiance at the Ngāpuhi marksmen. In the midst of all this hilarious, rowdy performance the Ngāpuhi marksmen took careful aim and fired a deadly volley. Several of the performers fell back dead and dying, some with ghastly wounds. Other would-be performers were mounting the parapets at the same time. Those in the trench below were too stunned for the moment to understand what had happened to those who had fallen. Presently several more fell back off the parapet. Consternation soon turned to fear—fear of something these Waikato had never even imagined. When at last they realised that the dead and dying had been struck down by some secret weapon that only the Ngāpuhi possessed, the Waikato began to panic, and the panic spread.

IV

At this stage Te Wherowhero and his party returned, and were resting when the first wave of panic-stricken men and women rushed past in a wild dash to reach the exit at the southern end of the *pā*. For the moment Te Wherowhero thought that a breach had been made by the Ngāpuhi. Calling on his companions who were resting near him to follow, he moved off to the northern end of the *pā*. Finding that it was still intact he told Te Kanawa to go back and restore order at the southern end where the panic-stricken men and women had gone.

By now, however, practically the whole garrison was stampeding out of the *pā* and, to add to their fright, Te Wherowhero and his men had fired a couple of volleys which had wiped out the Ngāpuhi marksmen, but the excited men and women thought it was the Ngāpuhi who had entered the *pā*. Te Kanawa tried to stay the mad rush, but there were hundreds of people now frantically struggling to get beyond the *pā* across the deep outer ditch.

Another party of Ngāpuhi by this time had crossed over the Mangapiko and was moving across the flat where their dead comrades were lying. This company of the enemy had observed the evacuation of the northern end of the *pā* and surmised that something had gone amiss for the defenders, and they were crossing over when Te Wherowhero and his men fired the volleys that wiped out the first lot of marksmen. The second company of Ngāpuhi moved toward the *pā* without knowing the fate that had befallen their comrades. They were more intent on ascertaining the reason for the mad rush of the garrison from the northern end of Mātakitaki.

V

In the meantime at the other end of the *pā* the first of the garrison had managed to cross by the narrow bridge over the outer ditch, and were now running wildly off in the direction of Mangauika Pā, some five or six miles away across the Waipā on the eastern slopes of Pirongia. Those who followed rushed madly across the narrow bridge in increasing numbers. Some were so desperate that they attempted to jump across the ditch, but it had been constructed to prevent anybody being able to do just that, and in attempting the impossible they fell back. In the bottom of the ditch they found that the steep, smooth sides made it difficult for them to get out in a hurry. At the bridge the position soon became chaotic. All thought of wife, sister or child was forgotten in the mad rush out of Mātakitaki. By now, too, any attempt to cross the bridge was out of the question. The crowd was so dense that scores were continually being jostled into the ditch. Those on the brink were pushed in; others trying to get out were pulled back by those who hoped that by climbing upon the bodies of the fallen they would be able to make their escape. Very soon the ditch, especially around the bridge, was full of struggling men and women. Hundreds were trampled to death or were smothered.

VI

At the northern end of the *pā* Te Wherowhero and his trusty warriors again fired some volleys and the second company of Ngāpuhi was halted in its tracks. Te Wherowhero and his men had now exhausted their ammunition and it was at this moment that Te Kanawa appeared and reported what was happening at the other end of their *pā*.

A third and much larger party of Ngāpuhi was now approaching across the flat. On seeing their dead and wounded comrades, and realising that it was not safe to move too close to the *pā*, the Ngāpuhi fanned out and took cover. About 100 Ngāpuhi then approached in short dashes and in open order. Te Wherowhero kept a watchful eye on them, and also on those at the far end of the flat who were now being reinforced by the rest of the Ngāpuhi. The whole of the enemy force appeared to be concentrating on this sector. Te Wherowhero thereupon ordered his men to move further back into the inner defences of the *pā*, and here they waited.

The *pā*, except for Te Wherowhero and his band of about 100 men, was now deserted. An eerie silence settled on the scene. Those who had managed to escape were now well on their way through the scrub, or had swum across the Waipā river and were on their way to Mangauika Pā. Te Kanawa was very worried about his mother Te Rahuruake; and likewise Te Wherowhero about his young wife, Whakaawi, who was an expectant mother at the time.

The 100 or so Ngāpuhi moved close up to the *pā* and as they could not hear any voices they cautiously climbed the outer ramp and peered over the parapet. Not a soul was in sight. Presently about 50 Ngāpuhi warriors leaped down into the trench inside the *pā*, laughing and joking as they did so. Then, like a bolt from the blue, Te Wherowhero and his men rushed at them from three sides and in a few moments the Ngāpuhi were knocked down right and left. No sooner had these invaders been dispatched than several more appeared on the parapets. These men were unarmed as they had left their weapons to be handed up by their comrades below. A few lightning blows from Te Wherowhero, Te Kanawa and the others, and a score or more Ngāpuhi were killed where they stood, or were hurled back down the ramp.

This upset the Ngāpuhi and they retired right back across the flat. By now Te Wherowhero realised that he could not hold out for long. There was also the danger of the enemy sending out scouts to ascertain exactly what had happened at the other end of the *pā*. Te Wherowhero therefore took full advantage of the temporary respite from the enemy's attempts to enter the *pā* and he and his men hurriedly left, taking the 90 guns with them. They made for Mangauika Pā where they rested that night.

VII

The next day Te Wherowhero and Te Kanawa rallied some more of their men and with a company of about 150 strong they returned to the scene of battle. While they were cautiously approaching Mātakitaki they ran into a force of Ngāpuhi and in a sharp engagement they killed many of them and put the rest to flight. The Ngāpuhi were now in occupation of the *pā* and on learning that Te Wherowhero was in the vicinity the Ngāpuhi leader decided to remain in Mātakitaki until his men were rested. This inactivity on the part of the enemy enabled the Waikato refugees from Mātakitaki to get away in the direction of Ōtorohanga. The Mangauika Pā was by this time full and it was necessary to seek refuge further afield. Some of the Waikato fled in the direction of Kāwhia.

The Ngāpuhi spent the following day in scouring the countryside near Mātakitaki and they captured a number of stragglers. Among those taken were Parekohu and Te Rahuruake, Te Kanawa's sister and mother. On learning who they were Hongi Hika treated them with every respect and when he vacated the *pā* he left them there with ample food for several days.

VIII

In the meantime Te Wherowhero rejoined the shattered remnants of his people near Ōtorohanga. He also had his wife Whakaawi with him now. The Maniapoto tribes retired into their fortified *pā*, and when Te

Wherowhero and his people reached the big *pā* at Totorewa at the junction of the Mangaorongo stream with the Waipā river, they found this *pā* was, like Mangauika, also full. The Maniapoto leaders offered sanctuary to Te Wherowhero and his wife, but he declined, preferring to remain with his people to the end. He was advised to proceed to Pamotumotu, a Ngāti Matakore *pā* near the Rangitoto ranges. All the Maniapoto *pā* in the vicinity of Totorewa and for miles to the south were fully manned, so Te Wherowhero made for Pamotumotu. On arrival there, however, he found that this *pā* was full. Te Otapeehi, a Ngāti Matakore chief, suggested to Te Wherowhero that he go with him to another *pā* of his Ngāti Matakore tribe on the upper waters of the Mōkau river. When Te Otapeehi made this suggestion Te Wherowhero pondered for some time. Te Otapeehi was not known to him. At last Te Wherowhero asked Te Otapeehi, *"Tērā rānei ahau e maru i a koe?"* (Can you shelter me?). Te Otapeehi replied and said, *"Āe. ka maru koe i tāku pūreke. He kahu-pītongatonga, whakatari-hauhunga. Ka maru koe!"* (Yes, my cloak will shelter you; it is closely woven and made for wintry weather. It will indeed shelter you!)

A specially selected band of 140 warriors of Te Otapeehi's people then left Pamotumotu and went across country to the Mōkau valley and finally reached Ōrongokoekoeā Pā on the banks of the Mangaongaonga stream, a tributary of the Mapiu. It was here sometime later that Whakaawi gave birth to a son.

After the capture of Mātakitaki Hongi rested there for a time and then went on to attack Mangauika Pā. This *pā* also fell to Hongi Hika and his men and a large number of prisoners was taken. The Ngāpuhi were now masters of the Waikato and the Waipā as far as Pirongia. After the fall of Mangauika the Ngāpuhi army divided into two sections. One section under Huiputea, one of Hongi Hika's ablest leaders, went in a southeasterly direction to Ōrāhiri near Ōtorohanga, and there he made his camp and established his headquarters. He captured a large number of women here, and these he kept for the entertainment of himself and his men.

Hongi Hika turned to the west and marched over the southern shoulder of Pirongia mountain, and then on to Kāwhia by way of Te Rauamoa and the Tirohanga-Kāwhia track. The rest of Hongi Hika's activities in Kāwhia belong to his history. Te Wherowhero in the meantime settled down in the *pā* of Te Otapeehi's people, at Ōrongokoekoeā (the place where the song of the long-tailed cuckoo was heard).

ŌRONGOKOEKOEĀ

The Place where the Song of the Long-tailed Cuckoo was heard

Te Manu ki tapu a Tāne;
E, Manu!
Nau mai; e waha i taku tua!

Nō te Whakatapatapa Manu

The Sacred Spirit of the Birds of Tāne,
O thou Bird Spirit!
Draw nigh, and be thou borne aloft
On these mine shoulders!

From the Invocation for the Preservation of Birdlife

CHAPTER 9

ŌRONGOKOEKOEĀ

I

Ōrongokoekoeā[1] situated at the end of a long ridge with steep slopes of crumbling stones on three sides, and with formidable earthworks, was an impregnable *pā* of the Ngāti Matakore, sub-tribe of the Maniapoto. Shortly after Te Wherowhero and his people arrived there Te Huiputea, who was Hongi Hika's second-in-command, reached the vicinity at the head of 200 fully armed Ngāpuhi. He reconnoitred the adjacent *pā* of Te Haupeehi and then come on to Ōrongokoekoeā. Both *pā* were fully manned and because of their strength the fortifications were not attacked. The time was now mid-winter and there was no food to be had, and the Ngāpuhi leader had no alternative but to return to his headquarters at Ōrāhiri near Ōtorohanga.

Time went on, and Te Wherowhero's men having recovered their morale after the crushing defeat at Mātakitaki were now anxious to obtain some satisfaction for the Ngāpuhi invasion. Word had been received that the Ngāpuhi under Te Huiputea occasionally sent out companies from their headquarters at Ōrāhiri to scour the countryside, and that they had captured a large number of prisoners and were well supplied with food.

II

Spring came and the Ngāpuhi were still in Ōrāhiri. By this time the Maniapoto, who had mostly kept to their fortified *pā* since the Ngāpuhi invasion, had started to make plans for driving out Te Huiputea and his men who, as rumour had it, were intending to settle in Maniapoto land and had sent back for reinforcements and colonists. Te Otapeehi and Te Wherowhero at the head of 140 men made up equally of Ngāti Matakore and Waikato, now departed from Ōrongokoekoeā leaving a fairly strong garrison behind to guard against any surprise attack from Ngāpuhi raiding parties. Proceeding northward they came out at Waipari stream near Ōtorohanga and within striking distance of Te Huiputea's headquarters. Here Te Otapeehi met a woman who had escaped from the main body of the Ngāpuhi, who were then camped in the open on the banks of the Waipā river at Ōtorohanga. Te Huiputea was with this company. On questioning the woman, Te Otapeehi learnt that the Ngāpuhi were indulging in an orgy of debauchery with the women they had captured. Te Wherowhero thereupon told the woman to return to the encampment and to tell her companions that ere the rising of the sun they would be rescued.

In the meantime these women were to exercise all the subtle and fascinating witchery of which they were capable and they were to arouse the passions of the Ngāpuhi warriors with the sorcery that "seems half to yield, yet flies the bridal hour," and they were to continue to do so until well into the approaching dawn. The woman returned to the camp with the news.

III

That night, led by Te Otapeehi, the Ōrongokoekoeā. force approached the Ngāpuhi encampment. Te Otapeehi crossed the river under cover of darkness. He crawled underwater as he could not swim, leaving Te Wherowhero and the others to follow later. As had been prearranged, one of the captive women, a high-born Maniapoto whose name was Te Riutoto, came to the river ostensibly to get drinking water, and from her Te Otapeehi learnt that the Ngāpuhi were nearly all fast asleep. A few were awake, and had taken the precaution of tying to her wrist a string on which every now and again they tugged for Te Riutoto to give the answering jerk to indicate that she had not attempted to escape. Te Riutoto explained to Te Otapeehi the exact disposition of Te Huiputea's men and also the spot were they had piled their arms. This was at the foot of a *kahikatea*[2] tree around which the Ngāpuhi slept like "full-fed hound or gorged hawk, unapt for tender smell or speedy flight." Te Otapeehi, while talking to Te Riutoto, remained in the water close to the bank with his head among the water weeds, and it was while thus conversing that a thirsty Ngāpuhi came to the river. As he stooped down to drink and before he could utter a cry his head was pulled under the water and held there until he was drowned. Te Riutoto then returned to the encampment.

IV

As the morning stars rose over the Rangitoto ranges Te Wherowhero with his 140 men crossed the river and joined Te Otapeehi. Then stealthily approaching the encampment they prepared to carry out the bold plan of exterminating in one swoop Te Huiputea and his Ngāpuhi. Te Otapeehi moved forward like a shadow between the sleeping men. He was closely followed by four other Ngāti Matakore warriors, and presently they stood alongside the tree with their hands upon the pile of enemy arms.

The sleeping forms were barely visible in the faint starlight when Te Wherowhero opened the attack from all sides. Te Otapeehi and his four men immediately crashed their *mere* down on the heads of the Ngāpuhi lying at their feet. As others awoke still in a sleep-laden stupor, they instinctively moved toward their arms, but were speedily slain. The attack was swift and deadly, and in a matter of moments all the Ngāpuhi were prone on the ground *i te moe tē rena* (in the sleep from which there is no rising). Not a single man escaped.

V

The death of Te Huiputea and many other Ngāpuhi leaders who were in his section of Hongi Hika's army was a severe blow to the northern invaders. Te Huiputea was Hongi Hika's most dashing leader. A large quantity of ammunition also fell into the hands of the Maniapoto. A mere handful of Te Huiputea's men who happened to be away on a foraging expedition when the attack was made were the only survivors from this deadly retaliation. These men fled to Kāwhia to join Hongi Hika. With the 90 guns captured at Mātakitaki, the Maniapoto and Waikato now had Te Huiputea's armoury, and were in a much better position to challenge the great Hongi Hika and his *pū*.

But the astute Ngāpuhi leader was not now disposed to test out the fighting capabilities of the Maniapoto and their Waikato allies. He and his men had been living a life of ease in the Kāwhia lands for some months now. He was also a long way from home and his lines of communication were in danger of being cut. Hongi Hika decided to go while the opportunity offered.

VI

The news of the annihilation of Te Huiputea and his Ngāpuhi was received throughout the Waikato with jubilation. Hongi Hika did not waste any time. Immediately he received information of the disaster he set off for home. He was not going to give Te Wherowhero any time to mature plans for his further undoing. Returning the way he he had come, Hongi Hika went by forced marches and did not rest until he had crossed the Mangatāwhiri stream.[3]

As the Ngāpuhi passed downstream at Taupiri an old man of the Waikato stood on a hill overlooking a wide sweep of the Waikato river at that point. He stood and watched them paddle steadily. The old man had heard of Te Huiputea's defeat and, emboldened by what he thought was the enemy's dejected appearance, he began to make insulting gestures at them as they went by. He was quite a long way off and well out of gunshot range and he thought he was perfectly safe from the Ngāpuhi. He had his *taiaha* with him and he presently broke into a *haka*. He leaped and made violent passes with his *taiaha*. He sang a *kaioraora* or cursing song, interspersed with taunting calls at the Ngāpuhi. Among other things he yelled out was that if the Ngāpuhi were to return to Waikato land he would personally see to it that they were scattered "like filth" over the countryside—and he accompanied this threat with a significant and most insulting gesture.

The canoes rounded the bend. After his violent exertions the old warrior sat down to rest. He felt elated after launching those insults at the retreating invaders. It was good to curse and taunt the defeated foe, he meditated. How he was going to enjoy telling the story to his tribesmen on his return to the *pā*! But, around the bend, one of the canoes had landed and now, stealthily coming up the wooded gully, was a Ngāpuhi with the dreaded *pū*. The old man was rested and was about to make his way homeward. He stood up and stretched himself, and then stooped down to pick up his *taiaha*. As he did so the Ngāpuhi marksman took careful aim and fired. His aim was true and the Waikato slanderer of his people fell forward dead—shot in that part of his body he had exposed when making his last expressive taunt and insult.

Some of the Waikato were for following the Ngāpuhi, but Te Wherowhero was not in favour of this. The recollection of that panic at Mātakitaki and the dreadful consequences were too fresh in the mind of the Waikato leader, and he considered it advisable for his people to bide their time. Meanwhile he selected a group of leaders for future battles and went with them into Taupō country where they accompanied some Ngāti Tūwharetoa raids under their chieftain-warrior Te Heuheu II. Te Wherowhero himself spent the next four or five years mostly among the Maniapoto and made regular visits to confer with Te Heuheu, and to discuss future plans with the Waikato leaders who were rapidly making a name for themselves among the Taupō people as fighting men. The rest of the Waikato had scattered and were living in the forest ranges of the coastal regions and in the lands of the Maniapoto. Te Wherowhero kept a careful hold on them. He wished to see them with their morale fully restored.

VII

Te Wherowhero made Ōrongokoekoeā his headquarters. He found the life with Te Otapeehi and his people pleasant and restful after the arduous, hazardous and momentous period he had undergone. Te Otapeehi and the Maniapoto tribe were happy to be host to the great *ariki* (paramount chief) of Waikato.

The *hapū* or sub-tribes of the Maniapoto vied with one another in their contributions of varied foods from their tribal lands. Rereahu *hapū*, from Maraeroa and Te Tiroa, at the headwaters of the Waipā and Waimiha rivers, brought the tender fronds of *mamaku* (an edible tree fern), and in the season *kākā* (native parrot) and *kererū* (wood-pigeon). Ngāti Paemate, from Aorangi and Kahuwera on the Mōkau river, brought berry-fattened *tūī* (parson-bird). Ngāti Te Kanawa, Kaputuhi and other tribes, from the Mangati, a tributary of the Waipā, brought *piharau* (lamprey). Ngāti Rungaterangi and Ngāti Waiora and other Mōkau tribes brought from Awakino and Waikawau *wheke* (octopus), *kōura* (crayfish), *inanga* (whitebait), and all manner of shellfish. Succulent eels of all varieties were brought from every quarter. And there was no need for the Waikato *ariki* to pine for the silver-bellied eels of his lake country, for these were caught in thousands by the Ngāti Matakore and other *hapū* in the waterways of the great Te Kaawa swamps at the foot of the hill Kakepuku.

From the Hurakia ranges at the headwaters of the Ōngarue river, Ngāti Te Ihingarangi, Ngāti Raerae, Ngāti Hinemihi (all expert fowlers) brought *miro*-fattened *kererū*, either freshly snared or in calabashes as *huahua* (preserved in their own fat).

VIII

The presentation of the *huahua* by the last-mentioned tribes was attended with much ceremony. These *hapū* were past masters in the sacred lore of the *mauri o te tāhere-manu* (symbolic cult of the forest fowlers). Among these active hill-climbing people were the most expert bird-snarers and fowlers in the Tainui country. They were intrepid and expert fowlers, who climbed and set their snares on the trees that overhang the 1000ft. cliffs above the Ōngarue river amid the Rongoroa ranges.

We will accompany one of these *huahua* presentation parties as it approaches the *pā*. At the *pā* entrance the party has put down its burden and rested. (The main parts in the ritual accompanying the presentation are usually taken by the chief—also an expert and priestly fowler—

and the *tapairu* or priestess of the bird-snaring tribes. The latter also performed many other important ritualistic duties including the opening ceremony for the snaring season.) The party having rested, the priestly expert rises and approaches the calabashes. Addressing the spirit of dead birds he opens the invocation of the *whakatapatapa huahua* (the sacred chant for the slain birds) and at the end of the first stanza, he intones:

> *Te manu ki tapu a Tāne;*
> *E manu!*
> *Nau mai! e waha i tāku tua!*
>
> The sacred spirit of the birds of Tāne;
> O thou bird spirit,
> Greetings! and be thou borne aloft on these mine shoulders!

At this point the receptacles in which the birds have been preserved in their own fat are reverently raised and carried in silence for a moment or two. Then the priestess takes up the chant, and from this moment until the end there must be no break in the recital except for the responses at each ending of a stanza in the invocation. The cue for the response is given by the priestly expert or the priestess on a declamatory note:

> Priestly Expert (in a declamatory voice):
> *Ka whakairi?*
> And 'Tis raised up where?

> Chorus:
> *Ki runga o Hurakia koia!*
> Up on Hurakia over yonder!

It is necessary for all taking part in the ceremony to be on the alert for the responses, as any perceptible break between the challenging declamation of the priest and the responding chorus is an ill omen. Should the one chanting feel in need of a rest, the signal is given by a gesture to the other officiating priest or priestess to take up the chant at that point. A break in the recital would bring misfortune not only to the reciter but also to the tribe. In both cases ill luck would come in the form of the birds shunning the tribal forests and the family snaring trees. It would then be necessary to perform many propitiatory ceremonies to appease the spirit of the birds of Tāne, God of the Forests. At another point in the chant it is also most important to be on the alert. The priestly expert must have complete control of the recital lest some designing alien tribesman pronounce the *rotu* unchallenged. It was by such means, and by the theft of the *mauri* or talismanic stone image of the Kahuwera forest, that the *tūī* forsook their centuries-old haunts to go and foregather in the Rongoroa ranges.

The reader asks, "What is a *rotu*?" The author smilingly declines to enlighten him. There are now very few people who know what a *rotu* is, and the author is happy because he, as a responsible member of the tribes of Ngāti Raerae, Ngāti Ihingarangi and Rereahu, and the tribes-people themselves like to think that they are helping the present authorities preserve the birdlife of their ancestral forests, despite the depredations of sawmillers and others.

While the reader has been pondering the *rotu*, the *huahua* presentation party has reached the *marae* or courtyard of the *pā*, and several stanzas of the ritual have been chanted—quite an amazing feat of memory because there is no regularity of metre or any rhyming in Māori poetry. The verses vary in length. Thus, devoid of all these aids to memory, the Māori reciter relies entirely on euphony, his sense of rhythm, and his capacious memory.

The procession has been timed so as to reach the courtyard at the spot where the presentation is to take place and with still one stanza to be chanted. The calabashes are placed in front of the honoured chief, and the concluding stanza is chanted to its end. Then, as the final measure, the priest intones:

Hoki mai! Hoki mai, te manu ora!
Ki te maunga koia!

Comeback! Come back, O ye spirit of the living bird,
To the forest ranges—Ah!

And the response comes on a note of joy:

Ki runga o Hurakia koia!
Up onward to Hurakia over yonder!

IX

Te Wherowhero was indeed a happy man. He had the company of his blooming and charming wife Whakaawi who had given him so much joy in producing a son and heir. He idolised his wife and she was grateful and contented with the life at Ōrongokoekoeā, for she had come through a most anxious time since Mātakitaki. Te Wherowhero too had suffered untold agony of mind at Mātakitaki when he learnt of the seriousness of the panic. The Lord of Waikato was deeply grateful to the modest, but nevertheless purposeful warrior chief of Ngāti Matakore, Te Otapeehi.

On the birth of his son Te Wherowhero was delighted when the Maniapoto chiefs sought his permission to allow them to celebrate the occasion. On the day of the child's *tohi* [4] ceremony there was a large gathering of the tribes and there was much rejoicing. There was feasting, singing, posture and *poi* dancing the whole night through. Te Wherowhero also had Maniapoto blood, and he left the naming of his son to the Maniapoto chiefs, and they acknowledged the privilege by commemorating his gallant stand at Mātakitaki Pā in the name of this boy. They named Te Wherowhero's infant Tūkaroto, "he who stood undaunted within." [5]

NOTES ON CHAPTER 9

Note 1

Ōrongokoekoeā: The author in company with Mr. L. G. Kelly, an authority on Māori *pā*, visited Ōrongokoekoea on December 2, 1935. The *pā* then had quite a young forest growing on it, but the earthworks were almost as they were more than 100 years before.

Note 2

Kahikatea: (*Podocarpus dacrydiodes*, white pine). The tree mentioned in this account is still growing (1945). It is at the south end of the railway yards at Ōtorohanga.

Note 3

Mangatāwhiri: This is the name of the stream which flows into the Waikato river at Mercer. It figures in the later troubles between Māori and European and might be reckoned as the Rubicon of the Waikato.

Note 4

Tohi: The ceremony attending the severance of the umbilical cord, when the child was also named at the same time.

Note 5

Tūkaroto: Later, when the missionaries first came to Waikato, Tūkaroto was baptised Matutaera (Methuselah) and under this name he appears in many of the early records about the Waikato. After the death of his father and when he became the second Māori King, Matutaera as he was now called, went on a visit to Taranaki. While there Te Ua Haumene, the Hauhau prophet, bestowed on him the name Tāwhiao ("hold the people together"; or literally translated, "hold the world"). Later on again Tāwhiao was passing through Te Kumi, near Te Kūiti, and here a Maniapoto chief named Te Mahuki had started a new cult. As part of the service Tāwhiao was invoked as a god. Immediately after the service which he attended, and when he heard the supplication to him, Tāwhiao made a protest. As a high priest of the Tainui *Io* cult and an adherent of the Church of England, this supplication was not only distasteful to him, but was ludicrous in the extreme. Addressing Te Mahuki and his followers Tāwhiao said, "I was once named Tūkaroto, then I was baptised Matutaera, and then Te Ua bestowed the name Tāwhiao upon me. Now, in your service, I have heard you praying to Tāwhiao. As Tāwhiao is now the name of a god, I have decided to give myself a new name. Henceforth, I am to be known as Te A" (practically the same thing as Mr. A.) The name Te A never became popular, but in his own family circle it was used most frequently. (The Māori family, including the children, called one another by their first names; it was not until recent times that "father" and "mother" became more general.)

A ROMANTIC INTERLUDE

Tiatia whakaripatia te kai-wharawhara,
Kia pai au te haere i ngā tarawaha kai whitiwhiti
Meremere-Tāwera, te whetū takiaho mai o te rangi
Ko ahau ki raro nei ....

Nō Te Pātere a Ngāwaero

Thence, jauntily wearing each side mine head
The much-prized plume of the albatross,
I will travel far and wide;
While in the starry heavens shines forth Meremere-Tāwera;
And here below, resplendent and vying with her,
Will be none other than I! ....

From The Song of Ngāwaero

CHAPTER 10

A ROMANTIC INTERLUDE

I

Some time before the events related in Chapter 6 Te Wherowhero had married, and added to the number of his wives as becoming a high chief, Waiata, the elder of the two daughters of the chieftain Tūkōrehu. There had been no children of this marriage, and Tūkōrehu was anxious that this should be remedied if possible, and he decided that his younger daughter Ngāwaero should also marry the great chieftain of Waikato. The union was made the occasion for festivities on a lavish scale at Ngāruawāhia, the principal gathering-place of the Waikato tribes.

There are certain places in Aotearoa that seem to have a spell of strength and endurance cast upon them by primeval forces. Through the ages they do not appear to suffer any permanent harm from the depredations of mankind. In the Waikato is one of these places where the waters of the Waikato and Waipā rivers meet at Ngāruawāhia. For more than 12 miles above this point the clear and deep-flowing waters of the Waikato, in its westward course, appear to be bent on charging straight through the out-flung Hākarimata range. But as if in obedience to the quiet persuasion of the sluggish waters of the Waipā, it turns with renewed zest to the north, where for about three miles it rushes through Taupiri gorge to the west of Taupiri mountain. Around its detached and almost silent-flowing waters rise banks and terraces, on the top of which stretch for mile upon mile to the north and south to the distant hills, fertile plains interspersed with lakes and fens. This, then, was the setting for the romance of Ngāwaero.

II

Ngāwaero was a handsome maiden in the full bloom of young womanhood. Tall and statuesque, she was a fine specimen of that race of handsome men and women, the Ngāti Raukawa-Maniapoto blend. Te Wherowhero was in his forties and was beginning to put on weight. In this respect he was tending to the Waikato type of heavy built men. He was fully tattooed and, with his upstanding height of more than 6ft, he was a commanding figure. He had an open countenance, but when roused his penetrating look was overpowering. In repose he was inclined to be shy. His forehead and bold features, with the symmetrical curvilinear lines of *moko* (face tattoo) set him apart as an aristocrat of the aristocrats. He was a worthy son of his bold Polynesian seafaring ancestors.

Ngāruawāhia, on the occasion of the marriage festivities of Te Wherowhero and Ngāwaero, was the scene of animation and joy. There were *haka* and *poi* parties of entertainers from all the Tainui tribes. Among the visiting peoples were Ngāti Tipa, Ngāti Naho, Ngāti Amaru, Ngāti Pou and Ngāti Tamaoho from the lower reaches of the Waikato river; Ngāti Te Ata, Te Waiohua, Ngāti Tai, Ngāti Tamaoho and Ngāti Whawhakia of Manukau, Tāmaki and east of the same river.

There were Hauraki tribes of Ngāti Pāoa, Ngāti Tamaterā, Ngāti Maru and Ngāti Whanaunga. There came Ngāti Raukawa from the Kaokaoroa o Pātetere, of Waotu, of Maungatautari and of Wharepuhunga; and the kindred tribes of Ngāti Wairangi, Ngāti Hā and Ngāti Te Koherā of Ngāroto, Tuaropaki and Titiraupenga.

Hauraki plains people of Ngāti Hauā, Rāhiri and Wairere and Ngāti Korokī of the middle reaches of Waikato above Ngāruawāhia were present, and Ngāti Tūwharetoa of the lake Taupō and Tongariro mountain area.

There were Ngāti Maniapoto of Waiari, of Rangitoto, of Hauturu, Maraeroa, Hurakia, Kāwhia and Mōkau; the tribes of Rangiaohia, Waipā, Pirongia, Moerangi and Waitetuna of Ngāti Apakura, Ngāti Hikairo, Ngāti Hourua, Ngāti Reko and Ngāti Tamainupō.

The Kāwhia colonies of Ngāti Mahuta and Ngāti Hikairo also sent representatives, and Ngāti Te Wehi of Aotea harbour, and Tainui of Whāingaroa and the west coast up to Waikato heads were present as well.

The numerous and the most powerful of the Waikato tribes, Ngāti Mahuta—Te Wherowhero's own tribe—were hosts for this immense gathering. Among many of the chieftains who attended were Kukutai of Ngāti Tipa, Te Awaitaia of Whāingaroa, Te Heuheu Tūkino of Ngāti Tūwharetoa, Te Haupokia and Te Rangituatea of Ngāti Maniapoto, Te Waharoa of Ngāti Hauā, and Te Horeta of the Hauraki tribes. There were great quantities of food contributed by the tribes, but it was noticeable that one important delicacy was missing, especially for such an outstanding gathering. There was no *huahua*.

The people of Ngāwaero were noted fowlers and the visiting Waikato tribes and many of the coastal tribes had looked forward to a feast of *huahua*. Many of the chiefs made some comment about the absence of this dish. One of the chieftains, Kukutai of Ngāti Tipa, on his return home to the lower Waikato, made some rather caustic remarks about the *huahua*, and said, "*Ka hua au kei te tamāhine a Tūkōrehu rewa ana te hinu manu o ngā maunga!*" (Indeed, I thought that on the occasion of the marriage of Tūkōrehu's daughter preserved birds from the forest ranges would have been floating in their own fat!).

In those days it took time for news to get about and, in the meantime, Ngāwaero had settled down happily at Ngāruawāhia. Then one day as she rested in the porch-way of Te Wherowhero's house some visitors from downriver called. The women of the party talked and retailed the gossip of the river tribes. One of these women was related to Ngāwaero, and when the gossiping visitors had broken into small groups and she found herself alone with their hostess, she imparted the gist of Kukutai's disparaging reference about the *huahua*. The story ended and, with a deep sigh and an expressive shrug of her shoulders, the story-teller added, "*Tukua ake ki ahau, kua mate noa ake!*" (I was so overcome [with shame] I was as one already dead!)

III

Ngāwaero, the happy bride, was now hurt to the quick and she became restless. She, with her illustrious ancestry, was belittled, and something had to be done about it. At this time a messenger called to discuss with Te Wherowhero a projected expedition to Taranaki. The Maniapoto chiefs, had decided to call a meeting at Whatiwhatihoe near Pirongia for the purpose. The meeting was to take place in the early summer. On hearing of this Ngāwaero began to make her plans.

The fowling season was approaching and after consulting her lordly husband she set off for her father's home at Turata on the northern bank of the Pūniu river. She called on all her relatives and after they had heard her story it was decided to make a special tribal effort during the bird-snaring season that was about to open. Word was also sent out to her kinsmen at Maungatautari and Wharepuhunga. The season promised to be a bounteous one. The *miro* trees along the banks of the Mangaohoi stream were bearing heavily. The story reached the Ngāti Maniapoto of the Hurakia ranges, and they set about preparing for the snaring of *kererū* and *kākā* at Te Tiroa and Ketemaringi, while at Te Rongoroa *rākautūtū* (the snaring trees) were put in order for catching *tūī*. Ngāwaero's, Ngāti Te Koherā kinswoman Noaia, the tribal priestess, had sent a special invitation to her to visit Tuaropaki and Te Kakaho at the foothills of the lofty Titiraupenga peak for the opening of the fowling season.

Te Wherowhero also had occasion to visit the Taupō chieftain Te Heuheu Tūkino and, accompanied by a small party, he and Ngāwaero set forth. After the ceremonies at Tuaropaki and Te Kakaho the party went across the Tihoi plains to Waihora where they boarded the famous war-canoe Te Moata and were taken over to Te Rapa at the southeastern end of Taupō lake. The two high chiefs conferred on matters of mutual interest, while their wives retailed stories as women all the world over will do. Ngāwaero told the story of Kukutai's remark, and Te Heuheu's two sister wives, Nohopapa and Te Mare, were most sympathetic. At the first opportunity they obtained the permission of their husband for access to the famous family heirloom which was being lent Ngāwaero. This famous heirloom was a *tiki* of greenstone named Te Ngako which had been handed down through their grandfather Te Rangituamatotoru. This prized *tiki* was kept on the sacred island of Motutāiko and a special messenger was sent to fetch it. Te Wherowhero and his party then returned home.

IV

The meeting at Whatiwhatihoe was to be held in a matter of a few weeks and the preparations for it were being hastened. Te Wherowhero did not stay very long with Ngāwaero's people before he went back to Ngāruawāhia. The Waikato chieftain left his young wife with her people who were at that time completing the carving of a *waka manu* or a dug-out one-piece wooden vessel for preserved birds. The vessel was made from *tōtara* wood with projecting hand grips at each end and on the sides. It required, when filled, eight men to carry it. The *waka manu* was filled with *huahua*, as were several *ipu* (calabashes) which were filled to the brim with *kōkō* or forest berry-fattened *tūī*. The wooden *waka manu* was given a name and was called "Haowhenua" (the widespread food-gathering of the land). All was now in readiness for the meeting at Whatiwhatihoe.

On the day appointed Ngāwaero and her people set out from her father's home at Turata. The party comprised relays of stalwart young men for the transporting of the food vessel to Whatiwhatihoe, and there were also included in the party the best *haka* men for the posture dancing and waiata men and women for the singing. Dressed in the finest cloaks of the tribe, cheeks specially and gaily hued with *tākou* (red ochre) and plumed with rare *huia* feathers, the young high-born women of Ngāwaero's tribe presented an attractive picture. Ngāwaero was similarly robed, but in addition she wore the famous *tiki* Te Ngako.

The occasion was to be celebrated with song and story and the special *haka* displays for which her people were famous. The best orators were also in the company for recital of the tribal traditions and genealogies. The poets of Ngāti Paretekawa, her father's *hapū*, had been consulted and with their assistance Ngāwaero had composed a special *pātere* (action song) for the *huahua* presentation at Whatiwhatihoe.

V

At high noon, under a cloudless sky, Ngāwaero's party, after crossing the Waipā and resting some distance away from Whatiwhatihoe village, moved off on the last stage of the journey. When they reached the outer bounds of the village, the party paused, as they had been seen, and the tribes gathered at Whatiwhatihoe were assembling and preparing to receive them with the time-honoured welcome of the Māori. After the last wailing sound of the local women's welcoming chant had died away, Ngāwaero and her party moved forward a distance as the women of their tribe responded with the chants of greeting. Then the great food vessel was lifted up on to brown shoulders, with the proud Ngāwaero perched in front and sitting on a specially constructed seat. The party moved, forward slowly on to the main courtyard of the village. Ngāwaero, her eyes glistening, was the centre of attention as she sat up aloft with head slightly bent forward, her composure dignified and demure.

The appearance of this party betokened to all that a special presentation was to be made. An expectant hush settled on the assembled multitude. At a fitting moment, Ngāwaero proudly raised her head and with eyes aglow, she began to sing the opening lines of her song in which later the specially selected party of singers and posture dancers joined.

TE PĀTERE A NGĀWAERO

1

E noho ana i te papa tahi o taku koro,
Whakarongo rua aku taringa
Ki te hiha tangi mai o Kukutai!
Me aha koa i te awa whakawhiti ki Pūniu,

Tē pikitia i te pīnakitanga ki Turata, ko Te Arawai!
E kore, au, e Kahu, e aro iho;
He kai tata waiho noa i te huanui.
Ngā pikitanga ki Te Matau,
Kia marama 'hau te titiro auahi,
Kōkiri mai ki Mangahana; ko Te Huanui!
E kore au e peka noa
Kei ngurungurua 'hau e te tangata.
Me whakarangi-pūkohu e au ki Hurakia;
Hei a Te Whare, me whakatangi te korowhiti ki Titiraupenga!
Hei a Te Momo, tū ana 'hau i te pou tū papa o Te Raro!
Kia tākiri tū au i te wai o te huariki:
Ū ē, a rarā! Te whakamā i ahau, ē!

2
Me tohe tangata ki Hauhungaroa, ki Tuaropaki ko Te Kohika!
Mā te tangata e kī mai, "Ko wai te wahine e haere nei?"
Māku anō e kī atu, "Ko au! Ko Hine i pakia e te ngutu;
E kimi ana i te whare o Te Tuiri."
Mā Noaia e kī mai;
"Utaina koia ki te ihu o Te Moata,
Ngā uranga kei Te Rapa!"
Tū ana 'hau i te pou-toko-manawa o te whare o Te Riu':
Ko te whare rā, i parua iho ki te muka rāwhiti;
Ki te neko, ki te kaitaka, ki te pakipaki;
Kāti ka hoki mai....

3
E kore au e hoki noa i te tihi mōrunga ki Tokerau:
Me tohe ā-wairua ki ngā pūau o Tongariro,
Ko Te Rangimōnehunehu; ko tōna tuakana ko Tauteka!
Hei ngari mōhoku ki te nohoanga i a Te Whatanui.
Tiatia whaka-ripatia te kai-wharawhara;
Kia pai au te haere i ngā tarawaha kai whitiwhiti:
Meremere-Tāwera, te whetū takiaho mai o te rangi!
Ko ahau ki raro nei; me hoki komuri e au
Ki Motutāiko, ko Te Heuheu!
Kia wetekia te tau o Te Ngako ki au mau ai:
Hei aha rā? Hei ata mōku
Mō te wahine hakirara, ē!

THE SONG OF NGĀWAERO

1

1 Across an empty courtyard gazing,
  I sat at my lordly master's threshold:
  When both mine ears were assailed
  By the biting taunt uttered by Kukutai!
5 Straightway, without thought of the intervening river,
  I hied me off to Pūniu;
  And I did not turn aside to climb
  The gentle rise to Turata
  Where abideth Te Arawai.
10 (I will not tarry, O Kahu! As the food you offer
  Lies to hand alongside the tribal highway.)
  O'er yonder is the ascent to Te Matau;
  From that summit I shall clearly see the smoke rising
  In stately columns from Mangahana
15 Where abideth Te Huanui:
  (But 'tis not my purpose to turn aside here,
  Lest I be harshly spoken of by men.)
  From there, my gaze will go outward
  Through the hazy distance, to Hurakia,
20 Where abideth Te Whare;
  Who will sound the piercing signal
  To Titiraupenga to appraise Te Momo of my coming.
  With him I shall be privileged to stand alongside
  The upright snaring-post of Te Raro.
25 And there, proudly standing,
  I shall quench my thirst with the juice of the *huariki*!
  There, now, you see what comes
  Of this shameful jest on me!

2

  Now, let a messenger be sent
30 To Hauhungaroa and also to Tuaropaki,
  To fetch Te Kohika:
  Some men will ask,
  "Who is this woman travelling about?"
  I shall reply and say:
35 "'Tis I, the young woman whose story is on many lips?
  Seeking for the dwelling-house of Te Tuiri."

Noaia will then speak forth and say:
"Let her be taken aboard
And placed at the bow of Te Moata:
40 And let the course be set
For the landing-place at Te Rapa!"
There I shall enter, and take my place
By the centre-pillar of the house of Te Riu';
That ornate house laid out with cloaks
45 Of finest eastern fibre;
And adorned with *neko*, *kaitaka* and *pakipaki*:
With my mission fulfilled, I here do homeward turn.

3
I shall not, however, wend my homeward way
Without pausing on the summit of Tokerau:
50 From here I shall urge
My spirit to journey forth
To the delta-mouth of Tongariro
Where abideth Te Rangimōnehunehu and his senior cousin Tauteka;
These two will arrange for safe-conduct
55 To the dwelling-house of Te Whatanui:
There I will bedeck and adorn mineself;
Thence, jauntily wearing each side mine head
The much-prized plume of the albatross,
I will travel far and wide....
60 In the starry heavens shines forth Meremere-Tāwera
In all her splendour;
And here below, resplendent
And vying with her,
Will be none other than I!
65 I must here modestly retire to Motutāiko,
To the presence of Te Heuheu;
Where he will unfasten the cord
And hand over to me to wear
The valued heirloom Te Ngako!
70 For what purpose?
For my adornment of course!
I—the woman who was so belittled and despised!

The party of Ngāwaero had by now reached the centre of the *marae* and here the food vessel was slowly lowered and placed on the ground. After the traditional wailing ceremony the speech-making began.

VI

At last Tūkōrehu strode forward and drawing himself up to his full height he called across the *marae* to his son-in-law Te Wherowhero and made the *huahua* presentation to him in the time-honoured manner and in these words:

Ara! ki ngā Hau e Whā!
Ka hoki mai anō ki ahau:
Ara! ki ngā Iwi katoa e pae nei;
Ka hoki mai anō ki ahau
Ara! ki ngā Rangatira!
Ka rongo mai koutou,
Ka hoki mai anō ki ahau:
Ara! ki a Kukutai!
Ka rongo mai koe,
Ka hoki mai anō ki ahau
Ara! ki a Waikato!
Ka hoki mai anō ki ahau
Nā, taringa whakarongo!
Ara! ki a Te Wherowhero!
Oti atu! Oti atu !
Ka huri!

TRANSLATION

Behold! (pointing with *taiaha* at wooden vessel and calabashes)
These, I do present unto the Four Winds of Heaven! (pause)
They are returned unto me:
Behold! (pointing, etc.)
These I do now present unto all the Tribes here assembled! (pause)
They are returned unto me:
Behold! (pointing, etc.)
These, I do present unto the Chiefs! (pause)
Ye having heard,
They are returned unto me:
Behold! (pointing, etc.)
These I now present unto Kukutai (pause)
And ye having heard
They are returned unto me:

Behold! (pointing, etc.)
These, I now present unto Waikato! (pause)
Again they are returned unto me: (pause)
Do ye all now hearken unto me! (pause)
Behold! (pointing, etc.)
All these I now present unto Te Wherowhero!
With him they remain! They remain!
I retire!

As Te Wherowhero arose and strode across the *marae* to receive the gift of Ngāwaero and her people, Ngāwaero —who had dismounted and now stood at her father's side—moved over and awaited her husband alongside the wooden vessel and the calabashes of *huahua*. Te Wherowhero greeted his wife with the *hongi* (touching of noses). Then he turned to face the assemblage and made the formal presentation of the gift to the chiefs and tribes. At the conclusion of his presentation he smilingly turned to his happy wife and asked her to repeat her song. Her eyes were brimming with tears of joy as she threw her head back and started her song of joy and triumph. This time Ngāwaero joined in the *pūkana* (posture dance), a glistening greenstone *mere* which Te Wherowhero had passed her quivering in one hand. Her liquid brown eyes shone brightly as her beautiful young body swung and swayed, and her waving hands moved in time to the rhythm of her song in which the whole of her party joined. All the pent-up pride of her race entered into the half-alluring and haughty turn of her aristocratic head. It was indeed a great day for Te Wherowhero's young wife Ngāwaero.

NOTES ON CHAPTER 10

Song of Ngāwaero

(1) empty courtyard... lordly master's threshold: In reference to the Ngāruawāhia tribal headquarters of Te Wherowhero, after the tribes had departed.

(4) Kukutai: A great chieftain of the tribes of the lower Waikato, near the mouth of the river.

(5) intervening river: Waikato river.

(6) Pūniu: The river of that name, a tributary of the Waipā river. Haereawatea, the home of Tūkōrehu, was on the north bank of the Pūniu (southern end of the present township of Kihikihi).

(8) Turata: Formerly a village situated at the northern end of what is now Kihikihi township. This was the home of a chief named Te Arawai. The main tribal highway passed his home.

(9) Te Arawai: A relative of Ngāwaero, and the priestly guardian of the tribal bird-snaring forests fringing the banks of Mangaohoi stream.

(10) Kahu: The wife of Te Arawai.

(12) Te Matau: The first village to the south of the Pūniu river, and beyond Tūkōrehu's home.

(14) Mangahana: A small stream on the south side of the Pūniu river. This is a fertile area and was once closely settled by various members of the Matakore *hapū*. Much of the food supplies for the tribal gatherings at Whatiwhatihoe were obtained from the Mangahana district. This explains the reference in the song to Ngāwaero's reluctance "to turn aside, lest I be harshly spoken of by men." Her kinsmen here were very busy at the time and it would be imposing on them to mention her story to them in the expectation that they might make a contribution.

(15) Te Huanui: A Maniapoto chief.

(19) Hurakia: Part of the watershed on the western side of Lake Taupō. This extensive forest range was a famous bird-snaring locality.

(20) Te Whare: A priestly fowler of the Hurakia ranges.

(22) Titiraupenga: A high and bold peak to the north of the Hurakia. This was also a famous bird-snaring forest.

Te Momo: A chief of the Ngāti Te Koherā, a Raukawa-Tūwharetoa sub-tribe, the priestly expert of the *hapū*.

(24) Te Raro: The most important bird-snaring place in the Titiraupenga area. It was here that the tribal priestess of the bird cult performed the opening ceremony of the snaring season.

(26) huariki: Berry of the *pāpāuma* (*Griselinia littoralis*) tree.

(30) Hauhungaroa, Tuaropaki: Two well-known forest ranges adjacent to Titiraupenga; also famous as bird-snaring places.

(31) Te Kohika: A chief and priestly expert of the bird cult, and a cousin of Ngāwaero.

(36) Te Tuiri: A brother chief of Te Momo and Te Kohika.

(37) Noaia: A chieftainess and priestess of the bird cult; of the same family as Te Tuiri.

(39) Te Moata: A famous canoe of Taupō lake tribes.

(41) Te Rapa: Tribal village and former headquarters of Ngāti Turumakina sub-tribe of Ngāti Tūwharetoa tribe of Taupō. It was situated between Tokaanu and Waihī and was overwhelmed by a huge landslide in 1846 when the Lord of Taupō, Te Heuheu Tūkino II, was killed.

(43) Te Riu': In full, Te Riupawhara; a well-known warrior chief of the Taupō tribes.

(46) *neko*: A finely-woven and ornamental cloak.

kaitaka: A plain finely-woven robe with borders highly ornamented with *tāniko* geometrical designs.

pakipaki: A much-prized cloak made of one piece with attractive borders.

(49) Tokerau: A high hill on the Western side of Lake Taupō.

(52) Tongariro: The river of that name which flows into Lake Taupō near Tokaanu; now a world-famous trout-fishing river.

(53) Te Rangimōnehunehu, Tauteka: Both high chiefs of the Ngāti Tūwharetoa tribe.

(55) Te Whatanui: Famous Ngāti Raukawa chieftain who led his tribe to the Manawatū and Kapiti districts where, with the Ngāti Toa under Te Rauparaha, they conquered those fertile lands.

(60) Meremere-Tāwera: Meremere is the name of the planet Venus as an evening star; as a morning star it is called Tāwera.

(65) Motutāiko: Island in Lake Taupō.

(66) Te Heuheu: The name of the paramount chiefs of Lake Taupō. The Te Heuheu mentioned in the song was the second of that name. He was overwhelmed, together with his eldest son Te Waaka, and several of his hapū, Ngāti Turumakina, at Te Rapa in 1846. Te Heuheu was one of the ablest war-leaders of the Māori people. He was also a poet, and his compositions are among the classic ones of the race.

(69) Te Ngako: A much-prized *tiki* (a flat grotesque figure of greenstone worn on a string around the neck) of the Te Rangituamatotoru family. Te Heuheu's two sister wives were granddaughters of Te Rangituamatotoru.

SETTLING OF ACCOUNTS

Whakataka tō Hau ki te Muri;
Whakataka tō Hau ki te Tonga:
Kia mākinakina i Uta;
Kia mātaratara i Tai:
Kia hī ake ana te Ata-kura,
He tio... he huka...
He Hau-hunga!

Nō tētehi karakia tawhito

Cease thou, O East Wind;
Cease thou, O South Wind:
Let the murmuring breeze sigh o'er the Land;
Let the stormy Seas subside:
And let the Red Dawn come,
With a sharpened air... a touch of frost...
And the Promise of a Glorious Day!

From an ancient invocation

CHAPTER 11

SETTLING OF ACCOUNTS

I

For about a decade after the events described in the last chapter Te Wherowhero was almost continuously on the warpath. He had quite a number of old scores to pay off against various tribal enemies of his people. A full account of the expeditions that were led by him would fill a volume. For the present purpose it is proposed to compress the happenings of this eventful period within the limits of this chapter.

Te Wherowhero's military genius had fully ripened and his strategic and tactical methods were equal to every contingency that arose. It was during this time that he was given the name of Pōtatau or "doorway of night," a name which betokened the fear he had instilled into the minds of the enemies of his people.

II

Immediately following the defeat of Huiputea at Ōtorohanga and the precipitate retreat of Hongi Hika and his Ngāpuhi army from Kāwhia, overtures for peace were made by the Ngāpuhi leader to Te Wherowhero. The result of the meeting which subsequently took place was the giving in marriage of Matire, the daughter of the Ngāpuhi chieftain Toka (a senior cousin of Hongi Hika in the aristocracy of northern tribes), to Takiwaru or Kati, Te Wherowhero's younger brother. This was intended to be a permanent peacemaking or, as the Māori term has it, a *tatau pounamu* (a greenstone door).

Yet another, great Ngāpuhi warlord, the famous Pōmare—lately returned from the East Coast where he had fought against and with the tribes of that district—decided to make a man-killing raid into Waikato and Maniapoto territory. However, Pōmare's expedition was destined to be ill-fated. The Hongi Hika clan claimed that the disaster that overtook him was due to the fact that a sacred peacemaking was broken by Pōmare. In May of 1826 Pōmare was killed and his army decimated, only two or three men escaping from the battlefield at Te Rore (the snare) on the banks of the Waipā river. This defeat of the Ngāpuhi was immediately followed up by Te Wherowhero with a seaborne army to Tawatawhiti, in Ngāpuhi territory, where he inflicted a crushing defeat on the northern tribes.

This was followed in the ensuing year by an abortive raid by another Ngāpuhi warlord named Rangituke. His fleet of canoes appeared off Waitematā harbour in the autumn of 1827. A fierce battle was fought on the surrounding hills and on the landing-beaches. The Ngāpuhi were utterly routed and almost completely wiped out. Their leader was killed and, of the several large sea-going *kauri* war-canoes which had brought them to Mauinaina, only one escaped with 20 men to tell the tale.

The Waikato tribes were now joined by Ngāti Whātua of Kaipara and Tāmaki. Ngāti Whātua had just previously suffered a crushing defeat at Te Ikaaranganui by a Ngāpuhi force. The combined army went north in a fleet of canoes (some of which had belonged to Rangituke) and landed at Tawatawhiti. In the fighting there Te Wherowhero, who wore a red feather cloak during the engagement, further distinguished himself by killing several of the flower of the Ngāpuhi fighting men.

Later again, in 1832, another Ngāpuhi expedition, led by Pukerangi, invaded Waikato territory and marched up-river as far as Whangape lake. After some desultory fighting and finding that the full strength of Waikato was being rapidly mobilised against him he retired, and, embarking, he set off for Kawau island. Pukerangi was closely pursued all the way and was overtaken at the island by Te Wherowhero and his Waikato men. After suffering heavy casualties the Ngāpuhi fled across to the mainland. The Waikato followed and inflicted severe blows in the merciless battles that took place in and around Ngāpuhi territory at Whāngārei. After crushing the Ngāpuhi of that district, the Waikato followed a section of them, who had come through to assist the Whāngārei people, to Ngunguru. Here the Ngāpuhi were strongly reinforced, but this did not deter the Waikato fighters who in pitched battle inflicted the heaviest defeat the Ngāpuhi ever suffered. The dead were numbered in thousands, and the Waikato exacted more than ample payment for their crushing defeat at Mātakitaki at the hands of Hongi Hika. The Waikato also rescued several hundred of their tribespeople who had been captured by Hongi Hika at Mangauika and other places. After this taste of the fighting strength of Te Wherowhero and his people the Ngāpuhi were content to leave matters as they stood.

The account with the Ngāpuhi had been settled.

III

In addition to the feeling aroused by the fighting in the time of Te Rauparaha's stay with the north Taranaki tribes there were many "incidents" arising from time to time between these tribes and the Tainui people, particularly the Ngāti Maniapoto. There was quite a score to settle with them. Among Waikato and Maniapoto losses by death which called for payment were Maungatautari, a close relative of Te Wherowhero (mentioned in Chap. 1), Mama, Te Hiakai, Tikawe, and others.

An unusual interlude in the series of marches and counter-marches into Taranaki by the Waikato and Maniapoto was the 1826 expedition of Te Wherowhero. This invasion was made at the instigation of the north Taranaki chief Ngātata, of the Āti Awa tribe. He had a score to pay off against the southern Taranaki tribe of Ngāti Ruanui and he made a special journey to Waikato to enlist the help of Te Wherowhero and other Tainui chiefs. Some heavy slaughter was inflicted on the Ngāti Ruanui around the Tangahoe river district and many prisoners were taken, including the wife of the priestly chieftain and poet Turaukawa. After the fall of Te Ruaki Pā on the banks of the Tangahoe the Waikato fighters moved north and besieged the great *pā* at Waimate. The *pā* was impregnable and it was suggested that the garrison might be starved out. Hinewai, the Maniapoto chieftainess, whose brother Waata had taken one of the captive women from Te Ruaki as his wife, strenuously objected to this proposal. To emphasise her point she chanted an old taunting song, with topical allusions added for the occasion, and she postured in the *pūkana*. Her relatives remonstrated with her, but she went on. Then her brother Waata went up to drag her away, but she was a powerful woman and instead of her brother subduing her she felled him to the ground and sat on his back as he lay prone, picked up his *taiaha*, and went on with her song!

Hinewai's performance had a great influence on Te Wherowhero, especially later when Hinewai related that her brother's wife had told her that Ngātata's story which had induced the Waikato and Maniapoto to take up his cause was not quite true. At this juncture too the Taranaki defenders of Waimate Pā staged a performance by the young women of the tribe. A specially selected company of these young women appeared on the parapets of the *pā* and performed posture dances and action songs. Lightly clad—very lightly clad—and with calm and demure composure, with swaying bodies and quivering hands, they danced. As the performance went on these maidens infused more and more allure into their dancing, and they moved so voluptuously and seductively that the Waikato and Maniapoto youthful warriors lost their fighting ardour and became enamoured of the charm of Ngāti Ruahine maidenhood. From that time on the vigilance of the fighting men relaxed, and at last Te Wherowhero called on the chief of the *pā*. When the Taranaki leader appeared on the parapet Te Wherowhero addressed him, saying, "*Kātahi anō tāku rākau ka hoki mai. Ka hoki ake nei au e kore anō e ara mai te rau o tāku patu.*" (For the first time my weapon has returned unblooded. I am now returning and will never again raise my weapon in your direction.) Te Wherowhero never broke his word. Subsequent Waikato and Maniapoto raids into the south Taranaki district were made under the leadership of other chiefs.

In 1831 Te Wherowhero led a great war-party to Pukerangiora Pā. This was intended to wipe out the stain of the deaths of Maungatautari, Te Hiakai, Mama, and the others. The *pā* was besieged and finally carried by storm after the garrison had been weakened by hunger. The slaughter was on a large scale and several hundred prisoners were taken. It is said that upward of 1,200 were killed on the day the *pā* fell. On the following day a large number of prisoners was killed. Traitors among the local tribes betrayed those among the captives who had some part in the deaths of the Waikato and Maniapoto warrior-chiefs already referred to, and they were condemned to death. Several of these prisoners asked that they die at the hands of the great Te Wherowhero. It is said that the Waikato leader very reluctantly acceded to this request. Taking up a position near the entrance to the *pā*, Te Wherowhero despatched the captives one by one with his renowned *mere* named "Whakarewa" (borne aloft). After he had killed a few Te Wherowhero stopped, complaining that his arm was tired and, with down-cast head and tear-dimmed eyes, he moved away in silence. He absented himself from the army all that day, during which there were scenes of violence as some Waikato and Maniapoto relatives of the dead chiefs exacted revenge by killing the remaining prisoners and consigning them to steaming earth-ovens.

There were further raids by the Waikato into north Taranaki and Pukerangiora was again stormed and taken. There was also fighting at Moturoa in 1832, where the Waikato forces suffered heavy losses, and they retired leaving a large number of their dead on the field of battle. It was during this clash that the Waikato received word of the invasion of their lands by Pukerangi of Ngāpuhi.

In 1833 Te Wherowhero was back again at Moturoa at the head of a large army. On this occasion the local tribes entrenched themselves on the island fortress of Mikotahi. A siege was laid, but it proved ineffective as allied southern Taranaki tribes were able to bring supplies for the garrison by canoe at night. Muskets were freely used, but with little result. Finally peace was made, the outcome of pleas by Koropiko, a Kāwhia woman, who had married an Āti Awa man. To cement the peace several Āti Awa chiefs were handed over to Te Wherowhero as hostages.

After the surrender of these chiefs an incident took place that upset Te Wherowhero very much. He was escorting one of the hostages through the lines when he noticed a fellow chief whom he knew had a special grudge against the captive Taranaki. Te Wherowhero in an undertone told the Taranaki chief to hurry forward, and at the same time he clasped the chief's young son. The captive was pushing his way through some scrub when the vengeful Tainui chief came up behind Te Wherowhero and, as the Taranaki chief emerged on the far side, the Tainui threw his *mere* at his head, splitting his skull. As the dying chief turned over he looked up with a whimsical look on his face and said, "*He toa kōhuru tōu nā toa!*" (Your bravery is that of a murderer!) Shortly after this Te Wherowhero released the Taranaki captive chiefs and allowed them to return to their homes.

IV

Te Wherowhero's name does not figure in any of the fighting with the Te Arawa tribes of the Rotorua district. On his male line of descent he was an Arawa tribesman. There were also several other Arawa lines in his genealogy, and this circumstance apparently explains the absence of any mention of his name in the accounts of the Waikato fighting against the Te Arawa people. According to some Te Wherowhero was not very friendly with Te Waharoa, who led the Waikato and other tribes against Te Arawa, because of the excessive punishment inflicted, especially against the Ngāti Whakaue *hapū* of the Arawa at Ōhinemutu and Mataipuku in 1836. Te Waharoa, as a youth, was an Arawa captive and he was well cared for and was restored to his people; and Te Wherowhero considered this treatment should have received some consideration from Te Waharoa.

V

Up to about 1840 there were sporadic outbreaks of fighting among the Waikato, Hauraki and Maungatautari tribes. Te Wherowhero was tireless in his efforts to bring about friendly feelings between the tribes concerned. These troubles might very easily have developed into a general civil war among the Tainui tribes.

Te Wherowhero was now getting on in years and although still an active man his mind was now turning more and more to the arts of peace. He had been raised to the highest degree in the Tainui priesthood, and he spent a good deal of his time in the company of the Taupō chieftain Te Heuheu, who was also a high priest. For weeks at a time these two chieftains and other priestly elders of the tribes would discuss the ritual, and the esoteric teachings of the *whare wānanga*. These two warrior-chieftains had much in common, and they found each other's company congenial. It was at this time too that Te Wherowhero released all his captives, many of whom were chiefs of Heretaunga (or Hawkes Bay) tribes. These chiefs he accompanied as far as Taupō where he loaded them with presents before they left on their journey home. He had treated them as fellow chieftains and equals during their stay with him, and never allowed the Waikato chiefs to treat them other than with every respect.

Te Heuheu was very grateful for this treatment for, although he had waged war against the Heretaunga people, he was also related to them. Te Wherowhero stayed with Te Heuheu for several months on this visit, and he was there until about the middle of 1840. These two powerful chiefs were in Taupō when the Treaty of Waitangi was being signed, and neither of them was a signatory to this historic document. According to one account a Waikato chief offered to sign Te Wherowhero's name, but his offer was not accepted. Another story says that Te Wherowhero would not consider the matter because he had not been consulted before the other chiefs signed, especially those Waikato and Tainui chiefs. However, these accounts appear conjectural and it may well be that he and Te Heuheu had the same reason for not signing. Te Heuheu gave it, when pressed for his reason for not signing his allegiance to the British Crown, that he did not want his *mana* (prestige, power) to be considered as being inferior to that of a mere woman (Queen Victoria)!

THE STARS LOOK DOWN

Kia hora te Marino;
Kia whaka-papa pounamu te Moana;
Kia tere te Kārohirohi!

He Kōrero nā Rangitiria

Let the Calm be widespread;
Let the Sea glisten like the *pounamu*;
And let the Shimmer of Summer
Dance across thy path!

A Saying by Rangitiria

CHAPTER 12

THE STARS LOOK DOWN

I

Te Wherowhero had made his peace with all the tribes. At some time in 1840 he made his permanent home at Māngere. He also had a home near Maungawhau, now Mt. Eden,[1] and in the summer months he camped at Mauinaina, on the shores of the Waitematā harbour, near Kohimarama. From these places he often travelled on foot—later on horseback—to various parts of the Tainui lands.

II

He made a memorable journey to Ōtaki in 1840 with Te Heuheu Tūkino and other chiefs. The object of this visit was to invite Te Whatanui and his Ngāti Raukawa people to return to their ancestral lands at Maungatautari. But Te Whatanui decided to remain in the Manawatū and. Horowhenua-Ōtaki district on the lands they had conquered. Te Whatanui's reply to the delegation of chiefs was given in a song. In later years, when Te Whatanui's Ngāti Raukawa people made a claim in the Māori Land Court, that song proved to be their undoing. Their claim was opposed by the tribes who were in occupation and the principal witness for the opponents to the claim, when giving his evidence, sang the opening lines of Te Whatanui's song, in which the rest of his people joined. The European judges were taken unawares and for the time being the court was converted into a Māori assembly place with the singers and the witness emphasising their point in song and gesture. Ngāti Raukawa lost their case after the singing of that song, and the lines of it which weighed with the court were these:

Koia rānei, Raukawa,
Me hoki anō te whenua
Kua warewaretia nei e te Ngākau?

Indeed! O ye Raukawa,
Should we return to the land
That has been abandoned by the Heart?

III

Another journey undertaken by Te Wherowhero was to the lands of the far north. He was accompanied by a party of Waikato chiefs and by Te Kanawa, his comrade on many a hard-fought campaign. An amusing anecdote of the journey was related by Te Wherowhero on their return. The party had stopped at a place in the Kaipara district and one bright day a company of Waikato and Ngāpuhi chieftains sat around and conversed. They exchanged reminiscences of the past and of their fighting days.

The talk dwelt on Waikato raids into the North and the fighting in and around Tawatawhiti. A Ngāpuhi chieftain had a vivid recollection of a Waikato warrior who wore a *kahukura* (red cloak). His first question to Te Wherowhero and Te Kanawa was, *"Nā wai te kōkiri?"* (Who led the charge?) On this question being asked, Te Wherowhero who was sitting some distance apart, pretended he was dozing for he realized that the question referred to him personally. With his head down he remained silent. Now, Te Kanawa was a noted wit and the question appealed to him as a unique opportunity of scoring at the expense of Te Wherowhero. After a quick glance at Te Wherowhero who remained in a sleeping attitude, Te Kanawa turned to the expectant Ngāpuhi chiefs and in a stage whisper said *"Nāku!"* (Mine!) The Ngāpuhi chief again asked, *"Ko wai te mea i te kahukura?"* (Who was the one in the red cloak?) This again referred to Te Wherowhero. Te Kanawa after going through the same pantomime replied, *"Ko au!"* (It was I!) On this same journey Te Wherowhero took part in the conference in connection with the Declaration of Independence, and he signed this historic document on July 22, 1839.

IV

Te Wherowhero's tireless labours in bringing about a state of peace and goodwill among the tribes, bore fruit in most cases. In all these transactions he was mild and gracious. His military character ensured him the praise and respect of all chiefs, and was a circumstance which facilitated the happy outcome of his self-imposed task. He was honoured throughout the land. Graceful and dignified in his person, he endeared himself even to the tribes who had been ancient foes of his people. He was great without being arrogant. He maintained the dignity of his aristocratic lineage without giving cause for envy or jealousy over his success.

V

The arrival of the missionaries in his district was made the occasion for strong exhortations to his people to embrace Christianity. As a high priest of the Tainui sacred house of learning he was very interested in the new faith of the white man and, as he could not share the esoteric lore of the Tainui priesthood with his people, the religion of the missionaries offered an alternative belief that would be of spiritual benefit to the tribes. From then on and for the rest of his life he encouraged the missionaries in every way, but he never quite brought himself to the point of being baptised in the new faith. In this respect he and the Taupō chieftain Te Heuheu II remained steadfast to the ancient teachings of their priestly Polynesian forebears.

VI

Te Wherowhero was honoured by the early Governors of the infant colony. Governor Fitzroy paid him great respect, and later when Sir George Grey came as the new Governor, he and Te Wherowhero became firm friends. The great pro-consul was on several occasions the guest of the Waikato chieftain. Sir George Grey used to enjoy his stay among the Tainui chiefs, and he often spent weeks on end with Waikato and Maniapoto men of rank. He learnt much of the mythology and traditions of the Māori race from them. It is also said that the Tainui priesthood allowed him into inner teachings of the sacred lore of the Māori. This close association with Te Wherowhero and his people, and the knowledge he had of the loyal friendship of the chieftain, gave Sir George Grey many heartburnings during the troublous times of the 'sixties, as witness an incident during the march of General Cameron and his troops through the Waikato:

> The New Zealand Ministry of the day (Dec. 1863) thought, when General Cameron took possession of Ngaruawahia, that the time had arrived for peace to be made with the Natives. It was arranged that the Governor, Sir George Grey, should proceed to Ngaruawahia and interview those chiefs who were inclined to submit to the Queen's authority. On the appointed day a carriage and horses were ready to convey His Excellency on his journey. But the Governor changed his mind and decided not to go. The Ministry at

once waited upon the Governor, urging him to proceed on his journey. The result was that the carriage and horses were ordered back again. His Excellency, however, when about to step into the carriage, again altered his mind and would not go. The Ministry begged His Excellency to reconsider his determination, and after some time Sir George agreed once more to go, and again, at the last moment, finally resolved not to go. The carriage and horses were consequently sent back to the stables. The fickleness displayed by Sir George Grey upon this occasion can perhaps only be satisfactorily accounted for by himself (Featon 1923:108).

The author ventures the opinion that the Governor's "fickleness" can be explained for the reason that his conscience was stricken by the fact that the Ministry were bent on confiscation of the rich lands of the Waikato; and that the real culprits, if there were any on the Māori side, were the Maniapoto who had been responsible for the "incidents" which had been magnified until they were taken as a sufficient cause for war.

The incident just related was still in the laps of the gods, and we have to go back two decades to the time of the Hone Heke war in the north. At a critical stage in that struggle a Ngāpuhi party came through to Tāmaki and urged Te Wherowhero to join in a general uprising against the European. The Ngāpuhi said they were ready to descend on the town of Auckland. Te Wherowhero did not leave them in doubt as to his attitude. He told the Ngāpuhi leaders that he had implicit faith in British justice as administered by his friend Sir George Grey. He went further and told them that if they so much as made a move in the direction of Auckland he would himself march against them with the full might of his people. He immediately sent messengers to warn the Governor, and he himself did not relax his vigilance until the fighting in the north had completely died down. Sir George Grey was very thankful for the attitude of Te Wherowhero, as his firm stand against the Ngāpuhi undoubtedly averted a serious crisis for the early British colonists, and saved a good deal of bloodshed.

There is evidence of the unsettled state of the country at this period in the following excerpt from a despatch to the Colonial Office by the Governor (Sir George Grey) on August 20, 1847:

> I have to state to Your Lordship that within the last few days I have received alarming accounts from various quarters of the island regarding the excitement created in portions of the country most densely inhabited by natives.... I am not yet

in a position that would enable me to state whether actual insurrection upon an extensive scale is to be immediately apprehended; but I cannot entertain any doubt that the country is in a very critical state. I will lose no time in taking, such measures as are in my power to quiet the apprehensions which at present exist.... (*GBPP* 1847(899), Vol.XLIII).

And it was at this time that Te Wherowhero forwarded a letter to Queen Victoria couched in dignified terms and characteristic of a Polynesian high chief:

MAORI TEXT

He Reta na Te Wherowhero ki a Kuini Wikitoria

E Whae e te Kuini, whakarongo mai ki a matou korero, ki nga korero a nga rangatira o Waikato. Ma te Atua e mea kia u tau pupuri i ta matou kupu, me matou hoki i tau kupu mo ake tonu atu. E Whae, whakarongo, tenei nga korero kei te haere i konei tera o Minita kei te korero ka tangohia noatia atu te whenua o te Maori mo te kore take, ko enei korero hei whakapouri i o matou ngakau. Engari kaore matou e whakapono ana ki enei rongo korero, notema [sic] *i rongo matou ki te Kawana tuatahi ko te tuku i o matou whenua kei a matou ano te ritenga. Me ta te Kawana tuarua pera ano, nga korero i rongo ai matou, a me ta tenei Kawana hoki. Ratou katoa rite tonu te korero. No reira matou ka tuhi atu ki a koe kia aroha koe kia matou ki ou hoa e aroha atu nei ki a koe. Tuhia mai ou whakaaro kia matou, kia mau ai te rongo ki nga Maori o tenei Motu.*

O Madam the Queen, hearken to our words, the words of all the chiefs of Waikato. May God grant that you may hold fast our word, and we your word for ever. Madam, listen: News is going about here that your Ministers are talking of taking away the land of the Native without cause, which makes our hearts dark. But we do not believe this news, because we heard from the first Governor that the disposal of the land was with ourselves. And from the second Governor we heard the same words, and from this Governor. They have all said the same. Therefore we write to you that you may be kind to us, to your friends that love you. Write your thoughts to us, that peace may prevail among the natives of these islands (quoted Buick 1914: 336). (Translation by the Author.)

The action of the Lord of Waikato was warmly approved and strongly supported by the Church and the judiciary of the infant colony, and Te Wherowhero was joined by Bishop Selwyn, Archdeacon Maunsell, and Chief Justice Martin, and also by the Wesleyan Mission Committee in England. The talk of "taking away the land of the Native without cause" originated in an Imperial Enactment which was forwarded to the Governor by the Colonial Office, and which was accompanied by the Royal Instructions. Chapter XIII and Clause 9 of which read:

> No claim shall be admitted in the said Land Courts on behalf of the Aboriginal inhabitants of New Zealand to any lands situate within the said islands, unless it shall be established, to the satisfaction of such Court, that either by some Act of the Executive Government of New Zealand, the right of such aboriginal inhabitants to such lands has been acknowledged and ascertained, or those from whom they derived the title, have actually had the occupation of the lands so claimed, and have been accustomed to use and enjoy the same, either as places of abode or tillage, or for the growth of crops, or for the depasturing of cattle, or otherwise for the convenience and sustentation of life, by means of labour expended thereon (New Zealand Charter, 28/12/1846, under New Zealand Government Act, 1840, Chapter XIII, Clause 9: 9 & 10 Victoria cap.103).

The Charter was accompanied by a lengthy despatch from the Colonial Secretary (Earl Grey) in which he wrote, *inter alia*:

> The first and most important step which you will have to take with the view of introducing a regular system with respect to the disposal of land, will be to ascertain distinctly the ownership of all the land in the colony. The extent and limits of all which is to be considered as the property either of individuals, of bodies politic or corporate, or of the native tribes, must in the first instance be determined, and the whole of the remainder of the territory will then be declared to be the Royal demesne. The results of this inquiry must be carefully registered, and a regular record

henceforth preserved, showing to whom all lands in New Zealand belong. This measure has been repeatedly and earnestly inculcated on your predecessors, and I cannot too strongly repeat the same injunction (*ibid.*).

Now, on the face of it, the cause of all the trouble appears innocuous enough if not a laudable measure. But the British Parliament which had passed the Imperial Act was quite ignorant of the Māori customs appertaining to land and of the uses the Māori people made of their fishing grounds, forest lands, rivers, lakes, and fens. There was accordingly read into the proposed Constitution a threat of confiscation. The high dignitaries mentioned, and the Governor, were fully aware of the seriousness of the position and they found great difficulty in allaying the uneasiness of the Māori chiefs.

It will therefore be appreciated that it was most comforting to the Governor to know that Te Wherowhero was a true friend. The friendship and loyalty of Te Wherowhero was the more praiseworthy inasmuch as the Colonial Office of the British Imperial Parliament had failed to observe that in the Constitution "the rights to native lands were limited to those tribes whose chiefs had signed the Treaty of Waitangi." This limitation placed both Te Wherowhero and his kinsman Te Heuheu in a rather invidious position, neither of them having signed the treaty.

The immediate necessity for anxiety upon this point was happily removed by the prompt suspension of the Charter by Governor Grey who at the same time submitted to the Imperial Government "a more liberal and flexible Constitution" which was, as recorded by Mr. Lindsay Buick in his book *The Treaty of Waitangi* (1914: 343) "drafted upon the slopes and amidst the snows of (Mt.) Ruapehu" in the tribal domain of Te Heuheu, Lord of Taupō.

We will for our purpose now give an account of the visit of Te Hoariri (a high chief of the west Taupō forest lands of Tuaropaki and Titiraupenga) to Waikato to confer with Te Wherowhero, to whom he was related.

Te Hoariri: O Whero', the chiefs of the east and south have come to me and said that we should combine now to drive the Pākehā from this land.

Te Wherowhero: That must not be. My friend the Governor will not permit any wrong being done to us. And I have also written a letter to the Queen.

Te Hoariri: Is that all I am to say to the chiefs?

Te Wherowhero: Tell them that Pōtatau has set you up as Pilot (in Māori, *Te Paerata*) to guide the canoes through dangerous channels.

Te Hoariri: I think you are mistaken, O Whero'.

Porokoru (a Waikato elder of Te Wherowhero): O Te Paerata, Te Wherowhero has spoken his word. And why should you doubt the word of the Governor who is the friend of Te Wherowhero?

As the result of this conference and the saying of Te Wherowhero, Te Hoariri was henceforth called "Te Paerata" and it was as Te Paerata that he died in the heroic stand at Ōrākau nearly 20 years later (April 1864).

Using the name Te Paerata in place of Te Hoariri our account of the meeting with Te Wherowhero continues:

Te Paerata: I doubt not, O 'Koru (Porokoru), the word of the Governor, but I do doubt the motives of his Pākehā people. Dire calamities will come upon this land and upon your people, O Whero'. They do say that the Pākehā will open up roads in the name of the Queen through the land, and our people will be doomed. Bear in mind these words of mine, O 'Koru. Should these things come about in my time, know you that I will cast down this body of mine at the *ara rīpeka* (cross-roads) to stop it all. Before I sit down and before I return to my abiding-place in the uplands of Tuaropaki hear me in my song of sorrow:

TE WAIATA A TE PAERATA

Kauaka, e 'Koru, e tino nuia mai!
Ko wai tāu e koke kau nā koe
I waenganui o hewa?
He wairangi ko koe!
Tē riro te mamae ki te pū o taku taha;
Ka haere katoa ki te tau o taku ate rā!
Ko te atawhai ki au a te Tamaiti nei,
Mō āku haere ruahine i ngā rori nei:
He koha rā nāku;
Mā wai taku mea
E tiki mai e kokopi?
Mā Ngāpuhi i raro rā?
Ehara Wētere, he tangata waia ki au anake:
Engari Te Katipa hei oranga ngākau—

E koa nei au ki a koe,
He marama mate ka kōhiti kei runga!
Kei Whāingaroa rā
Ko Te Awaitaia;
Engari koe mā wairua e whakatata:
Nā Ue mai rānō, nā Ropi.
Me whakatangi te korowhiti ki Aotea — ko Pingareka!
Tahuri ki Kāwhia, ko Te Nuitone.
Koe ara rīpeka, he rau mangangatanga o te ngākau!
Kei Rotorua, ka ngaro Te Apoapo,
Te uri o Rangi-tohe-riri!
E tū ana Mōtai tangata
Ko Wiremu anake;
E mau ana te ingoa,
"Ko te uri o Te Waharoa".
Tahuri ki Waikato, ko Waata Kukutai; ko Takerei!
E tuhera ana a waenga he ara Kuini:
Māku e whakakopi, ka kopi mai, ī.

THE SONG OF TE PAERATA [2]

Thou hast no need to extol me O 'Koru!
Indeed, for whom art thou so keenly working
In the realms of fantasy?
For thou are quite infatuated!
5 As for me this anguish will ne'er move aside;
With one accord all came and within my heart do now abide!
And 'tis the mem'ry of the many kindnesses of this Son,
In my going and coming, weary'd with age, along these roads
That bids me show this regard for him.
10 'Tis asked, who else but he should
Go forth and close this gaping wound?
Is it to be Ngāpuhi abiding in the North?
Wētere cannot, for he but knows me:
Te Katipa, tho', gladdens the heart—
15 I do rejoice, indeed, in you,
A waning moon thou wert that now shines forth above!
At Whāingaroa abideth
Te Awaitaia!
But only in the spirit can you be approach'd!

20 And that harks right back to Ue and Ropi:
    Let then the piercing sound go forth to Aotea;
    Ah, 'tis Pingareka!
    Now let us turn to Kāwhia, there abideth Te Nuitone.
    Ah me, these many cross-roads bewilder the mind!
25 In Rotorua, gone is Te Apoapo,
    The descendant of Rangi-tohe-riri,
    "He who was Eager for the Day of Battle"
    Yonder stands one of Mōtai descent,
    Alone, he is Wiremu,
30 Bearer of the name,
    "The descendant of Te Waharoa"!
    Turn to (lower) Waikato; there is Waata Kukutai, and also Takerei!
    And in between (them all) is the pathway of the Queen:
    Peradventure 'twill be closed by me: and in closing it, close all!
    Ah me!

We are now in a position to present a balanced picture of the problem which faced Te Wherowhero and Sir George Grey in the first decade after the signing of the Treaty of Waitangi.

On one side the Governor was being pressed by the New Zealand Land Company and other interested parties to make available by "latitudes and longtitudes" by purchase (so-called) or otherwise the lands of the Māori tribes for European settlement. On the other side Te Wherowhero was faced with a no less difficult psychological problem. He had to resist the strong claims of blood ties and the ancient fighting spirit of his race, in the face of the call of the chiefs—given in speech and song—for a war-leader to unite the tribes against the European.

It was a most fortunate circumstance that the strong ties of friendship and mutual trust between the Governor and the Lord of Waikato held firm throughout this critical period.

For Te Paerata, and the other chieftains for whom he was the spokesman, it may be said that there was plenty of evidence to justify their forebodings of the future. As a matter of fact, read in the light of events that came to pass within two decades of the time we are at present dealing with, Te Paerata's speech and song proved to be an accurate forecast. By that time there had been a change in Government and although Sir George Grey was recalled to remedy subsequent trouble it was too late. It was not until the battle of Ōrākau had been fought, and Te Paerata and his eldest son Hone Teri had "closed the pathway of the Queen" (and in doing so had fallen on the field of battle and so "closed all") that the fighting in the land of Waikato was ended. "Dire calamities" did come upon the land and upon the people of Te Wherowhero as predicted by Te Paerata, but Te Wherowhero was not fated to see all this.

VII

Sir George Grey also took much interest in Te Wherowhero's son and heir Matutaera. In the case of his son the priestly Te Wherowhero had compromised with the missionaries and asked that he be baptised in the Church of England faith. In his meetings with the missionaries he had already been persuaded that there was nothing in the Christian faith that was, to his mind, at variance with the esoteric teachings of the Māori. He could not persuade the missionaries of this, but the Governor, from what knowledge he had of the Māori belief, agreed with Te Wherowhero; and it was this confirmation of his opinion by his good friend the Governor which led up to the baptising of his son. Te Wherowhero and his son were often guests of the Governor on Te Kawau island.

VIII

On one occasion, whilst living at Māngere, Matutaera had a strong desire to go into Auckland town, but he was short of money. He thought of a way of getting funds from his father's treasury. The treasurer was an aged man, and the young man decided he would intimidate him. One day he hid himself alongside the track the old treasurer took whenever he had occasion to draw or deposit moneys (usually sovereigns) in the treasury. The "treasury" consisted of a strong iron trunk which was hidden at the edge of a swamp. Only the treasurer and Te Wherowhero knew where the place was.

The annual income of Te Wherowhero's treasury was quite considerable. The extensive and fertile lands along the banks of the Waikato and Waipā rivers yielded great harvests of wheat, maize, potatoes, *kūmara*, and fruit; and pigs were reared and fattened by the thousand; fruit was abundant, and peaches of a size which have never since been seen were to be found in every village. A brisk trade with the town of Auckland had sprung up, and it had become the custom for some years for the tribal leaders and traders of that time to levy a tax on themselves, and to make substantial offerings to Te Wherowhero's treasury—a fitting tribute to one who had dared so much and exposed himself to so many dangers for the survival and preservation of his people.

To return to the escapade of the heir presumptive, Matutaera. He had that day heard his father give directions to the treasurer about withdrawing a large sum of money to finance a tribal gathering at Kohimarama. In due course the treasurer returned from a visit to the iron box carrying a quantity of sovereigns. Matutaera awaited him on the track armed with a *mere* and he did not waste time in soft words. The old man on seeing the son and heir was thrown into a panic. "I want some of that money," muttered Matutaera, and the lord's treasurer handed over the Kohimarama budget of sovereigns to the youthful robber. Matutaera took what he wanted and handed the rest back, with a warning not to say anything about the matter.

The old treasurer was in a quandary. As there was no auditor there was really no fear of the robbery being made known. Te Wherowhero himself never bothered about the state of his funds. Practically the only use the money was put to was the financing of tribal gatherings from time to time, and the purchase of presents for his fellow chiefs. Te Wherowhero lived a plain, simple and dignified life of a Māori chieftain, without pomp or pageantry. He was an affectionate husband and father, and his equal behaviour to all (including many captives who had been offered their freedom but had refused to return to their own tribes), and his humanity was such, that he endeared himself to everyone. His son, however, thought he was too parsimonious. Whenever he asked for money he had been lectured and earnestly urged to economise for the sake of the people who were to be his first consideration at all times.

The treasurer was very disturbed in mind. He was of the old school and considered everything belonging to the *Ariki* as being *tapu*. Finally he went to Te Wherowhero and told him all. The chieftain was very upset on learning of his son's lapse. He had long taught his son his duties as a chief, and he had also started teaching him the esoteric lore of Tainui. On this occasion Te Wherowhero was determined to teach his son a lesson he would not readily forget.

Matutaera had been back from the town a short while when he saw his father emerge from his house with a *taiaha*. The young man instantly divined that the treasurer had betrayed him, and he was rooted to the spot for a moment. His father was stripped for battle and was thoroughly roused. As he came toward his son, muttering dire threats, and with his tattooed face contorted with rage, the old warrior was a fearsome sight. Matutaera quickly thought of a temporary sanctuary, which was the *kāuta* or the communal cooking-house. His father was now so *tapu* that he could not enter such places. All houses where food was cooked were out of bounds to the priesthood. To the *kāuta* fled the young man. It was a big structure and it had two doorways. When Matutaera had gained this refuge his incensed father appeared outside the front doorway uttering savage threats. A sudden hush came over the gossiping women who were preparing the evening meal. Matutaera stood panting midway between the two doors. Te Wherowhero's *taiaha* flashed across outside the doorway as he went through his play of thrust and parry. After a time the old man paused and glared at his son. Then the young man's blood fairly froze within him when he heard his father call out to one of the tribesmen to come and fetch his son out of the *kāuta*. The man addressed hesitated about laying hands on the son of the *Ariki*, and this gave Matutaera his opportunity of escaping. Casting off his fear he braced his shoulders and made a dash for the back door, but his father had anticipated him and was already halfway around the *kāuta*. Matutaera paused in his stride and followed his father's progress through the open spaces between the wall-slabs of the building. He then made a dash for the front doorway and, brushing aside the half-hearted attempt to stop him by the tribesman who had been called, he sent him sprawling; and the next instant was running for dear life across the *marae*. Matutaera disappeared. About a week later a messenger arrived from Sir George Grey to tell Te Wherowhero that his son was with the Governor on Te Kawau island. Later the Governor himself called and he and Te Wherowhero discussed the matter of the fugitive, of whom the Governor spoke in the highest terms as to his behaviour since he had been with him. His Excellency also told the father that his son had confessed everything to him and was most contrite about the whole affair. Te Wherowhero was very pleased to hear of his son's exemplary conduct. He and Sir George decided that Matutaera should be exiled in Government House or wherever the Governor might be for a period of at least six months. Matutaera's period of banishment, in the circumstances, was not an unhappy one. At the end of six months he was recalled and was pardoned. After the reconciliation he had his face tattooed and he entered upon the life of a young chief. Matutaera had learnt his lesson. (He never tired of repeating the story to his own children to impress on them the duty of obedience to one's parents, and their duty to the people in all circumstances.)

IX

The Kohimarama meeting, referred to earlier, was duly held. Ngāpuhi, Ngāti Whātua, Hauraki, and Waikato chiefs were present. It so happened that at that time the vessel in which the great Te Rauparaha was being held as prisoner at the Governor's pleasure was anchored in Waitematā harbour. This was the outcome of the tragic affair at Wairau when a survey party in defiance of Te Rauparaha's warning trespassed on debatable ground and were killed. When Te Wherowhero heard that Te Rauparaha was aboard the vessel he made a request to Sir George Grey to allow the Ngāti Toa leader to come ashore on parole. The Governor agreed and Te Rauparaha was landed near Kohimarama.

Te Wherowhero awaited Te Rauparaha inside the great assembly house. Presently a ship's boat with the famous Te Rauparaha appeared off the beach. The news of his arrival attracted crowds who pressed forward on to every spot that gave a view of the landing place. Conflicting emotions throbbed in every breast. The chiefs, in the circumstances, were at first undecided what part to act. Should they receive Te Rauparaha with song and dance, or would silence be the better course? For a time nothing was decided. The boat came up to the landing place and the chief rose, then slowly and solemnly he came ashore, impressing a deep melancholy on every heart. Te Rauparaha approached the *marae* alone. Subdued sobbing was heard on every side. Men and women, Tainui kinsmen and strangers, all joined in one general scene of lamentation.

Te Wherowhero arranged with the chiefs that they were to spare the feelings of their renowned guest as much as possible. The knowledge that he was being held prisoner by the Government added to the grief which all felt. The proceedings on the *marae* were accordingly cut short, and Te Rauparaha was conducted inside the assembly house and into the presence of Te Wherowhero.

X

After the two erstwhile foes and military rivals gazed at each another for some time, they advanced silently in the *hongi* manner. Then Te Wherowhero conducted Te Rauparaha to a place next to him at the *tungaroa* (rear part of the house) where fine mats had been spread out. The other chiefs then came in one by one to pay their respects to Te Rauparaha.

Te Wherowhero all this time was taking stock of the Ngāti Toa leader. He wondered whether his morale had been lowered on account of his captivity. As each chief came in, Te Rauparaha would raise his head and look keenly at the approaching figure. (Many were the faces he had never seen before; some much changed since he had last seen them). A large number of the chiefs, when approaching the place where Te Rauparaha was seated, paused and carefully parted the fine mats, so that they might not tread on them. Te Rauparaha judged these to be lesser chiefs. A high chief was not likely to notice such objects as mats on such an occasion, reasoned the Ngāti Toa chief; and as these chiefs bent down to *hongi* with him Te Rauparaha would deliberately turn his face aside so that the salute of the *hongi* came on his cheek instead of his nose. Te Wherowhero noticed all this, and he turned to a chief seated alongside of him, and in a low voice said, "*Kei te mau tonu te hīanga o te korokē nei!*" (This man remains as refractory as ever!)

After a round of speech-making the company of chiefs engaged in general conversation. Now and again Te Rauparaha would turn to Te Wherowhero and ask, "Who might that be?" referring to one of the chiefs taking part in the talk. If the chief happened to be one whose name was known to Te Rauparaha, he would ponder for a moment or two. If the chief was one that he assessed as of high standing, he would nod his head in approval. If it was someone whose chiefly rank was not up to Te Rauparaha's estimation of status, he would murmur, "*E hara!*" (Of no account!)

XI

After the conversation had become animated with the recounting of past deeds and subjects of topical interest and matters of moment in the Māori world of that time, quips were freely bandied to and fro. Someone made mention of the question of the setting up of a Māori King. Te Rauparaha thereupon gave an account of how the matter was mentioned by an Āti Awa man who had been on a visit to England. He then went on to mention the various chiefs whose names had been brought forward in connection with the choice of the first Māori King. With a smirk on his expressive face Te Rauparaha listed the names of all the chiefs whose claims for recognition in this matter were being considered, and he concluded his recital without mentioning the name of the great Te Wherowhero. As he gave the last name he gave a side-long look at Te Wherowhero which indicated that he had purposely omitted the name of the Waikato chieftain.

Everybody noticed the omission and a silence that could be felt settled on the company. The chiefs were both curious and concerned to know how Te Wherowhero would react. They sat in silence and looked glumly into space; and now and again stole glances at the *Ariki*. When the silence was becoming almost painful Te Wherowhero slowly turned to Te Rauparaha and with a gracious smile on his face, and in his slow deliberate voice said, "*E mōhio anō ana koe, e Raha', kei te whai ngā rangatira o te Motu nei ko ahau hei kīngi?*" (Do you know, O Raha', that the chiefs of this land seek for me to be king?) The tension was instantly relieved. Everybody smiled. Then Te Rauparaha, with an assumed look of surprise on his. face, said simply, "*E kāo!*" (Indeed, no!) Te Wherowhero then observed smilingly, "*E kī ana rā rātou ko ahau te rangatira nui o te Motu nei!*" (Indeed, they do say I am the most powerful chief in this land.) To this Te Rauparaha said, "*Ka pēwhea hoki te mangumangu o Mōkau rā?*" (What about that dark-visaged man of Mōkau?) This was a reference to Takerei, the Mōkau chieftain of the Maniapoto tribe.

"*Ko te tangata tēnā o te ihu o te waka*" (That man occupies the prow of the canoe)[3] was Te Wherowhero's comment. Then, with a twinkle in his eye, and in a reminiscent mood, Te Rauparaha said, "*Āe, engari rā, kia kore te tamaiti iti potopoto o Ngāti Kahutōtara rā, pakapaka ana koe i roto i tāku hāngī i Ōkoki!*" (Yes; but were it not for that diminutive fellow of the Kahutōtara tribe you would have baked in my oven at Ōkoki!).[4] Te Wherowhero laughed louder than anybody else at this thrust by Te Rauparaha, and the whole company was in high good humour when the feast in honour of the visit of Te Rauparaha was announced, and the party later broke up.

The matter of the setting up of a Māori King was to drag on for several years. In the meantime Te Wherowhero lived a peaceful life at his homes at Māngere, Maungawhau and Kohimarama. When the occasion demanded he paid a visit to Kāwhia. The trading vessels which called there all paid harbour dues into the treasury of the *Ariki* as also did those which sailed into Manukau and Waitematā harbours.

On one of his visits to Kāwhia, he found that one of his female relatives had married the European captain of one of the trading vessels. This relative was Ngangiha who had married Captain Kent. Ngangiha was the first of his people to marry a European. Te Wherowhero thought he would pass an idle hour one day when he came upon Ngangiha and a company of her women companions. "I hear you are married to a white man," said Te Wherowhero, eyes a-twinkle. "Yes, and what of it?" the young lady answered, looking archly up at him. She divined he was about to take a rise out of her and she was ready. "Ah yes, of course," observed the *Ariki*. "How you must love him!" The young lady raised her eyebrows, and with an expressive shrug of the shoulders she said, "*Me tatau koia tā te* pō!" She had purposely made play on the name of the great warlord in her punning rejoinder. "Is it expected that one should recount the enjoyment of the night!" Whenever anyone thereafter used his name of Pōtatau[5] he would smile and say, "Ah yes, that name was once used by my *tuahine* (female cousin). Te Wherowhero had a subtle sense of humour and he often enjoyed a good joke, even if it was at his own expense.

During this period a settled calm prevailed in the tribal lands of Tainui. Te Wherowhero had as his constant companions the various priestly elders of the Tainui tribes. His son Tūkaroto or Matutaera was initiated into the mysteries of the Tainui sacred house of learning and in due course he passed through the several grades of the priesthood. At the initiation the father had acted as *tūāhuroa* or grand high priest. His son's priestly mentor was the Ngāti Māhanga high priest of the Papa o Rotu school, named Tūheitia.

XII

Ngāti Hauā, which was Te Waharoa's tribe, having observed a long period of inactivity, conceived a plan of expansion and had moved across the Waikato river and taken possession of some of the fertile lands of the Ngāti Apakura and other tribes living on the wide, lake-studded plain in the triangle of the Waipā and Waikato rivers. They began to cultivate the land, and this led to protests being made which eventually flared up into a lively clash of arms in which among others the Ngāti Hauā usurpers killed Rangianewa at Rangiaohia, the principal settlement of the Ngāti Apakura. Rangianewa was a daughter of Uruhapāinga, a younger sister of Pōtatau's paternal grandmother Te Kahurangi. Her death was deeply mourned by him. This incident, for a time, threatened to lead to a general outbreak of hostilities, but such a calamity was averted when Tāmehana Te Waharoa gave his daughter over to the Ngāti Apakura to cement the peacemaking.

In the tribal wars of the nineteenth century several captive chiefs had been taken by the Waikato and Maniapoto war-leaders. Te Wherowhero urged all his fellow chieftains to allow these captive chiefs to return to their own tribes. When he released the Heretaunga chiefs he specially sent a female relative named Tiria, and her European husband, to accompany them home to their Ngāti Kahungunu tribesmen. Some of the Tainui chiefs remonstrated with him, but to them he said, "Let these chiefs return; for who knows but that some day we may have need of their help."

The assistance and advice of Te Wherowhero was often sought by the early Governors of the Colony and on many important occasions he accompanied the Vice-regal party to distant parts of the country. In August 1841 he was in Wellington with Governor Hobson, Mr. Halswell, the Commissioner of the New Zealand Company, and Mr. George Clarke, Chief Protector of the Māori people. The purpose of this visit was to protect the interests of the Māori inhabitants of what is now Wellington city against the unreasonable claims of the New Zealand Company to certain reserves on which the Māori had their homes. Subsequently, (June 24, 1842) Lord Stanley, of the British Colonial Office approved the Governor's work in these words: "In your transactions with the Company you may rely at all times in my firm and full support of your authority as Governor against any exaggerated pretensions on the part of the Company or its agents" (in "Correspondence and Papers relating to New Zealand", *GBPP* 1842 [569], Vol. XXVIII, p.161).

During this visit Te Wherowhero learnt a lot about the transactions of Colonel Wakefield of the New Zealand Company; and later when Governor Hobson proposed that he (Te Wherowhero) should confer with the Colonel on the subject of the Waikato claims to Taranaki (Chapter 7). Te Wherowhero refused point blank, saying he distrusted Colonel Wakefield.

At Remuera in May 1844 Te Wherowhero with his Waikato kinsman Wētere gave a great feast in honour of Governor Fitzroy. A sham fight was staged for the entertainment of the Governor and European visitors. Two forces of warriors, each 800 strong, armed with muskets, tomahawks and native weapons gave a thrilling display. "The sight was indeed remarkable. It was wonderful to see women and children gaily dressed wandering about unconcernedly among four thousand New Zealanders, most of whom were armed, and many utter strangers as well as heathens," was how the Governor subsequently reported on this occasion (Governor Fitzroy to Lord Stanley, 25 May 1844, in "Despatches from the Governor of New Zealand", *GBPP* 1845 [247], Vol. XXXIII, p.8). After the sham fight came the division of the feast. The Waikato presented more than 1000 blankets to the visiting tribesmen. Fish, potatoes and a portion of the blankets allotted for each tribe were ceremonially presented by Te Wherowhero on behalf of his people. Two days later, Governor Fitzroy received Te Wherowhero and about 200 chiefs at Government House. Te Wherowhero was seated on the Governor's right hand, and the day was taken up in speechmaking, the Governor taking advantage of the occasion to discuss important matters with the assembled chiefs.

An unfortunate incident marred the end of the gathering. At the close of the meeting depredations on European settlers by a party of Ngāti Hauā of the Matamata district were committed at Papakura, 20 miles south of Auckland. Te Wherowhero immediately sought an interview with the Governor. Although none of his own tribe was implicated he felt disgraced and he offered to make restitution there and then. The Governor absolved Te Wherowhero from any responsibility in the matter and expressed his determination to seek compensation from Pohepohe, the chief of that section of Ngāti Hauā who were responsible. The chiefs expressed admiration at the Governor's reply. Te Wherowhero turned to a Ngāti Hauā chief who was present and said, "Tell your people that they have behaved like cowards and dastards. They deserve to be considered as dogs and treated as such by their tribes. And tell the Matamata people that I and the other chiefs hold ourselves as hostages to the Governor for their misconduct, and that it is owing to his goodwill, and entirely as a matter of favour, that I am now at large instead of being in prison."

Te Wherowhero pledged his people, if Pohepohe and his tribe did not make reparation, to be responsible for "pigs, flax and potatoes, and these would be given to any extent."

The Governor declined to accept this pledge, and said that he did not doubt that Tarapīpipi, the paramount chief of the Ngāti Hauā, would see that the right thing was done, as he was a professed Christian. Te Wherowhero was gratified at the Governor's attitude and said, "It is true that it was the former custom on such occasions to plunder on the way home, but with their knowledge of English customs, the conduct of the Matamata people was disgraceful." Tarapīpipi, some time later, was able to make restitution—he restored the stolen goods and handed over a supply of produce as compensation. When forwarding the goods Tarapīpipi sent a letter to the Governor: "Darker than the darkness of a gloomy night without stars is the gloom in my heart because of the conduct of these disreputable fellows," he wrote, "and I cannot describe the load of shame I feel because of this plunder."

In May 1847 Te Wherowhero accompanied Governor Grey to Wanganui. Wāka Nene of the Ngāpuhi tribe was also in the party. The occasion was an outbreak of fighting against the infant settlement which followed the execution of some Māori who had committed a murder and had pleaded guilty at a court-martial held immediately afterward. The Governor subsequently reported on the incident "...Not only did these natives (Te Wherowhero and Wāka Nene) accompany me to Wanganui for the purpose of co-operating with Her Majesty's forces, but I am sure that every officer who was there will bear me out in saying that we could not have dispensed with their services, and that nothing could have surpassed their activity and gallantry."

NOTES ON CHAPTER 12

Note 1

Te Wherowhero's home near Maungawhau: The spot where Te Wherowhero's house stood is in what is now Auckland City Domain. His great-granddaughter Princess Te Puea planted a tree on the site in 1939.

Note 2

The Song of Te Paerata

(1) 'Koru: In full, Porokoru, was a Waikato elder of Te Wherowhero. There is further mention of him in Book Two of this volume.

(7) this Son: This is a reference to Te Wherowhero, being here used as a term of endearment, and not in the sense of nephew, cousin once removed, etc. (See Whakapapa).

(12) Ngāpuhi: The northern tribe which under Hongi Hika was a scourge to many of the southerners in the inter-tribal fighting until the latter tribes also became possessed of firearms. Under Hone Heke, Ngāpuhi challenged the military might of the European shortly after the inauguration of British sovereignty in 1840.

(13) Wētere: High chief of the Mōkau district. Although of high lineage Wētere, or Takerei as he was often called, never took a prominent part in the deliberations of the Tainui chiefs—hence the words, "he but knows of me."

(14) Te Katipa: A Manukau harbour chief of Ngāti Te Ata tribe. So far as the Māori cause was concerned in the troublous times of the 'sixties, Te Paerata's eulogistic lines in the song were misplaced, for this chief became a "loyalist" and was made a major by the British.

(18) Te Awaitaia: He was a well-known Tainui chief of Whāingaroa harbour area. He is mentioned several times in Book One, Chapter 5, and in the succeeding Book Two, Chapter 6. It is said he was a rather vain man, hence the line, "only in the spirit can you be approach'd."

(20) Ue and Ropi: Names of ancestors of the Tainui tribes. The implication here is that Te Awaitaia was so aloof that the only way one could claim any connection with him was through genealogical lines.

(23) Te Nuitone: A Kāwhia chief.

(25) Te Apoapo: An Arawa chief and a relative of Te Paerata.

(29) Wiremu: Best known as Wiremu Tāmehana, the so-called Māori king-maker.

(32) Waata Kukutai: A high chief of the lower Waikato. This chief also became a "loyalist" and was made a major by the British. Under his name of Kukutai he is mentioned in Book One, Chapter 10.

Takerei: In full, Takerei Te Rauangaanga, a close relative of Te Wherowhero. He was a large landowner who lost all in the confiscation by the Government of the lands of Waikato after the Waikato war. He did not long survive his misfortunes.

(34) Peradventure 'twill be closed by me: Te Paerata also belonged to the Ngāti Paretekawa sub-tribe, and was a close relative of Rewi Maniapoto, the famous Raukawa-Maniapoto war leader. In this line of his song Te Paerata disclosed that he had a prophetic vision, for with the fall of Ōrākau in April 1864, and his own death in the fighting there, the war ended. The warlike Maniapoto, who disagreed with the choice of Ōrākau as a site for the crucial battle, awaited General Cameron in the specially prepared *pā* of Paratui, near Hangatiki. They had also disposed various forces in advantageous positions to crush the British forces (on the pattern of Hingakākā Battle—Book One, Chapter 1). Instead of attempting an invasion of the lands of Maniapoto, however, the British "dug in" at Te Awamutu and carried out a wholesale confiscation of the lands of the Waikato (including tribal lands in which the rights of the "loyalists" were inextricably mixed with those of the so-called "rebels"). The Maniapoto among whom were no "loyalists" got off almost scot free, losing only a small strip of their tribal lands between the Mangapiko and Pūniu streams.

Note 3

prow of the Canoe: The Mōkau country is looked upon by the tribal orators as the *ihu* or prow of the Tainui "Canoe" area; Tāmaki isthmus in the north is the *kei* or stern, and Mangatoatoa, on the banks of the Pūniu river, near Kihikihi, is *waenganui* or amidships.

Note 4

that diminutive fellow: A reference to Manukorihi who distinguished himself in the fighting in north Taranaki. (See Book One, Chapter 7.)

Note 5
   Pō-tatau: Might be translated as "the doorway to the realms of night." This name was bestowed on Te Wherowhero as a tribute to his fighting qualities and skill as a warrior. In the sense used by Ngangiha, in the incident recounted here, it was given the alternative meaning of *tatau* (to count), hence *pō-tatau* (count the night).

GENEALOGICAL TABLE FOR CHAPTER 12

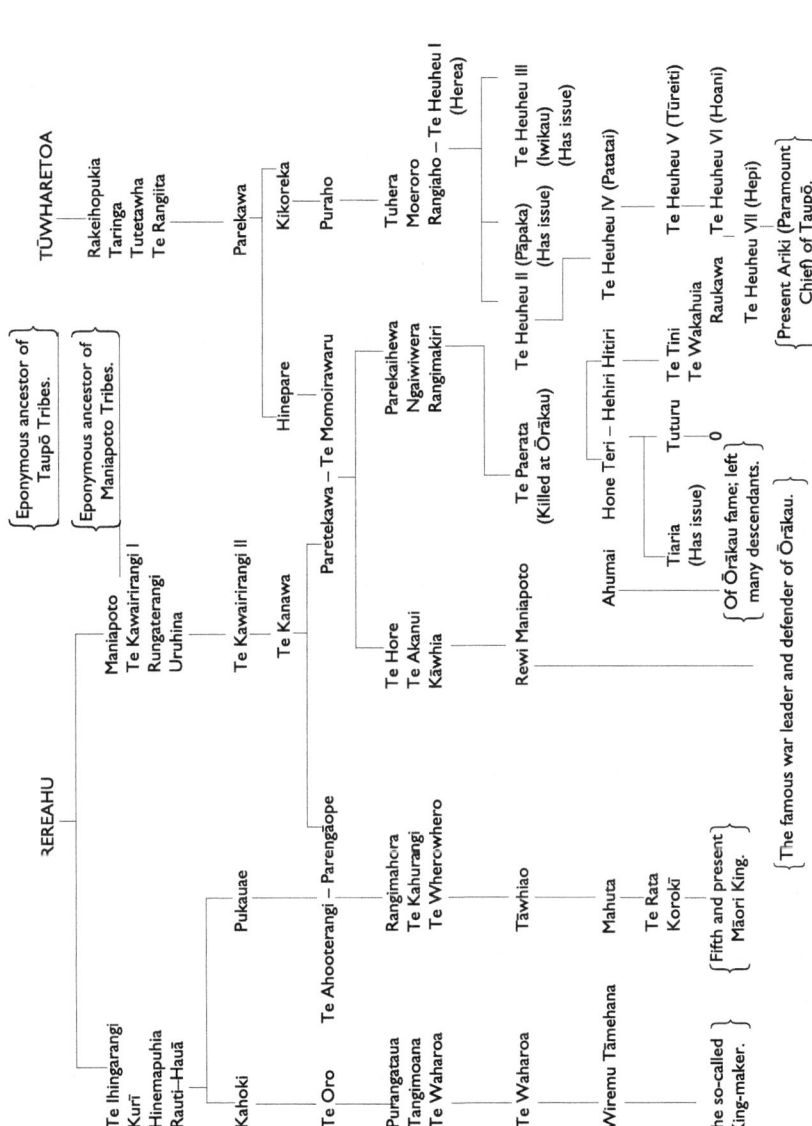

END OF BOOK ONE

Te Wherowhero

Reproduced from the coloured engraving in hs published volume
"The New Zealanders" by George French Angas.

BOOK TWO

PŌTATAU

Te Kīngi Māori Tuatahi

The First Māori King

THE GENESIS OF AN IDEA

The Setting-Up of a Māori King

INTRODUCTION

The Māori text on which the Author has based Book Two is a typical example of the Māori storyteller's art. In telling a story the skilled orator often purposely leaves gaps in the narrative as an invitation for questions from his audience. By such means he ascertains the interest excited and the degree of appreciation evoked by his tale, but in this translation, however, the Author may have defeated the story-teller's object and spoilt his technique. The narrative deals almost exclusively with the proceedings leading to the setting-up of Pōtatau Te Wherowhero as the first Māori King. The Author has endeavoured to "preserve the rather naive manner in which the Māori historian —referred to as "The Scribe"—tells the story, and words bracketed indicate that they have been inserted to clarify rather obscure passages in "The Scribe's" account. In later chapters—lest the reader finds the style somewhat tedious to follow—"The Scribe's" story will flow more smoothly.

CHAPTER 1

THE GENESIS OF AN IDEA

Let "The Scribe" speak—

To begin with, the reason why Pōtatau was set up as a King: It was the Europeans' (own) idea, and the Māori people embraced it. Commencing with the year 1845. (That year) Governor Grey went to (visit) the Queen. The question the Queen asked Governor Grey (was): "To your knowledge which chief has the (most) power in Aotearoa?" Grey answered, "Te Wherowhero of Waikato is the chief with (most) power." The Queen (then said), "When you arrive (back in New Zealand) be quick about setting him up as King of Aotearoa."

There was a Māori there, who was a friend of Grey's, and he heard of this matter. (The name of this Māori was) Piri Kawau. He was of Āti Awa (tribe) of Taranaki. His was the letter to Wī Tako[1] (to say) that the Queen had agreed for a King to be set up for New Zealand: And it was because of that letter that (the Māori people) got (the idea) of setting one up at the *upoko* or head of this country.[2]

Now, it was the desire of that man that the *kīngitanga* (kingship) should be taken by one of the chiefs of the upper[3] part of this country. He ignored (the one) the Queen had selected. (In time) this idea became widespread, around the upper part of this country. At that time there was a European (named) Davis[4] in Auckland, and it was he who supported the setting up of a Māori King, and he also (later) explained the idea to Pōtatau and Tāmehana Te Waharoa.

At that very time the word of Tāmihana Te Rauparaha went forth to his father, Te Rauparaha, that he (Tāmihana) be set up as King of Aotearoa. On hearing of this Mātene Te Whiwhi (chief of the Ngāti Raukawa tribe of Ōtaki district) had his word (and he said):

It would not be right! It (the kingship) should be presented
to Topia Tūroa (a high chief of the Whanganui tribes).

When Topia (was offered the kingship he) said:

I am not agreeable. My mountain is Matemateaonge; my sea is Whanganui; and the fish in it are *toitoi* (a fish which sleeps in shoals in fresh-water lakes), *parikoi* (sucker fish) and *inanga* (whitebait).

Now Tāmihana Te Rauparaha was very persistent that he be (made) King.[5] He left for England to (see) the Queen (and with the idea) that he be made King. When he went (he only) got halfway (there) and came back.

Then Topia got (the idea about) the kingship being offered to Te Heuheu[6] (of whom it was said):

> Tongariro is the Mountain;
> Taupō is the Sea;
> Te Heuheu is the Man.

He was also the chief who (lived) in the middle of this island, and (at) the meeting-place of the (human) currents from one side and the other.[7] It was observed that the fish in that sea were *kōkopu* (a freshwater fish), *kōura* (a fresh-water species of crayfish), and *kōaro* (a blind species of the fresh water whitebait found in Rotoaira lake, at the foot of Mt. Tongariro).

Te Heuheu (on receiving this offer, in turn) offered the kingship to Te Amohau (high chief of the Ngāti Whakaue of the Arawa tribes). It was said of him:

> His Mountain is Ngongotahā;
> His Sea is Rotorua;
> And the fish in it are *kōura*; *kākahi* (a freshwater bivalve mollusc) and *inanga*.

(On hearing of Te Heuheu's offer) the words Te Amohau uttered were:

> Take (the kingship and give it) to Te Hāpuku (a high chief of the Kahungunu tribe of Hawkes Bay).

He (Te Amohau) said this because he was not the right one to be King. When it was offered to Te Hāpuku, the word of Te Hāpuku was that he, too, was not the one to be the King.[8]

It was (then) taken to Te Kaniatakirau.[9] When it was presented to him he said: "It is right I am a chief (and) the descendant of your ancestors; but what is wrong is that (my territory) is isolated. I will not agree," and that was Te Kaniatakirau's last word.

We will here add to "The Scribe's" narrative an East Coast version of another saying by Te Kaniatakirau with regard to the offer of the Māori Kingship:

> My Mountain, Hikurangi,
> Is not a mountain that travels.

And he also added, "I am already a King!"[10]

According to Taranaki sources the Māori Kingship was also offered to Tāmati Hone of the Ngāti Ruanui tribe and to Tītokowaru, his kinsman. After a conference with Tamaiparea of Ngārauru and other chiefs of the Taranaki people, the final decision was left to Tāmati Hone, and he decided to defer to the claims of the Whanganui high chief Topia Tūroa.

NOTES ON CHAPTER 1

Note 1

Wī Tako was a well-known chief of the Whanganui a Tara (Wellington district) section of the Āti Awa tribe, who went with Te Rauparaha from the Waitara district and assisted in the conquest of the lands of the southern tribes.

Notes 2 and 3

upoko or head, or upper part of "this country" refers to the southern end of the North Island.

Note 4

Davis was a Government interpreter and Māori linguist, and author of *The Life and Times of Patuone*, 1876. According to one account Davis also dictated Tāmehana Te Waharoa's famous letter about the Māori Kingship (7/6/1861).

Note 5

Tāmihana Te Rauparaha and Kingship: According to another account Te Rauparaha himself was against his son aspiring to be the Māori King, and said to him, "You and I cannot accept that position, for look you, Kāwhia, our ancestral land, we have abandoned!"

Note 6

Te Heuheu: The Te Heuheu referred to here was the second of that name. He was overwhelmed in a landslide in 1846. Later in this account, the other Te Heuheu mentioned was the younger brother, Iwikau, who took his elder brother's rank as paramount chief of

Taupō, and also the name Te Heuheu. (In this account Iwikau will be named Te Heuheu III.)

Note 7

(Human) currents is in reference to the fact that the genealogical lines of the Te Heuheu family connect with the tribes surrounding their territory.

Note 8

Te Hāpuku: One blot on Te Hāpuku's escutcheon was the fact that he was at one time taken captive in war and was assisted to escape by Te Heuheu II.

Note 9

Te Kaniatakirau was an East Coast high chief whose home was at Whāngārā. He was a descendant of the famous Hinematioro, renowned for her beauty and whose person was very sacred. She was virtually a Queen of the East Coast tribes, and was famed in song and story.

Note 10

This is as quoted by Sir Apirana Ngata to the Author.

GENEALOGICAL TABLE "A" FOR CHAPTER 1

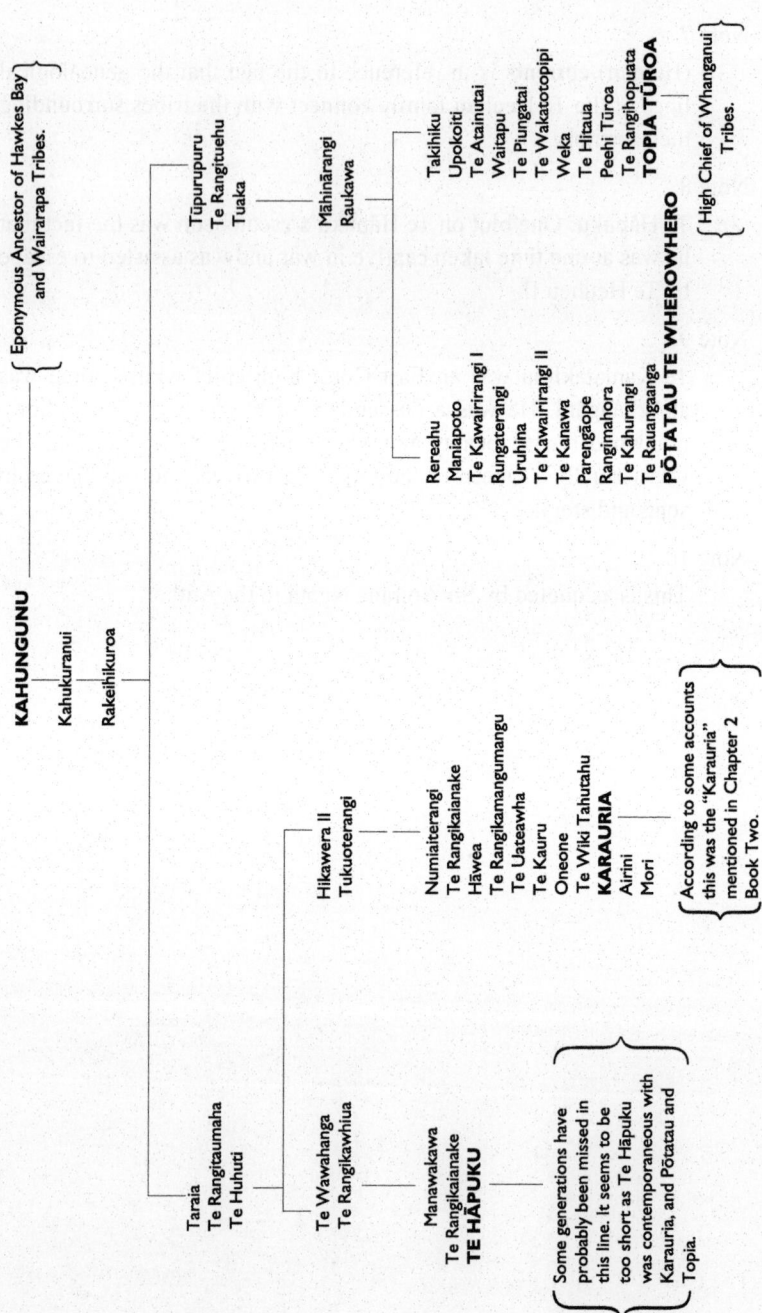

GENEALOGICAL TABLE "B" FOR CHAPTER 1

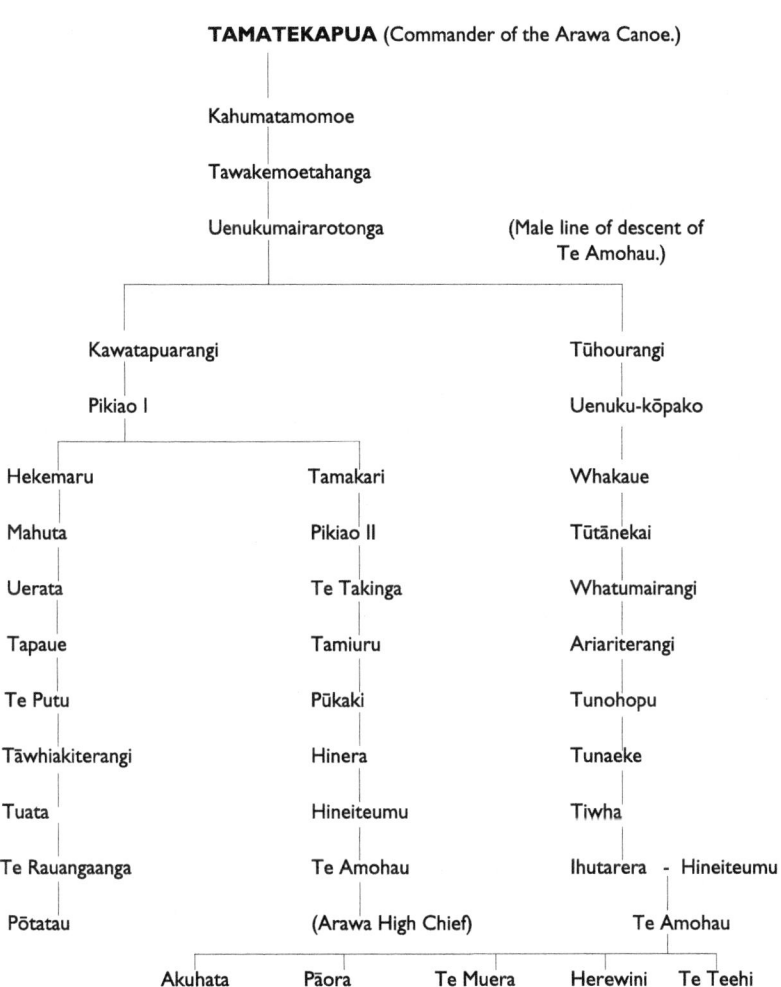

THE CHIEFS AND TRIBES DELIBERATE

Ko Taupiri te Maunga,
Ko Waikato te Awa.

Taupiri is the Mountain,
Waikato is the River.

CHAPTER 2

THE CHIEFS AND TRIBES DELIBERATE

I

A meeting was held somewhere on the east coast of the North Island (the exact place is not stated) when the offer was made of the kingship to the East Coast high chief Te Kaniatakirau.

From this point "The Scribe" takes up the story:

There was a chief there by the name of Karauria.[1] Everybody present agreed he was a powerful chief, and it was about to be decided to place the kingship on him. All the chiefs of the country who had spoken had agreed. Only one word remained. The word was a question, and the question was: "If there be a tribe or a man who objects, they should do so now. If not, the King is set up." (Now) there was a man there of Ngāti Raukawa whose name was Te Hukiki[2] and (he stood up and spoke) his word, saying, "I do not agree that this man be made King. But (I ask you) to return the kingship to Te Heuheu III." After he had spoken his word he collapsed.

The kingship was then returned to Te Heuheu and Mātene Te Whiwhi. Te Heuheu and Mātene Te Whiwhi then thought (it was time) to offer it to Pōtatau of whom the saying was:

> Taupiri is the Mountain;
> Waikato is the River.

and the proverb:

> *Waikato Horopounamu*
> Waikato, the swallower of greenstone.

Another proverb is:

> *Waikato Taniwharau,*
> Waikato of a hundred dragons
> *He piko he taniwha, he piko he taniwha*
> At each bend a dragon, at each bend a dragon.[3]

NOTES ON CHAPTER 2

Note 1
Karauria and Te Kaniatakirau and Pōtatau Te Wherowhero.

WHAKAPAPA (GENEALOGY)

POROURANGI   (Eponymous ancestor of East Coast tribes.)

Ueroa		Hau
Tokerau		Rakaipo
Iwipupu		Manutangirua
Kahungunu		Hingangaroa
Kahukuranui I		Hauiti
Rakeihikuroa		Kahukuranui II
Tūpurupuru		Tautini
Te Rangituehu		Karihimama
Tuaka	Te Aorangi	Tutaepena
Māhinārangi	Tupani	Whakinga
Raukawa	Takoro	Ngarokitepo
Rereahu	Tauaha	Marukawhiti
Maniapoto	Karera	Hineturaha
Te Kawairirangi I	Hinekura	Te Whakatatari
Rungaterangi	Ruapakura	Rangitumamao
Uruhina	Maroro	Te Kaniatakirau
Te Kawa	Horahora	
Te Kanawa	Pahura	
Parengāope	Karauria	
Rangimahora		
Te Kahurangi		
Te Rauangaanga		
Pōtatau Te Wherowhero		

Author's Note: According to Te Herekiekie Kerehi (John Te Herekiekie Grace) the place of this gathering was in Hawkes Bay and the Karauria mentioned in this account was the one traced out in the genealogical table given at the end of the preceding chapter.

Note 2
    Te Hukiki belonged to the Ngāti Raukawa tribe of the Manawatū section of that people. He was a near relative of the Raukawa high chief Te Whatanui. Te Hukiki and a fellow tribesman named Whioi, from Moutoa on the banks of the Manawatū river, were both selected by the sponsors of the Māori King movement to be a "College of Heralds" because of their profound knowledge of genealogies.

Note 3
    Dragons was a figure of speech used for the many powerful chiefs living along the banks of the Waikato river. "Swallower of Greenstone" is a reference to the many trophies of war won by the Waikato warriors on the field of battle. It was first coined after the Battle of Hingakākā. (See Chapter 1, Book One.)

SEARCH THE LAND,
SEARCH THE SEA

―――――――――

Hīnana ki Uta, Hīnana ki Tai

187

CHAPTER 3

SEARCH THE LAND, SEARCH THE SEA

I

The story by "The Scribe" continues:

It was in the year 1855 when Te Heuheu Iwikau went to take the word; that is, the kingship to Waikato, to Pōtatau. When Te Heuheu arrived (in Waikato) he handed over the kingship to Hone Papita, Te Paewaka and. Porokoru.[1] The word of Te Heuheu was, "Pōtatau Te Wherowhero is to be the King!" Te Heuheu left a hat with Hone Papita and Te Paewaka. Te Heuheu then went home.

Then Hone Papita, Te Paewaka and Porokoru went (to Māngere)[2] and took with them the hat and the kingship to give to Pōtatau. (On arrival) they said, "O Whero'! The word of the chiefs of the land is ended, and it is that you are to be the King." They (then) placed the hat on (his head). The word (of Pōtatau) was: "It is no good."

The Author interrupts to say that on this occasion the refusal of Pōtatau was also expressed in a song.

TE WAIATA A PŌTATAU

Tēnei ka noho, ka hihiri ngākau o tangata
Ki te mahi e takoto mai nei.'
Ki konā, e te Rau! taupū noa mai ai;
'A piki ake au ki runga te kiritai;
Ngā manu e wheko i raro o Rangiahua.
Hōmai ano koe, kia ringia iho
E tapu e ihi ana i a Rongo-whaka-hirahira.
Ki konā, e Tāne pani kara riri whanaunga,
He ngahere, pea, e whakanuia e te ngutu poto,
E pōkaia mai ana e te tamaiti niho koi,
Nāna i nohoia te Ihu o Tainui, te Waka o Hoturoa;
Nāna i harimai te kai ki te ao Māori.
He aha te atua kōrero i maua mai ai?
Mei huri kau ake ki muri ki tō tua mata.
Tua noa ana koera māhihi anake,
Takoto ana mai te rangi tā-whakarere i te rōhia,

Heoi te hirihiri e ngau ki Hauturu,
E ngau ki Te Whara, ki ngā puke i ahua;
Pohewa i takoto ki tawhiti.
"E ngoto rānei ō niho ki reira?"
Tēnā te kai ka ngaro te pae ki Hawaiki,
Ki te tupuranga mai o te kai, he kiore!

THE SONG OF PŌTATAU

Abiding with Mankind are many thoughts
For this Toilsome Thing that now lies here.
Remain you there, O ye Multitude! consumed by many desires:
And let me retire in pensive mood o'er yon outer palisading,
5   There to gaze in solitude at birds a-winging out there at Rangiahua.
Let me once more anoint myself.
The whilst I perform the sacred rites of Rongo of great renown.
Take away Tāne the orphan-maker and separator of kinsmen.
Perhaps, 'tis but a forest fantasy, coloured by hasty lips;
10 And that sharp-toothed youth, he seeks to encompass a
          subtle enterprise:
For he sitteth now at the Prow of Tainui, the Canoe of Hoturoa,
Which brought the food that grows in this land of the Māori.
Why dost thou bring this strange god unto me?
Hadst thou put it aside and left it behind thee,
15 These men would have striven in vain to fell the Forest Deep;
Meanwhile I, in deep content, would while away the livelong day.
Let those ardent and eager spirits assault Hauturu;
Yea, attack Te Whara too, those two upflung peaks yonder!
This proffered food receptacle would then be thrust afar off.
20 Verily, I ask, "Have you yet bared the teeth to attack there?"
Food a-plenty was forsaken and left in Hawaiki.
There, it did grow in great profusion.
In this enterprise, verily, I espy a food-devouring rat.

"The Scribe" resumes:

In the year 1856 (November) a meeting was held at Pūkawa (Lake Taupō). (The meeting was) called, "Hīnana ki Uta, Hīnana ki Tai" (search the land, search the sea). All the chiefs of this country went to that gathering. This was the first (of such meetings) that the Waikato people had attended. Their reason for going was to hand the kingship to Te Heuheu in accordance with the word of Pōtatau. On arrival (at Pūkawa) the Waikato (representatives) handed back the treasure (symbol of the kingship) of the chiefs to Te Heuheu. The words that were agreed upon at that meeting (with regard to the man to be set up as the King) were these:

(He was to possess) firstly, *mana* or prestige in all the land; secondly, *mana* over man; thirdly, to stop the flow of blood (inter-tribal wars); fourthly, the (Māori) King and the Queen (Victoria) to be one in concord and God to be above them both.

When these matters were agreed upon Te Heuheu took the hat[3] and placed it on Topia and said (to him), "You shall be the King!" But (Topia) declined (and) handed the hat back to Te Heuheu. Te Heuheu (then) handed it to Te Amohau. Te Amohau (also) declined. That hat was placed (by Te Heuheu?) on the head of each chief of this country in turn, but not one of them would accept it. The hat was handed back (by the chiefs) with the remark that Pōtatau and Te Heuheu were (the right ones) to have it. Te Heuheu thereupon placed the hat on the head of Taieti[4] for him to take back to Pōtatau.[5]

NOTES ON CHAPTER 3

Note 1

Hone Papita, Te Paewaka and Porokoru were three Waikato elder chiefs of the time of Pōtatau, who were related to him, and are referred to later in this account as his *mātua* or uncles.

Note 2

The home of Pōtatau at Māngere was near the stone building, the Church of England.

Note 3

the hat, which figures so often in this narrative, was described as a white bell-topper.

Note 4

Taieti was a Waikato chief and a relative of Pōtatau. Taieti was better known as Pātara Te Tuhi, the editor of the Māori King circular *Te Hokioi*.

Note 5
Pōtatau and Pūkawa meeting: A very pressing invitation was extended to Pōtatau to attend this meeting, but he did not appear at Pūkawa. He actually started for Pūkawa on horseback, but very reluctantly, and after travelling some miles on the way he fell off his horse (purposely it is said) and complained that it was too painful for him to proceed farther. He thereupon deputed Taieti to go on to Pūkawa with the hat.

NOTES ON THE SONG OF PŌTATAU

(2) Toilsome Thing: This is in reference to the Māori Kingship. Pōtatau was well-advanced in years and his life of ease at Māngere was one that he had fully earned. One can understand that to be loaded with the cares of kingship was a job that a philosopher like Pōtatau would not welcome. He could also envisage the burden that would be placed on his people in providing supplies of food for the tribal gatherings that would go with the position. As a matter of fact, the Author is of the opinion that the other chiefs who had turned down the offer of the kingship did so because they felt that their tribal resources would not be equal to the strain of keeping up the position of King.

(5) Rangiahua: The name of a beach near Kohimarama, Waitematā harbour.

(7) Rongo: God of Peace.

(8) Tāne the orphan-maker: Tāne or the male here refers to the warlike activities of man.

(9) a forest fantasy: Pōtatau here expresses doubt as to whether the idea of the Māori Kingship is genuine.

(10) sharp-toothed youth: A reference to Tāmehana Te Waharoa, whom Pōtatau disliked, and had not forgiven for the death of his relative Rangianewa, at Rangiaohia.

(11) Tainui: The canoe in which the ancestors of the Waikato, Raukawa, Maniapoto, and other west coast tribes of the North Island of New Zealand arrived in Aotearoa about the year 1350.

Hoturoa: Commander of the Tainui Canoe.

(12) Which brought the food: Tainui traditions have it that Hoturoa's wife Whakaotirangi was one of the leading women of the Māori migrants to Aotearoa who brought the *kūmara* or sweet potato and succeeded in propagating it in their new home.

(13) strange god: A further figurative reference to the Māori Kingship.

(15) the Forest Deep: A reference to the many chiefs and tribes throughout the land. Paraphrased, this and the preceding line might be given thus:

"Now, if you chiefs of the Waikato had ignored this kingship idea, and left it alone, the moving spirits or promoters of it would have finally become exhausted (like one struggling through the forest undergrowth) in travelling the land and arguing about this matter with the many chiefs and tribes."

(17) Hauturu: A range of high hills in the much-forested country of the Nehenehenui (now better known as the King Country). This range serves as the main watershed between the coast and the tributaries of the Waipā river.

(18) Te Whara: Another range of hills in the Nehenehenui country.

(19) food receptacle: A disparaging reference by Pōtatau to the hat and the offer of the kingship.

(20) bared the teeth to attack there: From this reference to Hauturu and then to the quotation above, Pōtatau shows that he felt that he and his people of the Waikato were under an obligation to the Maniapoto. There was the Huiputea defeat—and the fact that the Maniapoto (unlike the Raukawa) had never disturbed the peace between the Waikato and themselves. Pōtatau also had senior cousins among the Maniapoto chiefs. He felt that among the Maniapoto chiefs would be found one who would be acceptable for the position of Māori King.

(21) Food a-plenty: As previously stated, a number of chiefs had refused the kingship principally because they feared that the food economy of their tribal territories would not be able to sustain their kingly status. And it is to this aspect of the matter that Pōtatau refers.

(23) rat: Here the Waikato chieftain-poet likens the institution of kingship to the food-destroying rodent.

THE PRO-CONSUL AND THE BISHOP

Grey: Let your (Māori) Kingship be put down.

Selwyn: Let your flags be lowered.

CHAPTER 4

THE PRO-CONSUL AND THE BISHOP

I

The story is continued by "The Scribe"

(It will now be related) what Pōtatau and (Governor) Grey said to each other before (Pōtatau) was confirmed in his kingship.

Grey: "Let your (Māori) Kingship be put down."
Pōtatau: "I cannot do that. It is not mine. It belongs to the chiefs of this country!"
Grey: "If you (the Māori people) persist, I will (start) war against (your people in) this land. I will fight for seven years, and you (the Māori) will then be lost."
Pōtatau: "Indeed! If you fight for seven (years) I will resist for eight (years); for nine; and more: I, the Māori, will not die!"
Grey: "O Pō'! I possess a cow that has had numerous progeny. When it drinks it will keep on drinking until all the water is gone."
Pōtatau: "(That is) if it is but a pool of water. But if it is a spring that comes out of the heart of the land it will not run dry."
Grey: "Ah! but if we two fight, what food will you have?"
Pōtatau: "There will be *roi,*[1] *para,*[2] *mamaku,*[3] *hīnau,*[4] and *pōhue.*[5]"
Grey: "Ha! When those are gone, what food will you have then?"
Pōtatau: "You!"

This is all. This (account) is ended.

II

At this time, too, Tāmehana Wiremu Te Waharoa held a meeting at Pēria.[6] (At that meeting) the Bishop (Selwyn) said, "O Wī'! let your flags be lowered. If you do not heed, I will return over the seas with my widows. Beware, lest this territory become a land of trouble."

Wiremu Tāmehana Te Waharoa (often called Tāmehana Te Waharoa and Wiremu Tāmehana; but the latter name will be used from this point on) stood up and answered (the Bishop):

> Listen! Listen, O ye tribes from above and from below; from this coast and from that coast! I thought the waters of each stream and river all flowed on to their gathering-place. Do they not murmur and shout until they are engulfed in the mouth of the *parata*.[7] These (streams) are not unlike the (human) currents of various peoples. They all seek rest in God. When I worship God I am not rebuked. Now, with regard to the name King it is said I am (in the) wrong. Why? Look you now to the laws of (lands) over the seas: Of Tahiti is Pōmare; of Wiwi (France) is Buonaparte; of Russia is Nicholas, and of England is Queen Victoria. Now, am I a stranger in this land? It is (therefore) right I should set up a King for me. Look, it is (written) there in Deutoronomy, Chapter 17, verse xv:
>
> "Thou shalt in any wise set *him* king over thee, whom the Lord thy God shall choose; one from among thy brethren shalt thou set king over thee, thou mayest not set a stranger over thee, which is not thy brother."

III

In that same year a meeting of Ngāti Te Ata (tribe) was held at Waiuku. Many chiefs of Waikato, including Pōtatau, went there. His (Pōtatau's) words (at that meeting) were:

> Hearken, O ye people! All that I possess[8] I am gathering together and committing to the flames. In the past your god was Uenuku; and ye also ate of man; now it is the Great God in the heavens. It is not a treasure that may be bought. It is a treasure offered freely in the light of day. It cometh from heaven above to the land beneath. I have only three (things to offer you): Firstly, hold fast to the law; secondly, hold fast to love; thirdly, hold fast to the faith.
>
> Nothing else matters much.... No nothing, nothing. (It is better that one) be black without and white within. Indeed, the white skin, the red skin, and the dark skin all bathe in the same water; and the white thread, the red thread, and the dark thread, all are threaded on to the one needle.[9]

Thus spoke Pōtatau. (Then he added), "*Waiho ake au kia haere ki aku mātua i te Nehenehenui. Mō rātou tēnei taonga, te Kīngitanga.*" Let me go to my elders of the Nehenehenui. This treasured thing, the kingship, is for them.)

Pōtatau's answer reached the Maniapoto people (of the Nehenehenui) and they decided to call a meeting at Hauāuru near Ōtorohanga. The Maniapoto chiefs who called the meeting were Te Kanawa, Tuhoro and Hauāuru, who were Maniapoto relatives of Pōtatau. As the Maniapoto had heard of what Governor Grey had said to Pōtatau, and also of the speech of the Bishop at Pēria (now called Waharoa, in the Matamata district), the Maniapoto decided to call their meeting "Te Puna o te Roimata" (the well-spring of tears).

NOTES ON CHAPTER 4

Note 1

roi: A bread made from beaten *aruhe* or the roots of the *rarauhe* or bracken fern.

Note 2

para: The tuber of a species of orchid, used as food.

Note 3

mamaku: An edible tree-fern.

Note 4

hīnau: A tree with edible berries.

Note 5

pōhue: A trailing plant used by the Māori as vegetable food.

Note 6

Pēria is in the domain of the Ngāti Hauā tribe, of whom Tāmehana Te Waharoa became the chief after the death of his father Te Waharoa.

Note 7

parata: One of the denizens of the ocean, the opening and shutting of whose mouth was said to cause the ebb and flow of the tide.

Note 8

All that I possess: Pōtatau here refers to his sacred and priestly status, which he would besmirch if he accepted the much-debated position of King.

Note 9

Pōtatau's Waiuku speech: This is the longest recorded speech of Pōtatau. There was much speculation at the time as to whether Pōtatau would accept the kingship at the Waiuku meeting. Prior to this meeting and at this gathering, chiefs from various parts of the country were urging him to accept without any further delay. Many delegations had come to Waikato for this purpose. His success in bringing about a state of peace among several warring tribes was one of the principal reasons which impelled the chiefs to urge on him the acceptance of the position of Māori King. The speech was his reply to the chiefs.

THE WELL-SPRING OF TEARS

―――――――――

Te Puna o te Roimata

CHAPTER 5

THE WELL-SPRING OF TEARS

I

Says "The Scribe":

In 1857 a meeting was held of the Maniapoto people at Haurua. This was the meeting that was called "Te Puna o te Roimata." (At that meeting) the words of the chiefs were of one accord, and that was Pōtatau (was to) be the King. The people's mind being now settled that Pōtatau was to be the King, the word of Pōtatau went forth (and he said):—"I expect I will (now) be spoken to and be told: 'Stand up!' and I stand up. 'Applaud!' and I applaud. 'Stretch forth your hand!' and I stretch forth my hand. Enough as to this. Let me now go (back) to my elders, to Hōri Te Waru, Porokoru, Turimanu, and Te Paewaka."

II

"The Scribe's" account of the Haurua meeting is short and ends with Pōtatau's speech, and from this point the Author takes up the story from Maniapoto tribal sources.

The Maniapoto chiefs who took leading parts in the meeting at Haurua were Tuhoro, Te Kanawa and Hauāuru. They issued the notices of the meeting and acted as hosts.

On the arrival of Pōtatau and the Waikato party they had ceremoniously presented the hat and formally handed over the kingship to Hauāuru and he, in turn, handed it over to his elder (his father's first cousin) Tanirau. In turn the hat, which had by now become the symbol of the kingship, was presented to Tuhoro, Te Kanawa, Te Wetini, and Haupokia.

The Maniapoto chiefs deliberated on the matter, and it was unanimously decided that Pōtatau was the logical choice. It was also agreed that the decision of the Maniapoto was to be announced by Tanirau, because he was *tuakana* or senior line of descent in the tribal genealogy. Hauāuru, who was *tuakana* to Tanirau, had deferred to the latter because he (Hauāuru) on his male line of descent belonged to the same Waikato *hapū* or sub-tribe as Pōtatau.

III

The tribes were assembled on the *marae* at Haurua when Tanirau came forward wearing the hat and accompanied by a company of singers. A verse from the songs they sang was:

Tuhoro, Te Kanawa,
Nā Hauāuru!
I tū ai te Kīngi
Ki Haurua ē ī!

O Tuhoro, Te Kanawa,
It was Hauāuru!
Who raised-up the King
At Haurua!

After announcing to the assembly the decision of the Maniapoto chiefs, Tanirau advanced across the *marae* to the place where Pōtatau was seated. Pausing in front of Pōtatau, Tanirau took off the hat and, in a loud voice, called out:

Ko koe hei Kīngi! Hei Kīngi! Hei Kīngi!
You are to be King! Be King! Be King!

As he pronounced "King" for the third time, Tanirau placed the hat on the head of Pōtatau. Looking up at Tanirau Pōtatau said wearily:

E Ta'; kua tō te rā....
O Ta'—Tanirau—the sun is about to set....

Pōtatau meant that he himself was too old to worry about being made the King. To this remark Tanirau replied:

E tō ana i te ahiahi;
E ara ana i te ata:
E tū koe hei Kīngi.

It setteth in the evening;
To rise again in the morning :
Thou art raised-up as King!

Tanirau intended by this speech to make known the decision of the Maniapoto chiefs, that the Kingship was to become hereditary. After remaining silent for some time, with Tanirau standing awaiting his reply, Pōtatau at last looked up and said simply, "*E pai ana.*" (It is good.) Tanirau then retired and Pōtatau rose to give utterance to the words already penned in "The Scribe's" account. At the end of his speech Pōtatau sang a song.

HE WAIATA AROHA NĀ PŌTATAU MŌNA

E noho ana i te ranga māheuheu
O te ngutu o te tangata,
E wani atu rā he taranga hau;
Ka hāpainga ki te poti ngutu;
Hei hikihiki atu
Ki te pahī taua ki te tonga.
Kei Repanga ngā manu mōhio;
Ko Mumuhau, ko Takereto;
I tīraua ka waiho te ngaki.
Titiro mai ka eke i rua-hine,
Ka tokotoko ko te ripa tauārai
Ki ngā mahi i kauhoe i taku ohinga.
Tēnei tonu ka te heheu mai
Ka hoki au ki te 'hine,
Ko aku rongo kia puaina te ripa ki Mauina'.
E hara tāua i te taringa ki te whakarongo
Whakamōhoutia ka waiho hei raru
Ki ahau ē ī...!

PŌTATAU'S SONG OF SORROW

1   Oft these times, in pensive mood, I sit
    With thoughts heaped up
    Like the entangled weeds that do lie:
    My name now always on the lips of men—
5   Borne here and there with the winds that blow,

As 'twere a passing jest on frivolous lips,
'Tis carried even unto the distant South.
At Repanga, 'tis said, live two wise birds
Called Mumuhau and Takereto.
10 And here am I like unto them;
Pecked at and agitated by all the land.
Who will work and clear this weedy soil?
For look you, I am now grey and worn with years;
The last horizon has moved up quite close;
15 Youthful and zestful days are but a memory,
And my fretful soul is now at rest from all these.
Give me the life of women a-weaving,
As they gossip and around them children play.
Tho' my fame would then be environed
20 By the peaceful shores at Mauina'.
It would indeed be a joy for me and mine:
You and I should not have heeded
The oft-spoken seductive words,
Which, methinks, will but lead to endless sorrow
25 For me.... Alas, Ah me!

NOTES ON CHAPTER 5

Pōtatau's Song of Sorrow

(7) the distant South: Pōtatau here makes a reference to the fact that the King Movement had emanated from the southern tribes.

(8) Repanga is the Māori name for one of the small islands to the south of Aotea or Great Barrier Island.

(9) Mumuhau and Takereto were mythical birds able to foretell the coming of stormy weather. In a metaphorical sense *mumuhau* means an eddying wind, and *tā keretao* is a wooden puppet figure, which is made to perform in a most diverting manner by holding it at the end of a string with its feet barely touching a pliable board. By striking the loose end of the board the figure is made to dance and throw its limbs about. This is another of the several figures of speech applied by Pōtatau to the idea of the Māori Kingship.

(20) Mauina': In full, Mauinaina, which is a place near Kohimarama on the shores of the beautiful Waitematā harbour.

WHAKAPAPA (GENEALOGY).

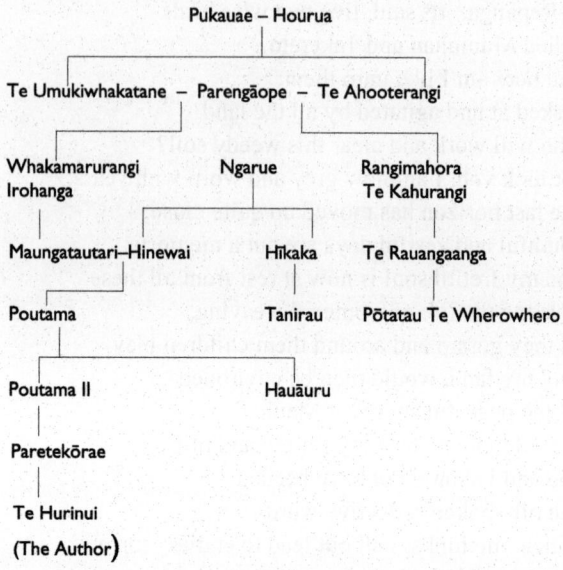

THE BIRDS OF STRONG FLIGHT

Ngā Manu Tarakaha

CHAPTER 6

THE BIRDS OF STRONG FLIGHT

I

In this chapter the Author takes up the story to fill a gap in "The Scribe's" narrative.

At the period under review, Pōtatau was being urged by some of the chiefs to raise a war-party against the Ngāti Hauā tribe, Wiremu Tāmehana's people, for the killing of Rangianewa (Book One, Chapter 12). The thought that the death of this relative had not been avenged had often rankled in Pōtatau's mind and he felt very bitter toward Wiremu Tāmehana and his people. It is said that when Pōtatau heard of the Pēria meeting (Book Two, Chapter 4) he could not conceal his distrust of and enmity toward Wiremu Tāmehana. Pōtatau suspected the Ngāti Hauā chieftain of duplicity and suggested that Wiremu's support of the King Movement was inspired more because of his fear that Pōtatau if he did not accept the Kingship would seek payment for the death of Rangianewa, rather than out of any conviction that the institution of a Māori King would be beneficial to the Māori people. When he heard what Tāmehana had said in his speech to Bishop Selwyn, Pōtatau scornfully remarked, "*E mōhio ana tēnā tangata ki tāna mahi.*" (That man—Wiremu Tāmehana—knows what he is doing.)

II

It is recounted that when Wiremu Tāmehana appeared on the *marae* at Paetai to address the gathering it was the first time Pōtatau had set eyes on him since the killing of Rangianewa. As Wiremu advanced on to the *marae* to deliver his speech he gave one quick furtive glance in the direction of Pōtatau. The Lord of Waikato sat back and stared at Wiremu with a fierce penetrating look. It was a tense moment. Tāmehana nervously put his hand to his mouth and fixed his eyes on the two flagpoles that had been erected on the *marae*. He stood in silence for some moments and then bracing himself he began his speech.

As he spoke Pōtatau relaxed somewhat, but looked intently at the speaker and listened in profound silence to what Wiremu Tāmehana had to say. All the chiefs present knew of the strong feeling between these redoubtable warriors. Pōtatau's restraint and Wiremu's courage in the ordeal was the subject of animated discussion in the villages for a long time afterward.

Tāmehana was a great orator. It was noticed that as he spoke a sense of quiet dignity and patient gravity seemed to suffuse the face of Pōtatau who, having gradually removed his eyes from the speaker, sat looking downward cupping his chin in his hand. Pōtatau offered no comment and remained silent throughout Tāmehana's oration. He seemed to be pursuing some fugitive thought through the address, and to let every other thing go by as if the speaker and he were alone in the world.

III

There were many chiefs and speakers at the Paetai meeting. The family of Pōtatau was noted as being one of few words, arid on the occasion of the Paetai meeting Pōtatau's address was very brief. He compressed most of the thoughts he had in mind into a song.

TE WAIATA A PŌTATAU TE WHEROWHERO

Ka raranga ngā hau o te Muri,
Ka raranga ngā hau o te Tonga;
Ka whakapuke koa ngā tai o te Awa;
Ka whakamoea ngā patu ki te Whare.
Kia mihi atu au
Ki te ipo tai-tama;
E kīia mai nei,
"He kākano whakauuru tupu noa ki te Marae"
He hanga hou hoki
Te pani taua e hoki ki te ora,
Te korakora rere a Mahuika,
Piri noa ake ki te kahikōmako!
Totoro te paoa ki tawhiti.
He manu makere i te rawe,
Ka tau te pōkai kākā—
Tau noa ki te motu.
Koia ka rere ngā manu tarakaha!
Rūnā e te manu kura.
Koia ka noho ngā tūturiwhatu;
Nō mua rā, ē, nō te Whetū

E piri ana ki te marama;
Taranui koe here ki te rangi!
I a koutou e noho mai nā,
Ka mamao au ko tawhiti.
"E kore te kī e whai i te tua' o Hekemaru"
E kīia mai nei,
"Mōkai nohoanga iti
Paengarau a Waiwaia"
Tūranga rau o Aitu!

THE SONG OF PŌTATAU TE WHEROWHERO[1]

1   The West Winds do hither gently blow,
    The South Winds too a caress on me bestow;
    But like the Swollen River
    Many thoughts within me rise:
5   Your *mere* discarded and mine
    Within the tribal House now lies.
    Ah me! 'tis with heavy heart
    I now salute you all
    O my gallant and youthful kinsmen!
10 Will ye always heed my call?
    Know ye, that, in the hearts of impetuous leaders.
    No thoughts for ye they cherish;
    "As scattered seed; strewn o'er the courtyard"
    So 'tis being said, ye will lie
15 And there will surely perish.
    The years that come and go,
    Seem bewildering and so strange;
    And now all around us,
    There has been wrought a wondrous change!
20 Has it not been decreed that,
    The fugitives from the Fields of War,
    To the Freedman's life we lead,
    We must all perforce restore?
    Because of this, methinks,
25 All manly thoughts now have fled,
    And in defiant rage,
    To the *kahikōmako* tree hath sped—
    Like the flying spark
    From *Mahuika*'s sacred fire:

30 Perchance, ye, that stand afar off,
    Saw the smouldering flame expire!
    Ah me, the once Captive Bird,
    And now escaped Decoy,
    Will lead the *kākā* flock,
35 And his many cunning arts employ!
    Peradventure, in the Forest a space to rest—
    The New Life to enjoy.
    The Birds of Strong Flight
    Will follow the Bright-plumaged One
40 And ye Tattooed Ones, Chieftains all,
    Ye will be left desolate and undone.
    Remember ye those other days?
    When like the bright evening star,
    Ye vied with the moon,
45 And in the heavens, I saw ye from afar!
    As ye around me foregather,
    And my spoken thoughts with yours entwine,
    Afar off my inward self hath gone:
    And of me, a true son of Hekemaru's line,
50 Ne'er let an angry word my path pursue!
    Tho', methinks, 'twill oft be said,
    "Like an humble one,
    Circumscribed will be his lowly bed:
    Lo! the fearsome dragon, Waiwaia, ashore
55 Hath drifted and there, inert, lies he outspread."
    But ye, who dared with me a Hundred Deaths,
    On the blood-soaked fields that ran red,
    Will abide with me, abide with me unto the end!

IV

Wiremu Tāmehana was without doubt a very resourceful man. He had intellectual powers above the ordinary and it was due to these that he was able to make such a mark in the history of his time. Before coming to the Paetai meeting he had visited the Ngāti Apakura tribe at Rangiaohia and had there handed over his favourite daughter Te Raumako as a peace offering, and thus made his peace with that people. During the meeting Pōtatau heard of this grand gesture and this knowledge led to a peacemaking between the chieftains—although Pōtatau remained to the end of his days rather wary of the Ngāti Hauā leader;

V

Among the chiefs present at Paetai was Te Awaitaia of Whāingaroa, the same Te Awaitaia who won renown at Taharoa by killing Raparapa (Book One, Chapter 9). Te Awaitaia sought to dissuade Pōtatau from accepting the offer of the Kingship and said, "You will be misunderstood by most people, and you will be blackened in the eyes of the world!" To this Pōtatau said, "*Āe, e pango ana i waho, e mā ana i roto.*" (Yes; black without, but white within.) Te Awaitaia then sang a song expressing his sorrow.

Te Heuheu Iwikau, who was also present, then said, "*Ka rere te tangata, ko wai a ia?*" (If a man flees, who will he be?) This angered Te Awaitaia and he said, "I am a descendant of Muriwhenua, the slayer of men!"

Pōtatau quietly interposed and said, "Why use such words to your elder?"

The sequel to this passage of words was to come in the time of the second Māori King, Tāwhiao, the son of Pōtatau, when Te Awaitaia threw in his lot with the Government, was given the rank of major, and actively assisted the forces under General Cameron in the advance into the lands of the Waikato. It was the defection of Te Awaitaia and other Waikato tribes which exposed the flank of the Waikato men defending their ancestral lands. In addition to Te Awaitaia, two other powerful Waikato chiefs turned traitor to the Māori cause, but in the aftermath it was found impossible to disentangle the lands of the so-called rebels from those who were called loyalists, and the confiscations included large areas of land belonging to Kukutai and Te Wheoro who went over to the Government side. These two chiefs were also given swords and made majors in the British forces under General Cameron.

VI

At the Paetai meeting Te Wherowhero acted as peace-maker between various sections of the Waikato. During these proceedings someone remarked to him, "What have you to say about the Maniapoto?" To this he replied, "*E pai anō Te Nehenehenui; he wai kōharahara.*" (They are all right as our troubles with them are like the raindrops on the forest leaves of the Nehenehenui.) By this he meant there was no deep-rooted cause at that time for which he would expect the Maniapoto people to disturb their good relationship with the Waikato. Having said that he turned in the direction of Te Awaitaia and said to the assembled chiefs, "*Ka pā tāu ko Tainui a Whiro, ngunguru te Pō, ngunguru te Ao!*" (Now, if you were to ask me about the Tainui of Whiro, it rumbles and rages by night, and it rumbles and rages by day!).²

NOTES ON CHAPTER 6

Note 1
   The Song of Pōtatau Te Wherowhero

(1) West Winds... South Winds: This is in reference to the tribes from the West Coast and southern districts who had come as a deputation to the Paetai meeting to pay homage to Pōtatau and to urge him to accept the Kingship.

(3) Swollen River: Waikato River:

(27) *kahikōmako* tree: *Pennantia corymbosa*.

(29) Mahuika: In Māori mythology Mahuika was the goddess of fire, and when the mythological hero Māui obtained her secret by deceit, she pushed him and in her rage threw her fingernails—in which the spirit of fire was kept—into some trees, including the *kahikōmako* tree.

(32) Captive Bird... Decoy: It is said that this is in reference to Wiremu Tāmehana whose father Te Waharoa was at one time a captive of the Arawa tribes of Rotorua.

(34) *kākā*: *Nestor meridionalis*, native parrot. The Māori fowler found the *kākā* a comparatively easy forest bird to decoy.

(38) The Birds of Strong Flight: Pōtatau here makes reference to some of the chiefs whom he expected would throw in their lot with the white man.

(39) Bright-plumaged One: A figure of speech for the bright red uniforms of the British forces.

(49) Hekemaru: An ancestor of Pōtatau and noted for being very sensitive to any affront to his dignity. He had been known to retrace his steps when on the warpath in order to chastise some tribe or chief who had fancied themselves safe from his anger after insulting him when he had passed on his way.

(54) Waiwaia: A tribal *taniwha* or dragon of the Maniapoto tribe. It lived in the Waipā river near Ōtorohanga.

Note 2
   Tainui: The tribal name of Te Awaitaia's people.
   Whiro: The personification of evil.

THE KING IS RAISED UP

Ka whakawahia te Kīngi

CHAPTER 7

THE KING IS RAISED UP

When Pōtatau arrived at Rangiaohia (on his return from Haurua) all his elders were there. "The Scribe" relates that he spoke to them thus:

Listen. The minds of the people of this land have been settled, and it is that I am to be the King. Now, you are to tell me whether I am to agree to accept the position of King, or not accept it at all. If I am to decline I will return the treasured possession of the tribes.

His elders replied: "The word of the tribes is that you are to be King; ours is to support what the tribes have decided."

II

In 1858 the first Waikato meeting was held at Paetai near Rangiriri, on the east bank of the Waikato river. The Waikato and Ngāti Hauā tribes attended. At this meeting two flagpoles were erected. Flying from one was the flag of the Queen of England, and from the other was the flag of the Māori King.

Wiremu Tāmehana said at the meeting, "Those who want the Queen are to proceed and stand under the Queen's flag. Those who want the King are to go and stand under the King's flag."

When they left their places all the Waikato stood under the Queen's flag.[1] They really believed that the Queen would protect them.[2] Finally, only four men stood under the King's flag. They were Hapi Hamaka of the Ngāti Naho tribe, Murupaenga (Ngāti Tipa), Pukewhau (Ngāti Hine), and Te Kihirini Te Kanawa (Ngāti Ngahia).

III

In 1859 a second meeting of the Waikato and Maniapoto tribes was held at Rangiaohia. All the chiefs of this country went there. Pōtatau, too, was there. This was the meeting where he was made King, and was raised-up by Te Tapihana.[3]

THE RAISING-UP RITUAL OF THE FIRST MĀORI KING

High Priest (Te Tapihana): O Io! Thou Heavenly One!
    Name him,
    This son of ours,
    A son, indeed, he was to us;
    When You and I
    Strove manfully in our striving.
    He guarded our peaceful slumbers,
    And we slept soundly through the night.

    O Io! Thou Heavenly One!
    Name him,
    Name him—what?

First Chieftain (Te Awarahi, of Waikato) responding:
    Name him Ariki Taungaroa! (Chief of Chiefs).

No voice was heard to repeat this name. Te Tapihana remained standing. And then repeated the concluding lines of the invocation.

High Priest: O Io! Thou Heavenly One!
      Name him,
      Name him—what?

Second Chieftain (not named):
    Name him Toihau! (the Supreme Head).

Again there was silence.

High Priest: O Io! Thou Heavenly One!
      Name him,
      Name him—what?

Third Chieftain (not named): Name him Kahutaratara!
(the High Chief of Scattered Tribes).
And again there was silence.

High Priest: O Io! Thou Heavenly One!
Name him,
Name him—what?

Fourth Chieftain (Hōri Te Waru, of Waikato):
Name him the King!

Wiremu Tāmehana (the so-called King-maker):
Yes, name him King!

High Priest: Yes, name him King!
O Io! Thou Heavenly One
Name him,
This son of ours.
A son, indeed, he was to us;
When you and I
Strove manfully in our striving.
He guarded our peaceful slumbers
And we slept soundly through the night.

O Io! Thou Heavenly One!
Name him, name him,
Name him—King!

Chorus from Assembled Tribes:
Name him King! Name him King!

The cry was taken up and the people shouted, "A King! A King!" and when their cries ended Remi stood forth and said, "Blessed be the God of our ancestors, who hath come down from Heaven on a chariot of a White Cloud. Thousands upon thousands do proclaim him the anointed King on his Throne. Indeed, he has now been made King of all peoples throughout the land. Verily, let him be blessed. He cometh in the name of the Lord. Hosanna in the Highest!"

The people made obeisance and honoured Pōtatau three times. When the ceremony ended there came this chant:

There is a father now within the house:
The old world turneth away;

A new world cometh.
Thou art now possessed of
The honour that here abideth.
Let there be no more words—
Let there be no bitterness.
This (kingship) is like unto
A bold headland that cannot be set aside.
Bind on the strength of countless numbers;
Bind on the strength of thousands upon thousands:
Bind it on and make it fast!
'Tis now firmly held—firmly held!
And it will endure!

Morgan, the missionary, then stood up and addressed the people, saying, "Let us pray." But Te Tapihana took the prayer away (from the missionary) and in a loud voice chanted, "Forsaken now is Egypt, the land of Sin and Shame: A new home (we) now seek; as a resting-place. Halleluia to God! God save the King!" [4]

IV

At Ngāruawāhia, on May 2, 1859, was held the biggest and the last gathering in connection with the setting up of Pōtatau as the Māori King. All the chiefs of this country gathered there and Wiremu Tāmehana spoke these words about the kingship:

> Commencing at Pūkawa (Lake Taupō) the words were these: Firstly, the King be set up to hold the *mana* or prestige over the land; secondly, *mana* over man; thirdly, to stop the flow of blood. The Māori King and the Queen of England to be joined in concord. God be over them both!

Wiremu Tāmehana then advanced and placed the Bible[5] on the head of Pōtatau. That ended the raising-up ceremony and he was proclaimed as "King Pōtatau Te Wherowhero."

The King's flag was then unfurled. Tapaue[6] was its name. At this time the chiefs of the land came forward to do honour to him, saying, "Blessed be the King! You have come forth in the name of the Lord. Hosanna in the Highest!" [7] One old man there stooped low and crawled between King Pōtatau's legs. His name was Tauke, and he was a chief from Taranaki. The word of the tribes was: "Stand thou, O King Pōtatau

Te Wherowhero, as a *mana* for man; for the land; to stop the flow of blood; to hold the peace between one man and another, between one chief and another chief. The King and the Queen to be joined in concord." It was in this way, continues "The Scribe," that the Kingship was embraced by the Māori people, as an heritage for many generations and for ever. These are the land pillars (mountain peaks) that were then placed under the kingship of King Pōtatau Te Wherowhero as a token of the unity of the Māori people:

Karioi (south side of entrance to Whāingaroa or Raglan harbour); Taranaki (Māori name of Mount Egmont, Taranaki province); Kai Iwi (at Kai Iwi, between Pātea and Whanganui); Tararua (the Tararua range, Wellington province); Titiokura (between Lake Taupō and Napier, Hawkes Bay); Putauaki (Māori name for Mount Edgecumbe, Bay of Plenty district); Ngongotahā (on the shores of lake Rotorua); Te Aroha (near the present town of the same name in the Hauraki district).

To end this chapter, the Author here interrupts "The 'Scribe's" story to give the Māori text of the *whakawahi* or raising-up ritual of Te Tapihana, in the setting-up of King Pōtatau Te Wherowhero.

TE KARAKIA WHAKAWAHINGA I A
KĪNGI PŌTATAU TE WHEROWHERO

Te Tapihana: *E Io! e Rangi!*
                     Tapa mai rā ia
                     Tā tāua tama
                     I whakatama ai tāua,
                     I ō tāua nōnoketanga.
                     I nōnoke ai tāua;
                     I ō tāua momoetanga
                     I momoe ai tāua i te pō:
                     E Io! e Rangi!
                     Tapa mai rā ia,
                     Ko wai?

Rangatira Tuatahi (Te Awarahi): *Hei Ariki Taungaroa!*

Te Tapihana: *(Ka karakia anō.)*

Rangatira Tuarua: *Hei Toihau! (Ka karakia anō a Te Tapihana.)*

Rangatira Tuatoru:	Hei Kahutarara! (Ka karakia anō.)
Rangatira Tuawhā:	Hei Kīngi!
Wiremu Tāmehana:	Āe, hei Kīngi!
Te Tapihana:	(Kātahi ka whakatutukiria te karakia ki ēnei kupu) E Io! e Rangi! Tapa mai rā ia, Hei Kīngi!
Te Iwi:	Hei Kīngi! Hei Kīngi!

NOTES ON CHAPTER 7

Note 1

The action of the Waikato people in indicating their refusal of the Māori Kingship which had been offered to their High Chief or *Ariki*, was strictly in accordance with Māori etiquette—that a gift when first offered is to be refused and handed back.

Note 2

The Queen's protection: "The Scribe's" somewhat cynical comment indicates that he had the land confiscations—following the Waikato War—in mind when the lands of the "Loyalists" were included in the confiscated area with those of the so-called "Rebels."

Note 3

Te Tapihana: A chieftain and high priest of the southern Waikato tribes of the Rangiaohia-Ōhaupō district.

Note 4

Forsaken is now Egypt, or *Ka mahue a Īhipa:* From hymn No.130 in the Church of England Māori Hymn Book.

Note 5

the Bible: The Bible mentioned in the account of the Ngāruawāhia meeting is still in the possession of the Māori King family, and it has been used in the same way by being placed on the head of each of the four successive kings after King Pōtatau.

According to one account given to the Author, Pōtatau arrived at Ngāruawāhia mounted on a white charger, and just in time for the ceremony recounted by "The Scribe," and he remained on his horse until Wiremu Tāmehana came toward him with the Bible in his hand. When Wiremu was a few paces off Pōtatau threw to the ground the hat which he was wearing, and he then dismounted and seated himself on a slope nearby. He was thus seated when Wiremu Tāmehana placed the Bible on his head.

Note 6

Tapaue: A very famous warrior ancestor of Pōtatau. (See Genealogical tables.)

Note 7

"Blessed.... Highest": See Matthew, XXI; 9, etc.

THE STORM CLOUDS OF WAR

You be on that side, and I will be on this side. Let Mangatāwhiri be our boundary.

Pōtatau's boundary

CHAPTER 8

THE STORM CLOUDS OF WAR

In the time of his reign, says "The Scribe," King Pōtatau laid down a boundary between himself and the Governor, Sir George Grey, saying, "You be on that side, and I will be on this side. Let Mangatāwhiri[1] be our boundary. Do not encroach on this side. Likewise, I am not to set foot on that side."

Then he set a boundary for the Waikato people to the south, and this line was the Pūniu river. In proclaiming this boundary Pōtatau said to the Waikato tribes, "You must not step over this boundary. This is *pekehawani*!"[2]

The reason why King Pōtatau took these actions was because the Ngāti Maniapoto tribe had joined in the fighting in Taranaki,[3] and when the Maniapoto went on their way under the famous Rewi Maniapoto, Pōtatau said to the Maniapoto people, "*Haere hei kai mā ngā manu o te rangi!*" (Go, and become food for the birds of the air!)

Some of the Waikato peoples took no heed of what King Pōtatau said.[4] Their leaders were Te Wetini Taipōrutu, Wiremu Kapara, Hēmi Rīwai, Pāora Te Uata, and others. When this party went they were all killed.[5] That was their fate because they had disregarded the laws under which the King had been set up. King Pōtatau remained true to the ideals of the Māori Kingship.

NOTES ON CHAPTER 8

Note 1

Mangatāwhiri: The name of the stream that flows into the Waikato river near (now) Mercer.

Note 2

pekehawani: Literally to break a truce.

Note 3
    Maniapoto under Rewi in Taranaki: The Maniapoto inflicted a severe defeat on a British force in an engagement near Waitara at the end of June, 1860.

Note 4
    Wetini Taipōrutu and others: On the return of the Maniapoto from Taranaki they boasted that killing *Pākehā* (white men) was like *kato pūhā* (breaking off the stalks of sour thistle). But they did not go back to Taranaki with Te Wetini Taipōrutu and the others. The bulk of the forces that went with Te Wetini were from the Ngāti Hauā tribe, Wiremu Tāmehana's people. [November, 1860.]

Note 5
    Wetini Taipōrutu and others all killed: These men were killed during the assault they made on the British redoubt at Māhoetahi.

END OF BOOK TWO

BOOK THREE

MANA MOTUHAKE

Spiritual Prestige Set Apart

Te Paki o Matariki
THE MĀORI KINGS' COAT OF ARMS

In combination the two words *mana motuhake*, which have been selected as the title for Book Three, may have several meanings. The word *mana* could mean any one of the following: power, prestige, effectual, authority, control, binding, authoritative, take effect, psychic force, having influence, effective authority. The word *motuhake* does not present the same problem. It means separated, or set apart.

These words were chosen by the Māori King Movement for its motto and, as such, it figures on the coat of arms of the Māori Kings. The coat of arms is called "Paki o Matariki" (the widespread calm of the Pleiades). The design, the motto, and the name Paki o Matariki, was the work of two Tainui high priests of the Io religion. They were Tiwai Parāone of the Hauraki tribes, and Te Aokatoa of the Waikato and Raukawa tribes. The work was completed and approved in the time of King Tāwhiao after a long delay. The two priests showed great reluctance in undertaking the task. They probably had some qualms about reproducing any part of the mystic designs of the priesthood even for the Māori King's coat of arms, and it was only King Tāwhiao's insistence that finally brought the work to completion.

As explained by the high priests the symbolic meanings of the design were:

1. The double spiral design in the centre is an improvised depiction of the mystic drawings on the inscribed stone emblems of the Tainui priesthood (Book One, Chapter 3). It is a representation of the Creation, the series of strokes between the double lines marking off the various stages or epochal periods in the creation of the world.
2. The two figures on either side of the curvilinear design represent TE ATUATANGA (spirituality) on the right, and AITUĀ (misfortune) on the left.
3. The cross with the heart design at the base represents the new faith, Christianity, brought by the white man.
4. The seven stars at the top of the design—one large and six smaller ones—represent Matariki or Pleiades, the first appearance of which before sunrise indicated the beginning of the Māori year—about the middle of June.
5. The *nīkau* tree (*Rhopalostylis sapida*, New Zealand palm) and the *harakeke* plant (general name for New Zealand flax, *Phormium tenax*) on the right of the design represent the housing and clothing of the ancient Māori. On the left of the design is depicted the *mamaku* (an edible tree fern) and *para* (a species of orchid, the tuber of which was used as food) emblematic of the food of the Māori of Aotearoa.

To return to the two words, *mana motuhake*. In combination they have often been translated as "power apart," in the sense of self-government or imperium in imperio. As a political slogan it has been so used. I have, however, delved into this matter and, in my opinion, the meaning the high priests—among them King Tāwhiao— intended was: *mana*, spiritual prestige; and *motuhake*, set apart, and hence "spiritual prestige set apart." That is the Māori Kingship was set apart as the symbol of the spiritual and cultural life of the Māori. And this was exemplified in his belief in *tapu* (sacredness), the priestly *mana* (psychic force) of his chieftains who had been parties to the setting up of the Māori *kīngitanga* and in the Io religion of the race. It was with this conception in mind that I selected the words *mana motuhake* as the title for this section of this work.—Author.

WAIKATO

The River and the Land

CHAPTER 1

WAIKATO

I

By now the reader will have become reasonably well acquainted with the tribes of Waikato. It is, therefore, to the river itself and the land that the Author now directs attention.

In song and story the Waikato river has exercised its influence upon the land through which it flows and upon the people who live along its banks. The river has played an important part in the history of the Tainui people, and at one point—where it is joined by the Waipā river at Ngāruawāhia— an outstanding part. The river is more than ever destined to play a leading part in the affairs not only of the Waikato, but of the nation itself, with the development of electric power-stations along its course, from the foot of the dominating forest-clad Maungatautari at Karapiro and Arapuni, and upward against its current right back to its outflowing waters at Tapuwaeharuru (the resounding footsteps) at the northern end of Te Moana o Taupō (the sea of Taupō).

A Waikato tribal version of the naming of the river itself states that the name is descriptive, and that the river Tongariro—world-famous for its trout-fishing—which is snow-fed from the mountains Tongariro and Ruapehu and flows into Lake Taupō at its southern end, is also part of the Waikato river. But the Taupō lake people do not agree with this claim. The Waikato tribal account describes how the waters (*wai*) of the mountain river were captured or *kato* by the inland sea of Taupō. Thus we have *waikato* (the captive waters).

II

The river is familiar to most travellers through the southern Auckland district. From Mangatāwhiri (Mercer) southward to Ngāruawāhia, road and rail at present follow its eastern banks for several miles through a rolling countryside of fertile river flats, lakes, swamp lands and sluggish streams. A few miles to the east is a range of hills, covered with a varying growth of *rarauhe* (bracken), *mānuka* (the so-called tea-tree), *monoao* (a shrub), and indifferent forest growth. These hills end abruptly on the south with the towering peak of the sacred Taupiri mountain.

To the Māori—especially to the tribes of Waikato—Taupiri mountain is no ordinary high hill. It was the sacred mountain of their ancestors and, in the time of Pōtatau Te Wherowhero, was enshrined in the saying:

Waikato is the River;
Taupiri is the Mountain;
Te Wherowhero is the Man.

Almost leaning up against its steep western slopes is a lower peak called Taupiri Kūao (*kūao*, the offspring) which is now used as the burial place of the great ones of the Waikato tribes, and which was formerly an impregnable, fortified *pā*. Lower down is Te Mataotutonga, the site of the dwelling-place of Te Putu, Pōtatau's famous forbear.

It was to Te Mataotutonga that the captive chieftain Ngātokowaru, the Ngāti Raukawa would-be conqueror of the fertile lands of Horotiu near Ngāruawāhia, was taken when he expressed the wish that he desired to greet and gaze upon the countenance of the patriarchal Te Putu before he was killed. Te Putu was so *tapu* that those who came to pay their respects to him had to salute him in the *hongi* manner on his big toe. But, when Ngātokowaru was ushered into the presence of the great Waikato *ariki* (paramount chief), the Ngāti Raukawa chieftain ignored the outthrust foot of Te Putu who was reclining on his couch. Kneeling on one knee Ngātokowaru leaned toward the face of Te Putu as if to salute him in the *hongi* on the nose. As his face approached Te Putu's, Ngātokowaru reached for his hidden *tete* (wooden dagger) and with a savage thrust he stabbed Te Putu in the throat.

As he drove his dagger home Ngātokowaru called out: "*Ko te tete a Ngātokowaru! Tēnā e rangona! Tēnā e rangona!*" (This is the dagger of Ngātokowaru! It will he heard of! It will be heard of!)

As the blood of Te Putu gushed from the wound Ngātokowaru smeared himself with it. By so doing the Ngāti Raukawa captive chief, who was promptly killed on the spot, escaped the cooking ovens of the incensed Waikato for he had made himself *tapu* with the blood of their *ariki*. An interminable vendetta threatened to go on as the result of this killing. It was ended by the birth of Tuata, the grandfather of Pōtatau, in whose person the blood of Te Putu and Ngātokowaru was united.

Here is the *whakapapa*:

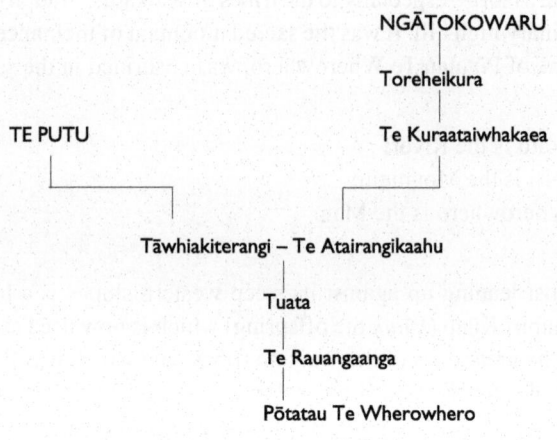

III

In ancient times the lakes, leisurely streams and the Waikato river never failed as sources of food and fish for the numerous tribes in the area, and the fertile lands yielded bountiful harvests of *kūmara*, *taro* and *hue*. Even today the old sites where *kūmara* and *taro* were grown can still be found, usually on the western banks of the river. But today the *hue* has given way to the pumpkin, marrow, onion and other introduced vegetables of the European. John Featon (1923: 14) records:

> The quantities of maize, potatoes, flax, and pigs that the Waikato [he is writing of the period 1850-1860] natives used to ship away and pour annually into the Auckland market would scarcely be credited. For transit to Auckland the route was down the Waikato River then up the Awaroa tidal creek not far from the Waikato Heads to Purapura, the landing-place close to Waiuku [Manukau Harbour]. The freight was then carted across the portage some two miles, and shipped in cutters or small schooners to Onehunga. At Purapura there was a bacon-curing establishment that was able to forward bacon to Auckland by the ton, equal in quality to the "best" Canterbury bacon of the present day [1911].

Sometimes cargoes of maize, wheat, potatoes, and flax were shipped direct from the Waikato to Sydney or other ports in schooners that used to cross the bar for that purpose. [A number of these trading vessels were owned and manned by the men of the Tainui tribes.] Those were halcyon days for the Waikato. Of money they were never short. The Waikato Heads provided them with an abundance of fish, from the schnapper to the dainty "guard"(?), whilst in the fresh water, higher up the river, shoals of whitebait and the esculent eel were to be had for the trouble of getting. Their plantations were luxuriant with maize, wheat, potatoes, pumpkins and kumaras, and their gullies swarmed with the wild pig and not a few cattle. For clothing, if they did not care to purchase that of European make, the flax plant rustled in the swamps and on the side of every river bed.

Perhaps no savage tribes that ever existed in any part of the globe had such an abundance of the good things of this world.

IV

The Author has never travelled the full length of the river, but he knows several sections of it and has frequently visited those parts below the Huka falls and the Aratiatia rapids, where for some miles it flows in a contemplative mood before it gathers impetus and rushes on past Ōrākei-Kōrako, Atiamuri, Pohaturoa and Waotu, and onward above Horahora with renewed zest until it assumes a more sober demeanour as it flows majestically past Kirikiriroa (now Claudelands at Hamilton). In recent decades the works of modern engineers have tamed the river at Arapuni and Horahora. At Arapuni, however, that European work was not allowed to proceed without interruption. At one stage of operations the ingenuity of the *tohunga* (experts) was taxed to the utmost in their efforts to harness the energy of the waters of the river, and a great *tohunga* had to be brought from the other side of the world—a hydroelectric expert from Sweden—to discover ways and means of quietening the outraged spirit of the Waikato river. It was not until the conclave of European *tohunga* (Public Works engineers) approached the problem in a conciliatory manner, and with care laid out in reinforced concrete a covering over the tormented and damaged side of the river, that the angry spirit again settled down in quiet content.

V

The river reach that will remain permanently in memory as the most characteristic part of the Waikato, is that magnificent sweep of fertile land lying to the west and south of Maungatautari mountain on the east, the Waipā and the Hākarimata range on the west, and the Pūniu and Mangapiko streams on the south. With Ngāruawāhia as the *tūrangawaewae* (footstool), where the waterways and ancient tribal highways converged, this landscape was the *manawatoka* or throbbing heart of the lands of the Tainui. The wide plains dotted with clear and sparkling lakes; the friable earth, the forest-clad ring of high hills teeming with wild bird life and the berry-fattened *kiore* (Māori forest rat); the wide skies which distilled in just the right amount the *ua mōnehunehu* (misty rain) and *kohu* (lowlying mists) in the springtime of the year—all these contrived to make this land a fitting place for priestly poets, chieftain warriors, husbandmen, artisans, hunters, forest snarers, fowlers of the fens, fishermen, canoemen, athletes, and lovers.

It is the landscape that Pōtatau looked upon as nobler than anything the rest of Aotearoa had to offer. The next time the reader passes through Ngāruawāhia let him pause on the bridge just below Tūrangawaewae Pā and contemplate at his leisure this noble landscape. If his soul is cleansed of all petty thoughts, the communion of sight, mind and nature will be enriched and the spirit will be enchained within this landscape framed and held by the distant mountain rims and the towering Hākarimata range above the flowing waters of the Waipā and the Waikato.

VI

The golden age among the tribes of this favoured land was between the years 1845 and 1860. It was a time of peaceful progress and industry, as is written in *The Old Frontier* by the late James Cowan (1922:14), and one could not do better than quote pen-pictures from this record of that eminent writer and historian of the Māori race.

Quoting from an unpublished manuscript of Rev. John Morgan, an Anglican missionary, Mr. Cowan records:

Wheat was introduced among the natives chiefly by the missionaries.... It was small in quantity for it was contained in a stocking, but it was sown and re-sown, and at present the increase from the little seed contained in a stocking is being sent by the natives to the Auckland market. Much is also ground by the Maoris in steel mills for their own use....

As a large quantity of wheat was now grown at Rangiaohia, and the natives had not purchased steel mills, I recommended them to erect a water-mill. At the request of Kimi Hori, I went to the millwright who was then building a mill at Aotea. In March 1846 a mill was built at a cost of £200, not including the carriage of timber, building of the mill dam, and the formation of the watercourse, all which were performed by the natives themselves.... Wheat is very extensively grown in the Waikato district. At Rangiaohia the wheat fields cover about 450 acres of land. I have also introduced barley and oats at that place. Many of the people at various villages are now forming orchards, and they possess many hundreds of trees budded or grafted by themselves, consisting of peach, apple, pear, plum, quince, and almond; also gooseberry bushes in abundance. For flowers or ornamental trees they have no taste; as they do not bear fruit, it is, in their opinion, loss of time to cultivate them.

The missionary, concluding his interesting narrative, described a visit paid to the district by the Governor, Sir George Grey:

His Excellency spent half a day at Rangiaohia, and expressed himself much pleased with the progress of the natives at that place. He visited the mill, which was working at the time. Two bags of flour were presented to him for Her Majesty the Queen, and they have since been forwarded to London. The Governor has since that time presented the Rangiaohia natives with a pair of fine horses, a dray and harness, and a plough and harness. He also requested me to engage a farm servant to instruct the natives in the use of the plough, etc. The value of the flour sent down this year from Rangiaohia and now ready for the Auckland market may be estimated at about £330. Of this sum upward of £240, was, or will be, spent in the purchase of horses, drays, and ploughs. Each little tribe is now endeavouring to procure a plough and a pair of horses, and the people expect during the next year to have at least ten ploughs at work. The rapid advancement in cultivation is the fruit of Sir George Grey's kind present to introduce the plough at those places. One of the chiefs at Rangiaohia has erected a small boarded house. He has also several cows, one of which he generally milks in the morning (*ibid*:16).

Mr. Cowan also quotes the narrative of a young man, Heywood Crispe, later a well-known Mauku settler and volunteer rifleman, who was one of a party of travellers from Auckland and Onehunga to Rangiaohia in February 1852. The Māori farm settlements were then at the zenith of prosperity, when produce prices were high. Mr. Crispe, in his narrative, said:

I can well remember the first sight we got in the distance of the steeple of the church at the Rev. Mr. Morgan's mission station at Te Awamutu, for some of the party were getting a bit tired when it came in sight, and it seemed to put new life into them. The natives at Rangiaohia had made preparations for a goodly party, as they had two days' racing in hand. They allotted us a large, newly erected whare, the floor being covered with native mats, and it was on them that we indulged in sweet sleep. There was a long grove of large peach trees and very fine fruit on them.... A large portion of the ground round the hill was carrying a very good crop of wheat.... It was of a very good quality, and some of the Waikato mills had a name for the flour they produced....

We spent several days in our camp on the Rangiaohia Hill, taking walks and viewing the country. We attended the races, which afforded some good sport, all being managed by the natives, assisted by some pakeha-Maoris of the neighbourhood. They were white men living a Maori life. Some of them had been well brought-up young men, rather wild perhaps, who had drifted away from home and taken up an idle life among the natives, getting regular remittances from their people at Home.

The Maoris provided all their pakeha friends with a most excellent meal on the ground, and peaches galore, as well as horses to ride. We rode some distance round to view the country, the Maori flour mills and cultivations. There were a lot of good cattle and horses about, and the crops of wheat and patches of potatoes were particularly good, although no bone-dust was used in those days. The Roman Catholics had a very nice place of worship at Rangiaohia, where regular worship was conducted. There were mission stations all up the Waikato and Waipa rivers in those days, and as far as Te Awamutu (*ibid*:18).

Mr Cowan goes on to relate:

Everywhere the Maoris of those days showed the travellers on their six weeks' trip the greatest hospitality. On the canoe voyage the pakehas called in here and there at native settlements and got a supply, of pork, potatoes, and peaches.

When the aged Potatau te Wherowhero was made King (1858) there were great gatherings at Ngaruawahia and Rangiaohia. At the latter place the Europeans in the district—the mission people, the traders, and artisans—were invited to the festivities. The abundance of food at Rangiaohia was probably the reason why the large village of Ngati Apakura was selected as one of the principal gathering places of the Waikato in 1858-60. Rangiaohia in those days was a beautiful place, with its comfortable thatched houses, shaded by groves of peach and apple trees, dotted along the crown of a gently-sloping hill, among the fields of wheat, maize, potatoes, and kumara, and its flour-mills in the valley.... (*ibid*: 18)

Mr. Cowan also mentions an old pioneer-colonist, Mrs. B. A. Crispe, the widow of Mr. Heywood Crispe. When she was a girl she attended Mr. Morgan's mission school at Rangiaohia in 1858. She described the aged and venerable Pōtatau as "a feeble old man, with his face completely tattooed; he wore a long black coat and dark cloth cap with a gold band round it" (*ibid*: 20).

Dr. Ferdinand Von Hochstetter, the famous Austrian geologist, on his expedition through the interior of the North Island in 1859, admired the settled aspect of Te Awamutu and the neighbouring country. He made an ascent of Mt. Kakepuku, setting out from Rev. Alexander Reid's Wesleyan mission station at Te Kōpua, and from the summit viewed the valley of the Waipā:

> The beautiful, richly-cultivated country about Rangiaohia and Otawhao [now Te Awamutu] lay spread out before us like a map. I counted ten small lakes and ponds about the plains. The church steeples of three places were seen rising from among orchards and fields. Verily, I could hardly realise that I was in the interior of New Zealand. (Von Hochstetter 1867: 318).

VII

This, then, was the land that nurtured Pōtatau Te Wherowhero; this was the river that revived his body and soul in the fretful days of lusty manhood; this was the life he was leading among his people when, in the Indian summer of his eventful life, he was called upon to assume the kingship of the Māori people; and these were the people who shared his joys and sorrows. This was Waikato of which he was *Ariki* Supreme.

RELIGION

Ko te pū, ko te kāuru:
Kei te hiahia, *kei te* koronga;
Ko Rongo-mā-Tāne!
Tūramarama a Nuku;
Tūramarama a Rangi:
Te Rangi e tū nei!
Te Papa a takoto!
Ngā tauira o ngā Wānanga!
Whakamau! Whakamau
Ki te ingoa o Io—
O Io i te Wānanga!

This is the *origin*, this is the *core*:
Let there be *desire*, (and) let there be *longing* (for knowledge)
It abideth with Rongo, The God of Peace, and with Tāne,
The God of Forests and Man!
(Though there be) but a vague light o'er the Land;
And but a faint light in the Heavens:
O thou Sky that stands Above;
O thou Earth that lies Beneath;
And all ye seekers of the Sacred Knowledge
Give heed! Give all heed
Unto the name of Io!—
Unto Io of all Knowledge!

From the Ritual of the Tainui House of Sacred Learning

CHAPTER 2

RELIGION

I

As high priest of the *whare wānanga*, Pōtatau could look back into the remote past—to the "Beginning of All" with Io, the Supreme Being. He could also contemplate with philosophic calm, in the light of the esoteric teachings of the priesthood, *Te Ao i tua o Rangi*, the World Hereafter.

In the closing years of his life King Pōtatau Te Wherowhero must often have meditated on the uncertainty of man's life. From many early dangers he had emerged safely and reached a period when he was able to enjoy a well-earned and tranquil life. Then came uncertain praise on his acceptance of the Māori Kingship. In so doing he had exposed himself to the jibes of impious men. Any justice or merit in his actions, or deeds carried out in his name, were misconstrued. But all in all, it is thought that Pōtatau had found life, an exhilarating adventure.

To compose and give peace to his fiery warrior mind he must often have recalled lines from the *Tohi whakauenuku*, the raising-up ritual of the high priesthood:

Whakarewaia rā
Ki runga te pakihiwi:
He hikitanga;
He hāpainga;
He ārewa;
He amonga!
   He Tauira!

Raise up aloft, up on to thine shoulders:
'Tis the lifting, 'tis the raising aloft; 'tis the carrying; 'tis the
bearing away! Thou art now a Tauira! [1]

Nature had taken its toll, and the reign of the first Māori King was destined to be a short one. It not only was brief, but also unhappy, and great disappointment and sorrow was to be the King's lot. And his people for many decades were to suffer untold misery.

The European had come to stay. Cooped up on Tāmaki isthmus, where the infant city of Auckland had sprung up, the white man, because of lack of employment and living room, was becoming discontented. The sight of Māori traders coming into town laden with the produce of their fertile lands, and the accounts of the flourishing farmlands of the Waikato tribal tillers of the soil, added to the sense of frustration and kindled feelings of envy. The European was now constantly looking with longing eyes over the rim of the hills above the Mangatāwhiri stream and over the flat lands along the banks of the Waikato; lands which stretched to the south until they merged in the forest lands of the Maniapoto tribe at the headwaters of Waipā river. Presently, in his land hunger, he was to cast about for "incidents" that would give him justification for invading the ancestral lands of Pōtatau and his people. Unfortunately for the Waikato these "incidents" were to be provided by adventurous bands of Maniapoto warriors within three years of the death of King Pōtatau.

Contemplating the present scene, Pōtatau marked that the stars in their courses indicated that dire events were to come upon the peoples of the land—upon Waikato. In the gathering gloom some other lines of the sacred raising-up ritual would be called to the priestly mind of Pōtatau:

Heketanga ngā mahi;
Ka heke ki te pūkenga a Rua'... [2]
Whakarongo, e Tama!
Ki te waha e tararau mai nei;
Nā runga ana mai, ē,
O te hiwi nui, ē,
O te hiwi roa, ē,
Tauārai mai nei;
He kape, pea, e Tamu!
I ā tāua nei kōrero...

The task will become burdensome;
Lo! the spirit descends unto the abode of Rua'...
Listen, o Son!
To the confused voices wafted hither
O'er the towering hill;
O'er the outflung hill;
Mayhap, O Son!
They seek to push aside our pledged, word...

Weighed down with new problems and with years—years that seemed "bewildering and so strange"—King Pōtatau Te Wherowhero had much need of spiritual solace. And this he found in the Io religion of his race.

II

The Māori priesthood of the house of sacred learning, like all mankind through the ages, was vitally interested in the questions: Who was and where was the dwelling-place of Io, the Supreme Being? How was the World created? How and when did Man, and all he means, come into being?

In the Io religion of the Tainui priesthood there was taught an esoteric version of the Creation, and in its teachings and ritual answers were given to these questions. And in the giving of the answers a high standard of philosophy is disclosed, which has eluded all European investigators of Māori lore for nigh on one hundred years.

In lifting the veil somewhat on this esoteric lore of his people the Author has been actuated by the idea that it would be befitting to *uhi* or clothe his account of the life of the high priest Pōtatau Te Wherowhero with the *tapu* raiment of the Polynesian religion of Io.

Tainui genealogical recitals have previously been published, but without explanatory notes and translations of the personifications, the publication of these recitals has only led to all manner of speculation as to the philosophy behind it all. The translations alone—which do not always conform to the dictionary meaning of the words—will be found to reveal a treasure trove of philosophic thought of a high order. Even in the original Māori text the meanings will more often than not defy the best of Māori scholars. It is, therefore, no small undertaking to track down the meanings of the archaic phraseology of the Māori priesthood, and in the present instance the quest extended over several years.

III

At the outset the declaration is made in the Io religion that the world evolved from Io, the Supreme Being; and his dwelling-place is at the apex and centre of Creation. And that Io himself evolved through eight stages from Te Kore or the Formless Void. In this deistic conception two elements were introduced and merged in Io, namely:

Te Ira tāne, or the male essence, which was personified in the celestial being named Hani, or the Questing One. Te Ira wahine, or the female essence, which was personified under the name of Puna, the Spring-well.

In the priestly ritual a highly descriptive account is given of the travels of Hani and Puna, along their separated pathways through Ngā Rangi tūhāhā, or the Be-spaced Heavens, in their ceaseless "search for a place where they could embrace each other." Although their pathways merged at the Ahurewa, the Sacred Mound or Altar of Io at the centre of Creation, they were here kept apart by Te Tumu, or the Concentric Pillar of Creation (literally, the Stump).

In their travelling to and fro—which actually commenced before Io was completely evolved—Hani and Puna were repeatedly frustrated in their search for a place where they could come together. It was not until the appearance of Ranginui e tū iho nei (the great Sky that stands above) and Papa tū ā nuku (the Earth that lies beneath) that Hani and Puna found the one place "in the whole of Creation where they could come together."

Hani and Puna came together on the bosom of Papa and propagated:

Firstly, things that live in the sea, including fish.
Secondly, things that live in fresh water, including fish.
Thirdly, things that live on the land.

The priesthood is careful to explain that these "things"; and the fishes were

> so implanted on the earth as food to sustain the *mauriora* or the life principle, by which the male and female of all species are nurtured, obtain life-giving blood, and so flourish and take form. By the *mauriora* the female gives birth, suckles her young and gives them sustenance. Indeed, all living things were thus nurtured on earth and had their being, and the means of sustenance for man—both men and women—who came into the world later, was thus provided. It was on account of all things related in this priestly recital that Hani and Puna were given these names:

Hani a te waewae i kimi atu,
Hani the Traveller and Questing One.

Puna he rau,
The Overflowing Spring-well.

IV

It is told that Hani and Puna were also responsible for the creation of Tikiāhua (the purposeful one who was created), and Tikiapoa (the purposeful one who was gathered together and moulded), by the banks of Hikarahi, or the Capacious Opening—"the river that divides the space between the earth and the sky"—and on the mountain which went by two names, Maunganui (the mountain of renown) and Maungaroa (the long mountain). Tikiāhua and Tikiapoa were fashioned from *uku pākeho*, or clay of limestone formation, which was called *reinga herea*, or that which has been impregnated with sacredness intensified. These beings were the first to be made in the likeness of Man. When Tikiāhua was completed, a heart was given unto it, and the heart was called Rangahau (the questing breath of life). When the heart was implanted, it was purified by Io with these words:

This is Rangahau,
The Questing Breath of Life;
It is Manawatina,
The Beating Heart;
It is Manawatoka,
The Throbbing Heart.

According to the teachings of the Tainui house of sacred learning it is the blood of Tikiāhua and Tikiapoa which inspires the soul of man, and urges him on to aspire and acquire the knowledge of the gods. The progeny of Tikiāhua and Tikiapoa, in the main, have remained unsullied by the sins of mortal man, and their dwelling-place is in the Be-spaced Heavens—although from time to time some have mated with the progeny of Rangi and Papa. We will have occasion to return to Tikiāhua and Tikiapoa later. In the meantime we proceed to recount the story of Rangi and Papa.

V

Rangi and Papa did not immediately come together after they were "begotten" by Te Aokimauī (the world turning left) and Te Pōkimauī (the night turning left), after they had striven mightily during the Epochal Period known as Ka Mārama te Ao (the world is aglow). But it was Hani and Puna who disturbed "the heavenly slumbers" of Rangi and Papa. (At this time Rangi and Papa were bi-sexual or a-sexual.) And we are told that when Rangi was rudely awakened by Hani he gave birth to a number of children:

1.	Tiororangi	The Piercing Cry of the Heavens
2.	Pipiri	The Coming Together
3.	Oho	The Awakening
4.	Ohonui	The Great Awakening
5.	Ohoroa	The Long Awakening
6.	Ohomauri	The Awakened Soul
7.	Ohomuturangi	The Awakening and End of Celestial Sleep
8.	Tārai	The Shaping
9	Pipī	The Oozing Forth
10.	Te Wariwariotū	The Banked-up Watery Mass
11	Tūterangiāmoa	The Bearing aloft in the Heavens
12.	Rī	The Screen
13.	Rā	The Sun
14.	Ruataraonga	The Sensitive Serrated Opening
15.	Tūkohuhui	The Great Banked-up Mist
16.	Rurutangiao	The Shuddering Sound of Space
17.	Tānepukurua	The Male with the Dual Stomach

The reason for the naming of the last-born offspring of Rangi was on account of the unusual circumstances, for he (Rangi) was a male and yet had given birth to children. In giving birth to the last-named, the second stomach of Rangi came forth. The birth of Tānepukurua was premature.

When Tānepukurua was born, the placenta and the afterbirth fell down on to Papa. This gave her such a start that she, too, awakened from sleep. In her sudden awakening, she also gave birth to several offspring:

1.	Keanuku	The Abrupt Sound from the Earth
2.	Kearangi	The Abrupt Sound from the Sky
3.	Whiriaiterangi	The Interlacing of the Heavens
4.	Rīwhenua	The Screen of the Earth
5.	Tukiakina	The Striving against the Obstruction
6.	Te Whauwhaunganui	The Great and Voracious Gulping
7.	Te Whiritaura	The Interlaced Strands
8.	Te Moanarire	The Deeps of the Ocean
9.	Tawatūtahi	The Solitary Tawa Tree
10.	Tāwauwau	The Prolonged Discontent
11.	Te Moreotewhenua	The Dreary Expanse of Land
12.	Motuwhāriki	The Mat of Severed Strands
13	Uoko	The Firm Receptacle
14.	Ueko	The Quivering Cultivating Implement

It was when the Earth Mother gave birth to these children and, as she turned in her labour, that the mountains were made, the waters were divided, and the declivities in the ocean were formed. When the Earth Mother grasped at the mountain peaks to support herself in her labour she took hold of the vegetation. When she released her hold on it some of the vegetation had been pulled upward, and these became the *tawa* tree (*Beilschmiedia tawa*) which still grows on the lonely ridges. The places where she had uprooted all the vegetation still remain bare. It was the straining on the mountain peaks by the Earth Mother that formed the cliffs and the steep mountain slopes of the earth. She had most severe labour pains when these things took place. These pains started when the Solitary Tawa Tree was about to be born. The births of her first two children were easy, as the Abrupt Sound from the Earth and the Abrupt Sound from the Sky came forth of their own accord.

After these children of the Earth Mother were born, the Sky Father gave birth prematurely to two more children. These two children fell down and alighted on the earth. Their names were Rimurehia (the enchanted seaweed) and Te Awekōpara (the soft downy plumage). It was Rimurehia who begat the vegetation of the sea and fresh-water lakes; and Te Awekōpara begat the plumage of all the birds.

When these two premature children of the Sky Father fell down to earth the noise of their fall reverberated to the heavens, and the earth quaked. The noise awakened Aituā (misfortune or the evil one) from sleep, and he clasped the Pou kōhatu (the limestone rock column) which was still suspended in Space. And there, he stood to obstruct the way of the Sky Father to the Earth Mother. Aituā had a fearsome aspect as he stood there to bar the way! It was then he was called Tūtangatakino (the man of fearsome aspect).

Io, the Supreme Being then spake, and said:

Lo! This is the Great Submergence;
'Tis the submergence of the Heavens!
Be propped up!

Lo and behold! The limestone rock column sways! Io stands aside; Aituā moves away; and Hani and Puna stand by. It was then that Rangi rushed downward to earth and embraced the Earth Mother. Thus they were joined. They slept together and became man and wife.

VI

Children were born to the Sky Father and the Earth Mother, and their names were:

Rongo, to whom was given the power over cultivated food plants of the earth. In his godhood he became the deity of Sound, and the god of Peace, Te Atua o te Maunga a Rongo.

Tānemahuta, to whom was given dominion over the birds and the trees of the forests; hence "the great forests of Tāne," Te Wao nui a Tāne. Tāne also has power over Man.

Haumiatikitiki, to whom was given power over all uncultivated food plants of the earth, such as fern root, and other food plants. He is still god over these.

Tāwhirimātea, to whom was given power over winds, storms and rain. In his godhood he holds sway over these elements.

Tangaroa, to whom was given the power over the fish in the ocean and fresh waters, and also all reptiles on land. He still retains the godhood over these.

Ruaimoko, to whom was given power over earthquakes, volcanoes and all thermal activities on land. He is the god of these things.

Tūmatauenga, to whom was given power over warfare and over mankind. His other names are:

Tūmatawhāiti	Tū' of the Restricted Vision
Tūkariri	Tū' the Quarrelsome One
Tūkanguha	Tū' the Active One
Tūkaitaua	Tū' the Consumer of War Parties
Tūmatateueue	Tū' the Grim-visaged One

Kahukura, who is also called Uenuku, the rainbow, which is visible to human eyes. In his godhood he discloses hidden things to Man. He is also protector of mankind. His other name is Kahukura Uenuku.

There were other children of Rangi and Papa, but these mentioned are the more important ones.

The priesthood closes this recital with the following lines:

As to all the Progeny
Of Rangi and Papa,
We will leave it to them
To enumerate their own family:
For they alone know them all.
I dare not attempt to tell...
They are too numerous;
Indeed, they are countless!

VII

The story of the lifting up by Tānemahuta, son of the Sky Father, to relieve the distressing conditions under which their progeny existed has often been told, and we will now proceed to the account of the fashioning of Hineahuone (the earth-formed maid).

After the Sky Father and the Earth Mother were parted Tāne' and his brothers began to fashion a Woman from a bundle of sea-grass shrub and earth at a place called Kurawaka (the crimson bowl). The name of the bundle of shrub was Rimurehia, who was one of the offspring of the Sky Father, before he embraced the Earth Mother. Tānemahuta possessed Hineahuone, which was the name of the Woman they had fashioned at

Kurawaka. Tānemahuta and Hineahuone begat two children, namely Tongameha (the secretive abashed one) and Rī (the screening one). Before Tānemahuta possessed Hineahuone, and during the time the Sky Father and the Earth Mother were in close embrace, Tānemahuta had mated with Kahukura and a daughter was born to the latter named Hineari (the fair maiden). (A bi-sexual conception is here, again introduced.)

Now when Hineari had grown up Tānemahuta took her to wife, and this so upset Hineahuone that she left him and became the wife of Tūmatauenga, Tānemahuta's brother. A child was born to Tūmatauenga and Hineahuone which was named Aituā, so called because of the unhappy married life of his parents. Tūmatauenga and Hineahuone finally parted, and she descended to the Under World, and henceforth she was called Hinenuitepō, "the Great Lady of the Night." She was accompanied on her journey thither by Hineari, who discovered that Tāne, her husband, was also her father. In the *whakapapa* of the Tainui and Te Arawa tribes, the descent of man from the Sky Father and the Earth Mother, through Tūmatauenga, is traced from Aituā.

VIII

The Tainui priesthood also have a long account of the Ascent of Tāwhaki (not Tānemahuta, as in the East Coast version) to Tiritiri o matangi, "the Sanctified Heaven of Fragrant Breezes, where he was given the Baskets of Knowledge which had been brought from Tikitiki o rangi, the Uppermost Heaven."

Tāwhaki having returned to the earth with the Three Baskets of Knowledge, there was much jealousy among Mankind.* Warfare arose. The Tāwhaki we speak of is the first Tāwhaki, the son of Rā (the Sun) who was one of the offspring of the Sky Father.

Through the ages the peoples of the world have shown resentment. toward any man becoming possessed of the treasures of the Baskets of Knowledge. They are governed by their feelings of envy, and will select those of shallow minds like themselves, or those who will give the *mānga* (chewed-over food). The people who continue for long in these ways will become possessed of languid souls. That is why the Sacred Assembly, Te Wānanga, has so arranged to make it difficult to enter into the Sacred House of Learning.

* As had been predicted by Rehua, one of the Superior Gods who dwells with Io in the Uppermost Heaven.—Author.

IX

In the foregoing account the story of "the World of Stars" has been passed over. The Tainui recital is quite a long one, and will have to wait for another time. For the present purpose the genealogy which is included in this chapter will have to suffice.

In the evolution of Man from the Sky Father and the Earth Mother, the generations down to Kaitangata, "the Consumer of Man" (in reference to carnal desires, not cannibalism) were—as indicated in the physiological names of the personifications in the genealogical table—of an animal nature. The first change from this pattern takes place with the union of Kaitangata and Whatitiri or Whaitiri (goddess of thunder); and by the time of their grandson Tāwhaki II there is a decided change, and he is called Tāwhaki (the husbandman). From this point we will again defer to the language of the Tainui priesthood:

> At that time the full enjoyment of the union of man and woman had been withheld from mortal man. It was not until Hāpai (the radiant and uplifting maid) came down (from the heavens) and was embraced by Tāwhaki, the son of Hema (the amorous one), that Man experienced the divine nature of his relationship with Woman. And, as to the generations of Woman, it was not until the time Pūhaorangi (he from the all-embracing heavens) came down (from the uppermost heaven) and embraced Māpunakiterangi (the pent-up love of heaven), that Woman realised there was goodness and a heavenly joy in her union with Man. It was because of her great happiness that she was given her second name of Te Kuraimonoa (the much-desired and glowing one).

X

In the teachings of the Tainui House of Sacred Learning it is given that:

> Kahukura Uenuku was set up as a symbol to (mortal) man of the godhood of Io. Io was so intensely sacred in himself that even the utterance of his name was avoided on all ordinary occasions. This is the reason why it was laid down that only to his symbol, Uenuku (the rainbow), were the common people to sing their sacred chants. It was the prerogative of the altar priests to recite the sacred chants to Io.

We will close this account by giving extracts from the ritual of the Uenuku cult:

Gather together the sacred powers
And abide in the faith of Uenuku:
Arm thyself with the Staff of the Gods!

Bind thy strength together;
Do not weaken,
Lest ye stand enfeebled
And be struck down!
Let the spirit of Tāwhaki the Great
Inspire and sustain thee:
Beware of Tē Mā, "The Unclean One".
He is always near!

Now here are the trangressions
Of Mortal Man:
The sin of *uru whakanunu*,
"The menacing and discontented murmuring:"
The sin of *kai a piko*,
"The Consuming of (human?) flesh;
" The sin of *hā piro*,
"The Offensive Breath."

There is also the sin of
Piko atu piko mai,
"Worship of this and that;"
For never ceasing is the embrace
Of man and woman;
And this oft becomes
A most grievous sin...

It is a sin to *pawhera*,
"Violate the chastity of women,"
It is a sin to *tiki kōpura*,
"Expose thyself in all thy nakedness."

Again it is a sin
When the sacredness of sacred things
Is treated as of little account,
And belief in the *tapu* (sanctity)
Is partaken of with the food we eat.

Give unto us abundantly,
Cause us to seek and search,
And to share the Treasured Knowledge!
Like the idle strands of the unfinished cloak
Of the woman weaver, now dead,
Gather up and make complete our shattered lives.
Yea, make it complete,
That it may give warmth
To the lowly and the great.

It is good to make it complete;
It is wrong to leave it unfinished,
And in the basket to lie unheeded:
It is wrong to carry Knowledge,
Like a useless burden round.
Cease such aimless labour!

Beware, and cherish the sacredness—
The sacredness of Sacred Places—
Lest the sacredness return
To its original abiding place.

Let *kakai* (unreasoning wrangles) cease;
Let *kōhuru* (outrageous and murderous deeds) cease;
Let *pūremu* (adulterous behaviour) cease;
Let *weriweri* (anger) cease;
Let *wene* (envious thoughts) cease.

Take hold of these teachings:
These are the *Pehipehi* (True Precepts)
These point to the *Ara* (The Way)
These are the teachings
Of the *Nihi* (The Contented Soul);
Of the *Matua* (The Parent)
These teachings are for
The *Aha aha* (all manner of men)
And thus I abide in the World
For ever and for ever!
Hou! (So might it be).

Because of the misbehaviour of the descendants of the Sky Father and the Earth Mother one part of the powers given to Tāwhaki was handed back to Uenuku (who was Tāwhaki's uncle) [and] to Io. Io, in turn, handed these powers over to the descendants of Tikiāhua and Tikiapoa. This was done to show mankind that it was possible to retain the essence, *mauri*, of the godhood of Io.

THE SACRED GENEALOGY OF IO
"DEISTIC"

TE AHO TUATAHI (THE FIRST STRAND)

1. TE KORE .... The Formless Void
2. KOTAHI TĒ KĪ .... The One Unspoken Thought
3. KOTAHI TE KŌRERO .... The One Spoken Word
4. KOTAHI TE WĀNANGA .... The One Sacred Assembly
5. TE KORE WHIWHIA .... The Intangible Formless Void
6. TE KORE MAKIKI HĪ RERE .... The Formless Void pierced by a Line extending into Space
7. MAKAKA .... The Sacred Curve
8. IO .... The Supreme Being

The Nights (Ngā Pō), or Epochal Periods, during which Io evolved through these eight stages were called: Te Pō ka ura (the night that glowed), Te Pō uriuri, (the dark green night), Te Pō kakara uri (the night that faintly gleamed), Te Pō aoao nui (the night with the aroma of sprouting things), Te Pō kerekere (the night of intense darkness), Te Pō tāmaku (the creation night).

Then, with the appearance of Io, came Te Āio nuku (the widespread calm). Io dwelt in harmony for countless ages during the Epochal Period called Te Āio nuku until the coming of the Night (Pō), or Epochal Period called Te Pō tiwhatiwha (the gleaming night) which heralded the appearance of Te Whetū (the world of stars).

THE SACRED GENEALOGY OF THE WORLD OF STARS
"COSMOLOGICAL"

TE AHO TUARUA (THE SECOND STRAND)

8/ IO

9/i TE WHETŪ ... The World of Stars

10/ii	TE RĀ .... The World of Suns	=	TAU ANA TE MARAMA .... Floating Moons
11/iii	AO NUI .... The Big Universe	=	TE PŌ NUI .... The Big Night
12/iv	AO ROA .... The Far-flung Universe	=	TE PŌ ROA .... The Far-flung Night
13/v	AO PAPĀ KINA .... The Bitterly Cold Universe	=	TE PŌ PAPĀ KINA .... The Bitterly Cold Night
14/vi	AO PAKŌ REA .... The Shattered and Expanding Universe	=	TE PŌ PAKŌ REA .... The Shattered and Expanding Night
15/vii	AO KI TUA .... The Separated Universe	=	TE PŌ KI TUA .... The Separated Night
16/viii	AO KI ROTO .... The Inward-striving Universe	=	TE PŌ KI ROTO .... The Inward-striving Night
17/ix	AO KI TAWHITI .... The Remote Universe	=	TE PŌ KI TAWHITI .... The Remote Night

THE SACRED GENEALOGY OF THE WORLD OF STARS – THE SECOND STRAND

18/x	AO RURU ……………………… The Brooding Universe	=	TE PŌ RURU ………………………… The Brooding Night
19/xi	AO ĀIO ………………………… The Becalmed Universe	=	TE PŌ ĀIO ………………………… The Becalmed Night
20/xii	AO WHERO …………………… The Reddened Universe	=	TE PŌ WHERO ……………………… The Reddened Night
21/xiii	AO MĀ ………………………… The Whitened Universe	=	TE PŌ MĀ …………………………… The Whitened Night
22/xiv	AO PANGO …………………… The Blackened Universe	=	TE PŌ PANGO ……………………… The Blackened Night
23/xv	AO WHAKARITO ……………… The Budding Universe	=	TE PŌ WHAKARITO ………………… The Budding Night
24/xvi	AO KUMEA …………………… The Perplexed Universe	=	TE PŌ KUMEA ……………………… The Perplexed Night
25/xvii	AO KI RUNGA ………………… The Ascending Universe	=	TE PŌ KI RUNGA …………………… The Ascending Night
26/xviii	AO KI RARO ………………… The Descending Universe	=	TE PŌ KI RARO …………………… The Descending Night
27/xix	AO KI KATAU ……………… The Universe turning Right	=	TE PŌ KI KATAU ………………… The Night turning Right
28/xx	AO KI MAUĪ ………………… The Universe turning Left	=	TE PŌ KI MAUĪ …………………… The Night turning Left
29/xxi	TE RANGI NUI E TŪ IHO NEI The Great Sky that stands Above	=	PAPA TŪ Ā NUKU ………… The Earth that lies Beneath

NOTES ON THE "COSMOLOGICAL" TABLE

Note 1

From Te Rā (The World of Suns), who mated with his sister Tau ana te marama (Floating Moons) each pair in the table mate likewise. The male line (or "sons" as the priestly recital has it) is on the left, and the table gives the first-born in each case.

Note 2

The Epochal Periods (Ngā Pō) during which the various worlds were born (the figures to the left indicate what world or universe was born during each epochal period, and correspond with those in the table):

i.	Te Pō tiwhatiwha	Gleaming Night
ii.	Te Āio rangi	The Celestial Calm
iii.	Te Āio papa	The Outspread Calm
iv.	Tumu kerekere	The Vibrant Pendulum [1]
v.	Te Papa kura	The Outspread Reddish glow
vi.	Te Papa mea	The Knocking sounds [2]
	Tū Te kuku rangi	The Indrawn Breath of Heaven
vii.	Tū kau whata rangi	The Elevated and Unheeding Firmament
viii.	Te Mahue	The Astronomical Fragments
ix.	Te Amo	The Supporting Pillar
x.	Te Tao	The Covered-in Heat
xi.	Te Tao werohia Apo	The Exploratory Piercing of the Covered-in Heat
xii.	Te Pōuriuri	The Dark-green Night
xiii.	Te Pō tangotango	The Night of Exceeding Darkness
xiv.	Te Pō tuki	The Night of Resounding Knocks
xv.	Te Pō whāwhā	The Groping Night
xvi.	Te Pō whakarongorongo Tapairu	The Night with the Tidings of the High-born
xvii.	Ka mārama ake te Ao	The World is dimly bathed in Light
xviii.	Hei runga nei tētehi Ao	There is a world Above
xix.	Hei raro nei tētehi Ao	There is a World here Below
xx.	Ka mārama te Ao	The World is Aglow

(1) Tumu kerekere: The conception here is that of a universe, shaped like a tree stump, suspended and swinging to and fro in space.

(2) Te Papa mea and Tū te kuku rangi: Te Ao papa kina (The Bitterly Cold Universe) and Te Pō papa kina (The Bitterly Cold Night) according to the priestly recital strove mightily during two Epochal Periods known as Te Papa mea (The Knocking Sounds) and Tū te kuku rangi (The Indrawn Breath of Heaven), and they begat Ao pakō rea (the Shattered and Expanding Universe)—a son—and Te Pakō rea (the Shattered and Expanding Night)—a daughter.

In all other cases one epochal period sufficed to bring forth each pair of cosmological brother and sister.

In every case, in this table, there is a begetting. Even "Io begat Te Whetū (The World of Stars)"; and Te Whetū "begat Te Rā (The World of Suns)"; although in these two stages there was no "striving mightily" before the begetting, as in all the succeeding stages.

THE GENEALOGY OF MAN
"EVOLUTIONARY"
TE AHO TUATORU (THE THIRD STRAND)

29	RANGI ... (The Sky Father)	—	PAPA ... (The Earth Mother)	
30/i	TŪMATAUENGA ... (The Grim-visaged Tū, god of War and Man.)	—	HINEAHUONE ... (The Earth-formed Maid)	
31/ii	AITUĀ ...		The Unfortunate One	
32/iii	AITU ERE ...		The Surprised Unfortunate One	
33/iv	AITU KIKINI ...		The Enfeebled Unfortunate One	
34/v	AITU TĀMAKI ...		The Deranged Unfortunate One	
35/vi	AITU WHAKATIKA ...		The Restored Unfortunate One	
36/vii	TE KORE ...		The Flaccid One	
37/viii	TE KORE NUI ...		The Deeply Flaccid One	
38/ix	TE KORE ROA ...		The Long-suffering Flaccid One	
39/x	TE KORE PARĀ ...		The Sapless Flaccid One	
40/xi	TE KORE TĒ WHIWHIA ...		The Destitute Flaccid One	
41/xii	TE KORE TE OTI ATU KI TE PŌ ...		The Flaccid One destined for the Realms of Night	
42/xiii	NGANA ...		The Striving One	

THE GENEALOGY OF MAN – THE THIRD STRAND

43/xiv	NGANA NUI	.......The Renowned Striving One.
44/xv	NGANA ROA	.......The Long-striving One.
45/xvi	NGANA RŪRŪ	.......The Impetuous Striving One.
46/xvii	NGANA MAOA	.......The Languid Striving One
47/xviii	HOTU WAI ARIKI	.......He with the Urge to Conquer.
48/xix	TĀPĀTAI	.......The Questioning One.
49/xx	TIKI	.......The Purposeful One.
50/xxi	TIKI TE POU MUA	.......The Purposeful One of the Front Pillar.
51/xxii	TIKI TE POU ROTO	.......The Purposeful One of the Inner Pillar.
52/xxiii	TIKI AHU MAI I HAWAIKI	.......The Purposeful One of the Origin.
53/xxiv	WHIROTETUPUA	.......The Evil-spirited One.
54/xxv	TOI	.......The Jaded and Tingling One.
55/xxvi	HĀTŌNGĀ	.......The Incoherent One.
56/xxvii	RĀKEIORA	.......The Adorned and Exuberant One.
57/xxviii	TAHATITI	.......The Unsettled One.
58/xxix	TAMAKITERANGI	.......The Son with the Heavenly Urge.
59/xxx	PIRO	.......The Conquered and Evil-smelling One.
60/xxxi	KAITANGATA	.......The Consumer of Man.

				WHAITIRI or WHATITIRI (The Goddess of Thunder)
61/xxxii	HEMA	The Amorous One	⎯⎯	URUTONGA (The Distractingly Voluptuous Maiden)
62/xxxiii	TĀWHAKI	The Husbandman	⎯⎯	HĀPAI (The Radiant and Uplifting Maiden)

255

THE GENEALOGY OF MAN
FROM TĀWHAKI TO THE TAINUI AND ARAWA ANCESTORS

"The Mythical to the Ancestral"
(i to x)   (From 73)

TE AHO TUAWHĀ (THE FOURTH STRAND)

62   TĀWHAKI (The Husbandman)   =   HĀPAI (The Radiant and Uplifting Maiden)

63/i   MATIRE HOAHOA .... The Enchanted Wand
64/ii   RUTU PAHŪ .... The Resounding Gong
65/iii TANGI PAHŪ .... The Wailing Gong
66/iv   NGAI .... The Panting Sob
67/v   NGAI NUI .... The Loud Panting Sob
68/vi   NGAI ROTO .... The Suppressed Panting Sob
69/vii NGAI PEHA .... The Proverbial Panting Sob
70/viii HAURAKI KI TE RANGI ..... The Dry Heavenly Breeze of Summer
71/ix   MĀPUNA KI TE RANGI ..... The Pent-up Love of Heaven
        (First name)
        TE KURAIMONOA .... The Much-desired and Glowing One
        (Second name)   = PŪ HAO RANGI .... The Celestial Being of the All-embracing Heavens

72/x   OHOMAIRANGI .... The One Awakened from a Heavenly Couch

73/xi   Ruamuturangi   =   Hapaikura

74/xii Tarao   Taunga = Rangitapu

75/xiii Tarawhaene   Tuamatua = Waiheketua

76/xiv Kokuotepo   Rakauri I   Houmaitawhiti   Rangitu

77/xv   HOTUROA   NGĀTOROIRANGI   TAMATEKAPUA

        High Priest and   High Priest and   Commander of
        Commander of   Navigator of Te   Te Arawa Canoe.
        Tainui Canoe.   Arawa Canoe.

The Tainui and Arawa canoes left Hawaiki circa 1350 for Aotearoa.

THE GENEALOGY OF A KING

"High Priests, Navigators, and Chieftains Bold And Brave Mothers of Men"

	HOTUROA	NGĀTOROIRANGI	TAMATEKAPUA
77	HOTUROA	Tangihia	Kahumatamomoe
78	Hotuope	Tangimoana	Tawakemoetahanga
79	Hotumatapu	Kahukura	Uenukumairarotonga
80	Mōtai	Rangitakumu	Rangitihi
81	Ue	Mawakenui	Kawatapuarangi
82	Raka	Mawakeroa	Pikiao
83	Kakati	Mawaketaupō	Hekemaru
84	Tāwhao	Tūwharetoa	Mahuta
85	Turongo	Rākeipoho	Uerata
86	Raukawa	Ruawehea	Tapaue
87	Rereahu	Parepounamu	Te Putu
88	Maniapoto	Tahinga	Tāwhiakiterangi
89	Te Kawairirangi I		

THE GENEALOGY OF A KING

#	(TAINUI)	(ARAWA priestly)	(ARAWA male)
90	Rungaterangi	Tūwhakahautaua	
91	Uruhina	Karewa	
92	Te Kawairirangi II	Te Tikiorereata	
93	Te Kanawa	Te Ketekura	
94	Parengāope I	Kōtare	
95	Rangimahora	Kauwhata	
96	Te Kahurangi – Tuata	Wehiwehi	
97	Te Rauangaanga – Parengāope II	Maniaihu	
98	PŌTATAU TE WHEROWHERO	Pareraumoa	Tuata
99		Te Ataiwhanake	Te Rauangaanga
100		Pakaruwakanui	PŌTATAU TE WHEROWHERO
101		Tokohihi	
102		Parengāope II	
		PŌTATAU TE WHEROWHERO	

A Senior and Priestly Line of Descent and Chieftain-Warrior Line. (TAINUI)

Priestly and Senior Arawa Line of Descent and Chieftain-Warrior Line. (ARAWA)

The Male Line and and Chieftain-Warrior Line of Descent. (ARAWA)

NGĀ KARAKIA WHAKAMUTUNGA
(He mea whakapoto mai.)

Ka tū he Manawa a-Rangi!
Ka tū he Manawa Whenua!
Hei ākinga kumu
Mō Hinetapu i te Papa;
Awhitia paitia ia;
Awhitia, puritia!
Kia ū; kia ū!
Hou!

He Taura kei te Ao nei
Hei aha koia?
Hei hutihuti ake,
Hei whakahoro iho;
Hei ninihi,
Hei āhurutanga nui!

He poke Hauhunga ka tangi ki te Whenua!
He Ia ka tere
He Oko ka eke kei runga:
Inumia paitia;
Kua poua atu hoki,
Tēnā rā kei ngā Awa nunui,
Kei ngā Awa ririki e tere ana!
Ka mau te kū,
Ka puta te Wai-ora ki te Ao!
Hōmai mā tēnei, mā tēnei!
Hou!

Ko Hani... ko Puna...
He putanga Wai Moana,
He Wai Nui!
He huihuinga Wai-ora nō ngā Ao
Ki te Ao-whenua nei...
Pau katoa ki raro nei;
Te Toi-ora o
Te Marama,

O Te Whetū,
O Ngā Rangi-tū-hāhā!
　Hou!

　Nā Io i ruruku;
　　He Mauri ora:
　　He Mana tapu;
　　He Iri kura;
　　He Iri rangi;
　　He Eketanga a Rangi;
　　He Apu tahi a pawa;
　　He Rōpu hau;
　　He Maikuku Mākaka;
　　He Apu 'Nuku;
　　He Āwhiowhio:
　　　Te tuinga a Io
　　　Ko te Tangata!
　Ka tū tonu ko Io te Ariki;
　　Hou!

Ko Te Kete o te Wānanga ka hikitia,
Kia ū te pupuri kei maringi ki waho;
　He hē nui hoki ēnei
Ko te marea, he pōrewarewa rātou
　Kei ngā kūaha tūtata tonu ngā wairua;
E kore e mau i a rātou te toi-tupu o te wānanga:
He tuarua tēnei o āku whakatūpato;
He nui atu i tō mua ake nei!
Kia ū! Kia ū !
　Hou!

THE CLOSING ODE

(Abridged)

The Heart of the Heavens has appeared!
The Heart of the Earth has appeared!
   Here, indeed, is an abiding-place for Hinetapu, "The
        Sanctified Maiden;"
   Clasp her lovingly when she appears; embrace her firmly:
Be steadfast; be steadfast!
      Hou! (So might it be.)

Now, there is a Rope in this World:
What is it for?
   To haul up,
   To let down;
   'Tis for the Timid,
   'Tis for us all!

The Eddying-winds of Frosty Days
They croon o'er the Land;
And the Current of Life; it flows strongly,
   Bearing hither the Bowl...
   The Overflowing Bowl (of Life)
Drink ...drink copiously from it,
For it hath been bounteously poured out.
The Great Rivers and the Little Streams (of Life)
   They are brimful and will flow on
   Strongly... unceasingly... for ever!
The Desire to live is thus sustained;
And the Waters of the World of Life are given abundantly,
   To this one, and to that one:
      Hou!

The Offspring of Hani and Puna
   They crowd the Waters of the Sea;
   Like unto a Flood of Great Waters!
It was, indeed, a gathering together
Of the Currents of Life from All the Worlds
On to the Soil Stratum of the Earth:

All the Essence of Life was poured forth;
    That of all the Moons,
    That of all the Stars,
    And that of all the Be-spaced Heavens!
    Hou!

It was *Io* who encompassed it all!
    The *Mauri ora*, "Life's Essence";
    The *Mana tapu*, "Sacred Power";
    The *Iri kura*, "Earthly Thought";
    The *Iri rangi*, "Celestial Thought";
The *Eketanga a Rangi*, "The Striving for the Heavens";
The *Apū tahi a pawa*, "The Questing Soul";
The *Rōpu hau*, "The Will to dare the Tempest";
The *Maikuku Mākaka*, "The Ritualistic Urge";
The *Apū 'Nuku*, "The Urge to Conquer the Land";
The *Āwhiowhio*, "The Enduring of the Swirling Winds";
    All these *Io* did contrive.
    Kō te tangata, "For man"!
    But *Io* remains the *Ariki*, "The lord and master of All"!
    Hou!

The Basket of the *Wānanga* will soon be lifted;
Let the hold of the Priesthood be firm,
    Lest the Burden be spilled out;
    For that would indeed be a great wrong:
    As the multitude of the uninitiated
    Are profane and unmindful—
    Preoccupied as they are with lesser thoughts,
    They are unheeding
    And will not cherish our Treasured sacred Knowledge:
This is the second time I have enjoined ye all;
It is stronger than that uttered aforetime:
Wherefore, be steadfast; be steadfast!
    Hou!

NOTES ON CHAPTER 2

Note 1
Tauira: Literally a pattern; but in this instance an adept, or initiate, or one admitted into the *Wānanga*.

Note 2
Rua': Abbreviation for Ruaimoko, the god of earthquakes (see para. VI).

COMMENTARY ON THE RITUAL AND GENEALOGICAL TABLES.

The material from which the greater part of the ritual in this chapter has been drawn is among the writings of the Author's adopted father (also granduncle) Te Hurinui Te Wano, who died in 1911, and is interred in the Maniapoto tribal burial ground at Te Kūiti.

His writings and a series of drawings indicate that he had some knowledge of the nature of the designs on the sacred inscribed stone emblems of the Tainui House of Learning. The Author hopes to be able to complete a comprehensive translation of these writings and a reconstruction of the sacred designs, and to embody the result in a work on the Tainui Io religion and esoteric lore.

GENEALOGY

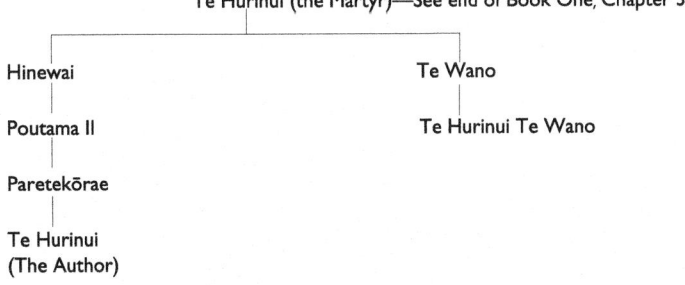

FATHER AND SON

Press'd with the load of life, the weary mind
Surveys the general toil of human kind.

CHAPTER 3

FATHER AND SON

"The Scribe" now concludes his narrative which was interrupted at the end of Chapter 7 of Book Two:

When the end was drawing near Pōtatau spoke to his son Matutaera and said: "O Son, my advice to you is: Hold fast to the *Nehenehenui*;[1] to the *Tāpōpokotea*:[2] and they will give you a safe place of refuge. As for me, *Ka pū te ruha; ka hao te Rangatahi* (the "old net" is worn and threadbare; a "new net" will now go a-fishing). In your days one bird will appear in the south, a *pītongatonga*.[3] Its home will be among the snows, its cry will be *titiro! titiro!* (look! look!). In my last rest take me to sleep with my people;[4] to my *rauru*;[5] to the *Tāpōpokotea*. There is little else for me now. Remember me always. It will give you courage. Be thou upright in all you do. Be strong, so that all portals may be opened unto you. Should war come upon this land, hold fast to the Nehenehui. Do not follow the carved ornamental canoe. Make fast your moorings lest they give way. Remain a fugleman on the humble *pukatea*[6] canoe. Be one with the *Tāpōpokotea* in the *Waonuiatāne*;[7] and lastly: Hold fast to the law; hold fast to love; hold fast to the faith. Nothing else matters much now—nothing else matters!"

Pōtatau welcomed the faith after the fighting against Ngāpuhi. He gave his people the choice of three religions—Wesleyan, Anglican, and Roman Catholic. Pōtatau never transgressed in all matters in which he was bound by man's oath. And he never sinned against God. He was a righteous king, and so he remained until he went to his fathers in his last long sleep.

NOTES ON CHAPTER 3

Note 1

Nehenehenui: A reference to the Maniapoto tribes.

Note 2

Tāpōpokotea: Literally, whitehead, a bird (*Certhiparus albicapillus*). Pōtatau uses this figure of speech in respect to the elders of the tribes, the grey-haired.

Note 3

pītongatonga: A small bird which builds its nest in the *toetoe* (rushes); also used as a term for a rain cloak woven with thick fibre. It is not very clear what was intended by Pōtatau in this saying. It has, however, in the intervening period, been used apocryphally to further their ends by various Māori prophets from among the Taranaki tribes including the late Wiremu Rātana, whose mother belonged to Taranaki. The references to "the south" and "home will be among the snows" have been interpreted by these prophets as pointing to the snowclad mountain of Taranaki (Mt. Egmont). There is in this connection a story (which is probably apocryphal too) about Wiremu Rātana camping on the slopes of Egmont, near the ancient altar at the foot of Dawson Falls, before he started on his faith-healing mission.

Note 4

The usual last wish of a Māori is to be buried with his parents in the ancestral burial cave or *urupā*.

Note 5

rauru: Literally, the end of the umbilical cord. This was usually buried in a sacred place near the ancestral home. In this instance Pōtatau expresses his wish that in death he be taken back to where his umbilical cord is buried—at the ancestral home at Taupiri.

Note 6

pukatea: A tree (*Laurelia novaezealandiae*).

Note 7

Waonuiatāne: The great forests of Tāne. Tāne is an abbreviation for Tānemahuta, the god of forests.

HAERE RĀ!

Farewell

CHAPTER 4

HAERE RĀ!

I

When Pōtatau Te Wherowhero departed this life on Sunday, June 25, 1860, he had been King of the Māori people for one year and 54 days. The news of his death ran like wildfire through the land, and the tribes gathered at Ngāruawāhia to pay their last tributes.

The tribesmen pressed around the couch on which the dead monarch lay, and the women of the tribes raised their anguished voices in lamentation. The rarest of mats were spread on the ground, and on them were laid tribal and family heirlooms and trophies of war—greenstone pendants, *mere*, whalebone weapons, elaborately carved *taiaha* and, of course, the *mere* called "Whakarewa." This *mere* was the sign of the worldly power of the House of Pōtatau, and is mentioned in Book One, Chapter 2.

As each company of tribal mourners arrived the Ngāti Mahuta tribe and the earlier arrivals would gather in a wide circle on the *marae* to receive the visitors with *maemae*, or special chants for the dead. The classical laments of the Māori race were sung over the illustrious dead. As the *tangi* (crying over the dead) died down the chieftains rose from their places, and in their turn, paced up and down and paid eloquent tribute in song and story:

> Stride forth boldly like a warrior of Tū';
> Let me gird on you this your waist mat:
> Whilst ye bedeck thyself with the waving albatross plume.
> Then suffer the women of the tribes
> To seek thy embrace as they did in days gone by.
> Alas! they now seek for thee in vain;
> For thou art gone from the warriors' ranks
> That now stand irresolute up there on Taupiri!
> Let your kinswomen lovingly caress you
> Those wavy locks, alas, will wave no more!
> And the sharpened blade of Whakarewa
> No more will flash afar!
> Proceed, O Sire, and pluck the sacred leaf
> On the altar at Te Papa-i-o-Rotu

O'er yonder below Karamu.
Go thence to meet thy renowned ancestors
Until ye stand there in the House of Tapaue.
They will spread for thee the famed red cloak,
And ye will abide there with the multitudes
In the far flung realms of Rehua.

In a voice charged with emotion the ageing warrior-chief Te Kanawa, who was Te Wherowhero's companion on many a hard-fought war trail, concluded an impassioned farewell oration with these words:

Sleep on, O Comrade, sleep on.
Sleep on the Couch from which there is no Rising;
And on the Pillow that will not fall....

You have gone by the Morning Tide,
I will follow on the Evening Tide....

On the day of the funeral, as the cortege moved off, a specially selected company of singers, wearing laurel wreaths in sign of deep mourning, followed slowly and to the accompaniment of waving branches they sang the Chant of Farewell:

Solo: *Kimihia, rangahaua;*
Kei whea koe, e Whero'
E ngaro nei?

Chorus: *Kei Taupiri!*
Kei Taupiri!
Kei te huinga o te Kahurangi,
Ka oti atu koe, e Koro, ē!

Solo: Seeking, searching...
Where art thou, O Whero'!
Who art hidden now?

Chorus: Up yonder on Taupiri!
Up yonder on Taupiri!
At the gathering of the departed Noble Ones,
Thou art indeed gone, O Sire, e!

This farewell chant was punctuated now and again by the deep-throated primitive *ngeri* (a vigorous chant) from the warriors of the tribes:

Solo: *Ripi, ripia!*

Chorus: *Hae haea!*

Solo: *Ripi, ripia!*

Chorus: *Hae haea!*
Tukitukia te upoko o Aituā!
O te Ngārara kai tangata!
Hue!

Solo: Slash and cut up, slash and cut up!

Chorus: Carve it up, carve it up!

Solo : Slash and cut up, slash and cut up!

Chorus: Carve it up, carve it up!
Crush in the head of the demon, Death!
The Dragon that consumes all mankind!
Hue!

II

What were the thoughts of that noble spirit as he stood on the brink of eternity? The answer to this question, as taught in the Tainui House of Sacred Learning, will be given presently in ritual and narrative form. As Pōtatau Te Wherowhero was a high priest of the *Wānanga*, the esoteric lore of the priesthood enabled him to see life steadily and see life whole. And judging from his poetical compositions, we think that he was endowed with some psychic force that had taught him a oneness with all nature. He had lived much in the wide open spaces; and in his vigorous manhood he had loved to feel the touch of the morning dew, and to smell the fragrance of his native soil. In his declining years he had chosen to enjoy the sunlight, and to follow the glow of the westering sun. The priestly philosopher Pōtatau did not fear death. The Priesthood will now tell us why:

KUA KAPEA ĒTEHI WĀHI KI WAHO

Te haerenga mai o te Tangata
I taiāwhio ka puta mai;
Te hokinga ki Te Tumu
E rima ōna Ara:

Te Ara ki Te Hono-i-wairua
Ka riro i Te Au-kumea
Awhitia i te Pou-toko-manawa,
Kei riro ana ia ki Wai-oti-atu!

Ka waiho ake nei te Ao-tū-roa; he ataata kau anō
Tū kau ana Te Wao-nui-a-Tāne':
He hikonga Uira ngā Tihi Maunga;
Papā te Whatitiri, te Tohu o te Mate!

Reia kua tū ki te Mata o te Whenua Hou
Ka mahue atu nei Te Hono-i-Wairua,
He Whenua nui, roa atu;
He Tangata kei reira, he Whenua pai;
He Tangata pai, he Nunui, he Roroa!

Ka takoto tahanga anō he Maonga Ua;
He Waipuke e mimiti ana;
Anō he Hukapapa e mimiti ana i te Rā...

Ka tū ka titiro, he Roto wai e takoto ana,
Ko ngā Manga e rere ana, he Rākau e tupu ana,
Ngā Tarutaru matomato;
He Whenua hoki tērā e hora noa ana te Kai.

Ka tū, hopukia i te uru nui o ngā Mātua
Unuhia i te takapū nui o ngā Whāea
Ko te Whāea ka awhi mai, awhi mai!
Kia ū, kia ū!

Ka whiti i te Awa
Ka haere i te One
Hōkai Papa! Pōkai Rangi! Pōkai Nuku!

Ka hurihia ki runga, kārewa, ka puta!
Ka tārewa, ka tūreia!

Tihe!
Mauri-ora!
Ki te Whei-ao!
Ki te Ao-mārama!

A SELECTION OF VERSES FROM THE TAINUI RITUAL

Man in his journey hither
Encircled Creation before his coming:
On his return to *Te Tumu*
"Creation's Concentric Pillar,"
He will travel by five ways.

Unresisting he will go
To *Te Hono-i-Wairua*;
"The Meeting-place of Spirits;"
Borne thither by *Te Au-kumea*,
"The Dragging Current."
There he will awake
And embrace the Centre Pillar;
Lest he be swept away
Into *Te Wai-oti-atu*,
"The Waters of Annihilation."

Mortal life is but a passing shadow;
[Only] The Great Forests of Tāne will endure:
The Lightning will flash across the Sky,
To strike upon the Mountain Peaks;
And the rolling Thunder will crash!
Omens these of Death!

He will proceed onward
From the Meeting-place of Spirits...
And he will behold the Face of a New World:
The Land stretches far and wide,
With People around about:
It is a most pleasant land,
The People are good; they are big and tall.

He will lay himself down to rest
In deep content.
Like the Calm after the Storm;
Like the Receding Waters of the Flood,
Or the Frost drawn off by the Sun.

He will arise...
Beside a placid Lake,
With limpid Streams flowing by;
Shady Trees, green and sedgy meadows all around.
A Land of Food and Plenty.

Our Forebears stand about...
And in deep content he will stand
And watch happy mothers weaving;
Weaving... and plaiting....
He will pick up a beautifully woven mat:
A mother—his Mother!
Will take him into her fond embrace.

He has crossed the Stream,
He has travelled along the Strand;
He has walked over the Land;
He has embraced the Heavens;
He has embraced the Soil
His spirit has soared aloft
And is one with all Eternity,
Bereft of all Earthly cares;
Emergent! Free!
    Tihe! (Sneeze lustily!)
    Mauri-ora! ('Tis the Essence of Life!)
    Ki te Whei-ao! (Into the Wide World!)
    Ki te Ao-mārama! (Into the World of Light!)

III

The description of the After World given in the abridged ritual relates to Rarohenga, the world below. The spirits after leaving this world, first of all proceed to Te Hono i Wairoa, the gathering-place of spirits, and foregather in the temple there called Hawaiki; the journey thither occupying five Pō (nights).

These nights, or epochs, are called Te Pōtēkitea (the hidden night), Te Pōtēwhaia (the pursuitless night), Te Pōtēwheau (the undeviating night), Te Pōtangotango (the night of utter darkness), Te Pōtēwhāwhā (the inert night).

The night on which the spirit leaves this world is called Te Pōkumea (the vertiginous night), and it is borne off on Te Auterenga (the steady current) which joins Te Aukumea (the dragging current) at the beginning of Te Pōtēkitea (the hidden night).

To reach Rarohenga from the meeting-place of spirits, the spirit leaves by the south door and enters the heaven known as Te Rēinga (the way of the multitude) and proceeds by way of Tāhekeroa (the long descent) to Rarohenga. Te Rēinga is the twelfth heaven, the earth being in the eleventh from the uppermost heaven.

From Rarohenga (the world below) the spirit may proceed directly to Tikitiki o rangi (the uppermost heaven) through Ngā Rangitūhāhā (the bespaced heavens) by Te Aratiatia (the stepped way); or it may be directed to Muriwaihou (the place of the purifying waters of the hereafter).

From Muriwaihou the spirit will take to the skyways, of which there are two: Te Angitamatāne (the skyway of the male) and Te Angitamawahine (the skyway of the female). On its way the spirit will pass Te Aratiatia and Te Toihuarewa (the suspended way), at different points on the journey. So on its journey, by way of the skyways, the spirit may be directed to either end of the stepped way or the suspended way—otherwise it will continue on its long and weary trail through the whole of Creation.

Even if the spirit is "swept into Te Waiotiatu" (the waters of annihilation)—these are the spirits of "those who have committed murder and other outrageous wrongs against mankind"—where they are tossed about for countless ages on the waters, they are rescued by Te Ihorangi (the umbilical cord of heaven) and his companion deity Māwakenui (the great and prolonged rainstorm). The spirit is then conducted to the presiding deity of Te Waiotiatu Mamaru (the overbearing and questing one). Under the abbreviated name Maru, Mamaru is also one of the "principal gods of the oceans throughout the creation. "In the temple of Te Waiotiatu, called Tangitewiwini (the place of dreadful and eerie lamentation), where Mamaru is the high priest, the rescued souls are purified, and then conducted back to the meeting-place of spirits, whence they proceed by the long descent. These spirits are not permitted to tarry in Rarohenga, but must proceed right on to Muriwaihou.

IV

After leaving Rarohenga or Muriwaihou the soul, after varying periods of celestial time—depending on the route taken—at last reaches the second highest of the be-spaced heavens called Tiritiri o matangi (the sanctified heaven of fragrant breezes). Those who in this world have lived a life spiritually in harmony with the behests of Io, will reach Tiritiri o matangi earlier than the others who have not been so mindful of the things of the *wairua* (the soul). Some souls will have gone directly from the meeting-place of spirits, through the east door and the right-hand north doorway, without descending by way of the long descent to Rarohenga.

In the sanctified heaven of fragrant breezes the attendant gods, the Apa puhirangi (the *apa* who are honoured in heaven), and the attendant goddesses the Apa kahurangi (the *apa* with heavenly raiment) will conduct the new arrival to Te Waiorongomai (the tranquil waters of the peace to come), for the purification rites. The spirit will then be conducted in turn to the three sacred temples of Tiritiri o matangi. These are Matanginui (the renowned temple of the fragrant breeze), Matanginaonao (the temple of the blossom-laden fragrant breeze), and Matangipuhi (the temple of the precious fragrant breeze). In these temples various ceremonies are conducted.

V

When the soul has been prepared in Tiritiri o matangi it is then ready to proceed on the last stage of its journey. In Tikitiki o rangi (the uppermost heaven), which is also called Te Toi o ngā rangi (the innermost of the heavens), the word of Io will go forth to Tinirangi (the caulk of heaven) the guardian of the sliding doorway called Te Pūmotomoto (the difficult and dividing way), who will admit the traveller into Tāwhirirangi (the guesthouse of the upper-most Heaven). Through the rear doorway, Ururangi (the entrance to the innermost heaven), of Tāwhirirangi, the spirit is conducted to Te Waiorongo (the tranquil and peaceful waters) where purification rites will be performed before admittance to the temple of Rangiātea (the splendour of the heavens). After the ceremonies there the soul will be taken to the sacred altar of Ahurewa (the sacred mound), where stands the pillar called Te Tumu (the concentric pillar of creation). The soul will then go on to the dwelling-place of the superior gods of Ruatau, Aitupawa, Rehua and Pūhaorangi. On the way to and from the sacred altar of Ahurewa, the soul will pass the courtyard Te

Rauroha (the limitless and widespread bounds of space) of the house of Io, called Matangireia (the much sought for fragrant breeze).

In the company of the superior gods mentioned, and in their dwelling called Whakamoeariki (the sleeping-place of high chiefs), the soul will sojourn as the guest of the gods, until the pleasure of Io is known and the summons comes to attend at the courtyard of Te Rauroha.

In this illustrious company there will be many great figures in the world's history. There will be many Polynesian heroes among the guests in Whakamoeariki to welcome the hero of this story, Pōtatau Te Wherowhero, the first Māori King. There will be many a tale told of high endeavour, of romance, and of human joy and sorrow. Indeed, many nights will pass unheeded in their telling....

KO TE MUTUNGA TĒNEI

THIS IS THE END

June 4, 1945

BIBLIOGRAPHY

The authorities listed hereunder were consulted in the writing of this volume. Where my account differs from that in the works mentioned the reader is not to conclude that I have mis-read or overlooked the authority in question. On the other hand, in such cases other versions have come under notice and the accounts have been carefully weighed and checked before deciding the point at issue. Tribal elders often settle these matters by quoting a song or a line from a song.

ANDERSON, Johannes C., 1928. *Myths and Legends of the Polynesians*. London: Harrap.
ANGAS, George, French, 1847. *The New Zealanders*. London: T. McLean.
BEST, Elsdon, 1924. *The Maori* (2 Vols.). Wellington: Board of Ethnological Research, for the author and on behalf of the Polynesian Society.
BUICK, T. Lindsay, 1914. *Treaty of Waitangi*. Wellington: S. & W. Mackay.
COWAN, James, 1910. *The Maoris of New Zealand*, Christchurch: Whitcomb & Tombs.
—— 1922. *The Old Frontier*. Te Awamutu: Waipa Post and Publishing Co.
—— 1934(?). *Legends of the Maori* (with Sir Maui Pomare). Wellington: Harry H. Tombs.
DAVIS, C. O. B., 1876. *The Life and Times of Patuone*. Auckland: J. H. Field, Steam Printing Co.
FEATON, John, 1923. *The Waikato War*. Auckland: Brett.
GORST, Sir John, 1864. *The Maori King*. London: Macmillan.
GRACE, T. S., [1928]. *A Pioneer Missionary among the Maoris, 1850-79*. Jointly ed. S.J. Brittan, G.F., C.W. & A.V. Grace. Palmerston North: G.H. Bennett & Co.
JONES, Pei Te Hurinui, 1945. *Mahinarangi (the moonglow of the heavens)*. Hawera: J. C. Ekdahl.
KEESING, Felix, [1928]. *The Changing Maori*. New Plymouth: Thomas Avery.
MCDONALD, Rod. A. *Te Hekenga, early days in Horowhenua*. Palmerston North: G.H. Bennett & Co.
NGATA, Sir Apirana, 1958. *Nga Moteatea* (Part I). Wellington: Polynesian Society.
—— 1961. *Nga Moteatea* (Part II). Wellington: Polynesian Society.
—— 1940. Tribal Organisation. In I. L.G. Sutherland (ed.), *The Maori People Today*. A General Survey. Christchurch: Whitcombe & Tombs Ltd.
—— 1940. Religious Influences (with I. L.G. Sutherland). In I.L.G. Sutherland (ed.), *The Māori People Today*. A General Survey. Christchurch: Whitcombe & Tombs.
RAMSDEN, Eric, [1942]. *Busby of Waitangi, H. M.'s Resident at New Zealand*. 1832-40. Wellington: Reed.
—— [1936]. *Marsden and the Missions*. Dunedin, Wellington: Reed.
REISCHEK, Andreas, 1930. *Yesterdays in Maoriland: New Zealand in the eighties*. Translated & edited H. E. L. Priday. London: Cape.
RUSDEN, G. W., 1895. *History of New Zealand*. Vol. II. Melbourne: Melville, Mullen and Slade.

SHRIMPTON, A. W. with Alan E. Mulgan. *A History of New Zealand.* Christchurch: Whitcombe & Tombs.
SMITH, Percy, 1898. *Hawaiki: the whence of the Maori.* Wellington: Whitcombe & Tombs.
—— 1910. *History and Traditions of the West Coast, North Island of New Zealand.* New Plymouth: T. Avery.
—— 1910. *Maori Wars of the Nineteenth Century: the struggle of the Northern against the Southern tribes.* Christchurch: Whitcombe & Tombs.
—— 1913. *The Lore of the Whare Wānanga* (Part I). New Plymouth: T. Avery
SUTHERLAND, I. L. G., (editor and contributor), 1940. *The Maori People To-day. A General Survey.* Christchurch: Whitcombe & Tombs Ltd.
TE RANGIHĪROA, Dr. P., 1929. *The Coming of the Maori.* (Lecture) Published New Plymouth: T. Avery
—— 1938. *Vikings of the Sunrise.* Philadelphia: Lippincott.
VON HOCHSTETTER, F., 1867. *New Zealand; Its Physical Geography, Geology, and Natural History.* Stuttgart: J.G. Cotta.

OTHER RECORDS CONSULTED.

AUTHOR	Manuscript Records of Tribal Genealogies, Ritual, Songs, and History.
GREAT BRITAIN PARLIAMENTARY PAPERS (*GBPP*)	1842 (569), Vol. XXVIII 1845 (247), Vol. XXXIII 1847 (837), Vol. XXXVIII 1847-48 (899), Vol. XLIII.
MAORI DEEDS OF LAND PURCHASES	1878, Vol. II, Deed I. Wellington: Government Printer.
NEW ZEALAND CHARTER	28/12/1846, Chapter XIII, Clause 9: 9 & 10 Victoria cap.103.
NATIVE LAND COURT (Auckland Office)	Waikato and Ōtorohanga series of Minute Books, containing minutes of the evidence of the following tribal witnesses:

Hakiriwhi	1884
Hari Te Whanonga (Maniapoto)	1892
Hauāuru Poutama (Maniapoto)	1886
Hōri Wirihana	1884
Te Kamaka	1884
Kaukiuta	1886
Te Naunau Hīkaka (Maniapoto)	1892
Te Ngakau (Hourua)	1882
Ngara (Apakura)	1882
Ngata (Waikato)	1884
Te Oro Te Koko	1888

Piripi Whanatangi (Korokī)	1884
Rewi Maniapoto (Raukawa-Maniapoto)	1882
Rihari Tauwhare (Hikairo)	1888
Tarahuia (Kauwhata)	1884
Tuarea Takoto	1886
Tuteao	1886
Tuwhenua Te Tiwha	1882
Wahanui Huatere (Maniapoto)	1886
Warena Te Ahikaramu	1884
Te Whaaro Kaitangata (Maniapoto)	1894
Te Wheoro (Waikato)	1886
Winiata Tupotahi (Maniapoto)	1884

TRIBAL SOURCES OF INFORMATION

Journal and *Whakapapa* (Genealogies) Book of the Late King Te Rātā (the fourth Māori King).

Ritual, *Whakapapa* and *Waiata* (Songs), Manuscript Records of the late Te Hurinui Te Wano (Maniapoto and Tūwharetoa tribes).

TRIBAL ELDERS

With names of Tribes and Addresses.

NAME	TRIBE	LATE ADDRESSES
Te Kiri Katipa	Tamainupō	Marokopa
Aihe Huirama	Maniapoto and Waikato (Te Ata)	Hiona, Ngutunui
Marae Erueti	Hikairo	Kāwhia
Peha Wharekura	Mahuta	Waahi, Huntly
Rauhinga Pikia	Hikairo	Kāwhia
Roore Erueti	Māhanga and Hourua	Moerangi, Whatawhata
Te Tahuna Herangi	Maniapoto	Ngāruawāhia
Taui Wētere	Hikairo	Kāwhia
Tūkōrehu Te Ahipu	Maniapoto, Raukawa, Whanganui and Tūwharetoa	Te Kūiti
Tuturu Hone Teri	Tūwharetoa and Raukawa	Te Motuiti, Foxton
Wehi Te Ringitanga	Maniapoto	Mangapeehi
Te Whare Hotu	Maniapoto	Ōparure, Te Kūiti

AN ARAWA GENEALOGY

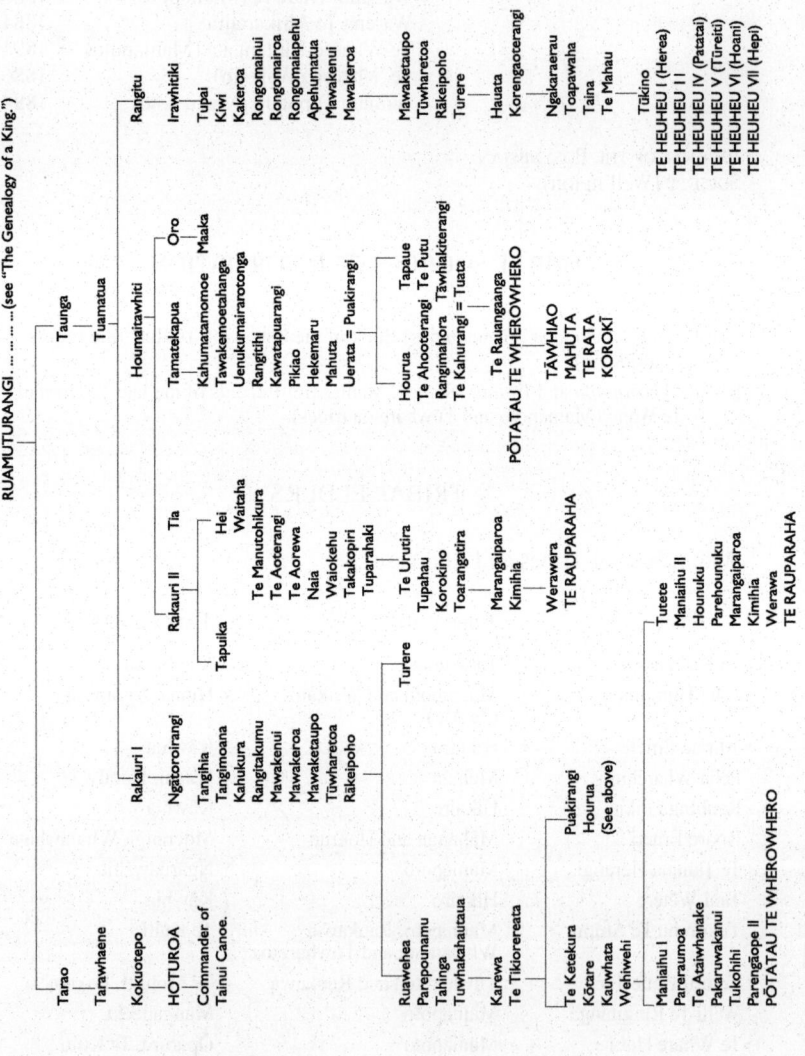

A TAINUI GENEALOGY

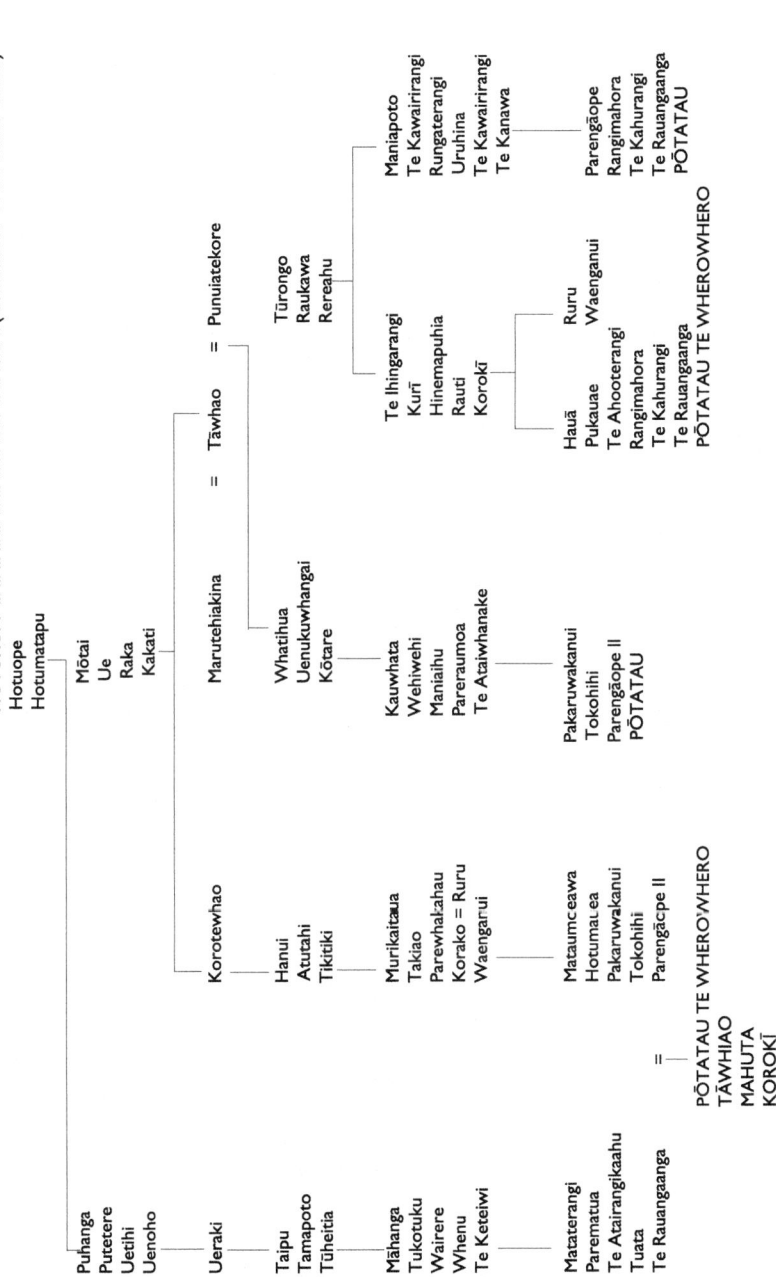

THE HOUSE OF PŌTATAU

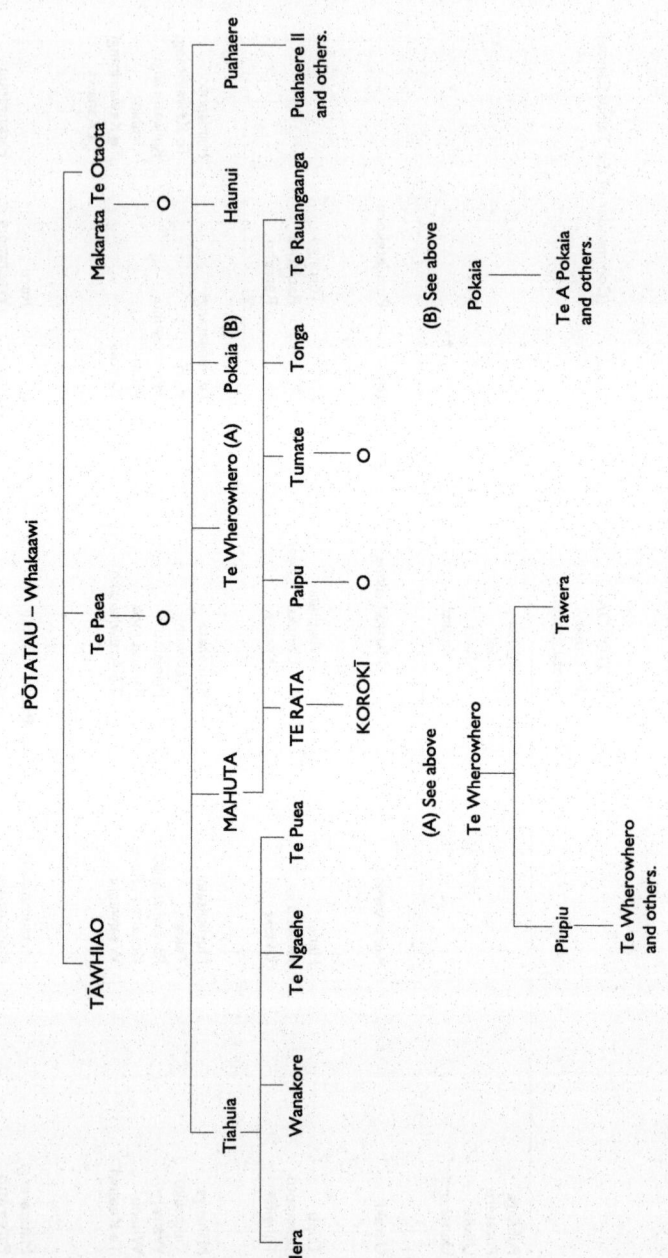

General Index

agriculture, advance in by Māori, 231
Ahooterangi, Te, 16 (a), 43; death of 44, 48
Aho Tuatoru, Te, 254
Ahurei, house of learning, 32, 34, 35, 36; sacred emblems of 35; Te Hurinui as high priest of, 36
Āio Papa, Te, 252
Āio Rangi, Te, 252
Aituā, 243, 254
Aitu Ere, 254
Aitu Kikini, 254
Aitu Tāmaki, 254
Aitu Whakatika, 254
Akamapuhia, Te, 56
Ākau, Te, 70
Ake, Te, 55
Albatross point, see Honipaki
Amo, Te, 252
Amohau, Te, 177; and Māori King movement, 189
Ao Āio, 251
Aokatoa, Te, 223
Ao Ki Katau, 251
Ao Ki Mauī, Te, 241, 251
Ao Ki Raro, 251
Ao Ki Roto, 250
Ao Ki Runga, 251
Ao Ki Tawhiti, 250
Ao Ki Tua, 250
Ao Kumea, 251
Ao Mā, 251
Aomārama, Te, killed, 42
Ao Nui, 250
Ao Pakō Rea, 250
Ao Pango, 251
Ao Papa Kina, 250
Aorangi, 122
Ao Roa, 250
Ao Ruru, 251
Aotea canoe, 21
Aotea harbour, 54; tribes occupying district of, 42, 129
Aotearoa, 176
Ao Whakarito, 251
Ao Whero, 251

Apakura tribe, in battle of Hingakākā, 7
Apoapo, Te, 157, 169 (n)
Arapae pā, 58; Moerua's wife at, 52; Te Rauparaha captures women at, 52
Arapuni, 229; power station at, 226
Aratiatia rapids, 229
Arataua, Te, 54; killed, 52
Arawa canoe, 20, 32, 34; commanded by Tamatekapua, 3
Arawa tribe, 146, 177; defeated by Ngāpuhi, 47; Te Rauparaha claims relationship to, 47, 90 (n)
Arawai, Te, 138 (n)
Arawaka, Te, killed, 79
Areiara, 21
ātahu, defined, 29(n)
Atiamuri, 229
Āti Awa tribe, 78, 81, 85, 87(n), 144, 146, 163, 176, 178 (n)
Au, Te, 58
Auckland, 176; Ngāpuhi prepare to attack, 152, Māori trade with, 159; Tāwhiao visits, 159-60; Te Rauparaha prisoner at, 162
Auckland City Domain, 168
Aurutu, 38
Awa river, see Waikato river
Awaitaia, Te, 55, 70, 71, 76, 129, 157, 168 (n), 208; homeland of, 76; fight with Raparapa, 76
Awakino, 122
Awakino river, 58
Awakino valley, 52
Awanuiarangi, 21
Awarua, 49
Awekopara, Te, 242
Awhirau, 21

battles, of Te Rauparaha, 46-50, 57, 65-7 of Kāwhia, 57-72
Best, E., 92
burial grounds, of Ngāti Toa, 74
Cameron, General, 92, 151, 169 (n), 208
canoes, arrival from Tahiti, 34
Chatham Islands, chief of, 38; Taranaki tribes flee to, 102

Clarke, G., 106-7, 166
Claudelands see Kirikiriroa
cloaks, 139 (n)
Coates, J., 107
coats of arms, see Māori and Coats of arms, desc.
Cowan, J., extract from *Old Frontier*, 230-233
Crispe, H., extracts quoted from, 232-233
Crispe, B. A., 233

Davis, C. O. B., 176, 178 (n)
dogs, as mascot of Waikato tribe, 67

Edgecumbe, mount, 215
Egmont, mount, 215
emblems, sacred, 34, 35-37, 92
Erueti, R., 30 (n), 76, 103 (n)

Fitzroy, Governor, 102, 151, 166, 167
food, of Māori, 122, 122, 193, 228; abundance of, 231-234
Forsaith. I. S., 107

Government House, Tāwhiao at, 161; Te Wherowhero guest at, 166
Grace, J. Te H. see Kerehi, Te Herekiekie
greenstone, legend of, 16 (n)
Grey, Sir G., 157, 176, 195, 219; friendship with Te Wherowhero, 151-152, 155; extract from despatch, 152; recalled, 158; houses Tāwhiao, 162; and Te Rauparaha, 162; Te Wherowhero accompanies to Wanganui,167; discusses kingship with Te Wherowhero, 193; inspects agriculture methods in Waikato, 232
guns, used by Te Pūoho, 69-70; Ngāpuhi use at Mātakitaki pā 110-115; first owned by Waikato tribe, 111, 119; of Maniapoto, 119

Haereawatea, Tūkōrehu's home, 138 (n)
Hahana., Te, killed, 48
Hakanoa lake, 25
Hākarimata hills, 25, 230
Hākarimata range, 128

Halswell, —., 166
Hamaka, H., 211
Hangatiki, 169
Hani, 239-240
Hape, 20, 42
Hāpuku, Te, 178 (n); offered kingship, 184
Harihari, 56; Ngāti Akamapuhia defeated at, 63
hat of kingship, 189; 190 (n), 198
Hatonga, 255
Hauāuru, 195, 199; kills Tūpoki, 53; at Haurua meeting, 198
Hauhungaroa range, 139 (n)
Haumiatikitiki, 243
Haunga, killed, 46
Haupore, 46
Haupokia, Te, 130
Hauraki district, 130; tribes from, 129, 146; at Kohimarama, 162
Hauraki Ki Te Rangi, 256
Hauraki gulf, Ngāti Pāoa of, 49
Haurora, 46
Haurua, 195; meeting of Maniapoto tribe at, 198-200
Hautehoro, Te, 99, 100
Hauturu, 129, 190
Haututu, see Kanawa, Te
Hawaiki, see Tahiti
Hawkes Bay, Tūrongo arrives in, 26; chiefs of released, 146
Heahea beach, 26, 29 (n)
Hei raro nei tētehi Ao, 252
Hei runga nei tētehi Ao, 252
Hekemaru, 20
Heketahutahuahi, Te, 85
Hema, 246, 255
Herekiekie, Te Kerehi, see Kerihi, Te Herekiekie
Heuheu I, Te, (Herea), 17 (n)
Heuheu II, Te (Tūkino), 3, 130, 131, 139 (n), 139 (n), 147, 1499, 150, 151,154, 178 (n); on raids in Taupō, 122, offered kingship, 177
Heuheu III, Te (Iwikau), 3, 178 (n), 183, 208; and king movement, 187, 189
Heuheu Tūkino, Te (Heuheu II), see Heuheu II, Te (Tūkino)

Hiakai, Te, 43, 47, 55, 59, 80, 95, 101, 144; war with Ngāti Toa, 43; assists in Te Rauparaha's escape, 81; killed, 97
Hiaroa, 33; establishes Kahuwera house of learning, 33
Hikairo tribe, at battle of Hingakākā, 7
Hikarahi, 240
Hikihiki, 47
Hikuparea pā, Te Rauparaha at, 46-7; mentioned, 51
Hikurangi, mount, 178
Hineahuone, 244, 254
Hineari, 245
Hineaupounamu, 20, 33
Hinematioro (queen of East Coast tribes), 179 (n)
Hinematua, 16 (n)
Hinewai, 38. 144-51
Hingakākā, battle of, 4-15, 24, 185 (n); sacred emblems lost in, 35-36
Hoariri, Te, *see* Paerata, Te
Hobson, Governor, Te Wherowhero accompanies, 166
Hochstetter, F. von, Dr., 233, 278
Hoea, 20
Hoewhakatu, Te, 38
Hohepa, 38
Hone Heke, 152, 168 (n)
Hone Papita, 187, 189 (n)
Hone Teri, 158
Hongi Hika, 47, 90 (n), 118, 142, 144, 168 (n); attacks and takes Mātakitaki pā, 110-115; takes Mangauika pā, 116; at Kāwhia, 116, 119; retreats to Mangatāwhiri stream, 120
Honipaka (Albatross point), 81; in Te Rauparaha's song, 82, 87 (n)
Horahora, 229
Horea pā, 26; position of, 29 (n)
Horeta, Te, 129
Hōri Te Waru, *see* Waru, H. Te
Horoure pā, 43
Horouta canoe, 21, 34
Horowhenua, Ngāti Raukawa reside in, 149
Hotumatapū, 20, 22

Hotumauea. 25-26
Hotumauea's leap, 29 (n)
Hotuope, 20, 22
Hoturoa, 20, 22, 32; as high priest of Ahurei house of learning, 32-33; allegedly buried in Muriwhenua, 88 (n)
Hou, 20
houses of learning—sacred, the Tāmaki, 32; Ahurei, 32; Te Papa o Patu, 33; teachings of, 34 *et seq.*; Kahuwera, 33: teaching in, 37
Houtaepo, 21
Hou-taketake, 86, 89 (n)
Huahua, 16-17 (n), 122-124, 129; in battle of Hingakākā, 7-13
huahua, ceremony of presenting, 122-125, 130-137
Huanui, Te, 138 (n)
Huiputea, 118-120, 142; leads Ngāpuhi to Ōrāhiri, 116; reconnoitres Te Houpeehi pā and Ōrongokoekoeā, 118 ; rests at Ōrāhiri, 118; force of annihilated, 119
Huka falls, 229
Hukiki, Te, 183, 185 (n)
Hurakia, 129, 138 (n); school of learning at, 33
Hurakia ranges, 122, 130
Hurimoana, battle of, 16 (n)
Hurinui, Te, accused of hiding sacred emblems, 35; killed, 35, 42; revenge for death, 42-43
Hurinui, Te (The Author), 38
Hurinui, Te (The Martyr), 38
Hurinui Te Wano, Te, 29 (n)

Ikatu, Te, 50
Ingoa, Te, killed, 49
Io, Māori god, 34, 236-238; theory of evolution from, 238-240
Irohanga, 16 (n), 22
Iwikau, *see* Heuheu III, Te (Iwikau)
Iwipupu, 21
Kaaro, 38
Kaheterauoterangi, 38
kahika bushes, 16 (n)
kahikatea (white pine) at Ōtorohanga, 125 (n)

Kahu, 20
Kahu, (Te Arawai's wife), 138 (n)
Kahukura *see* Uenuku
Kahukuranui, 21
Kahukurataepa, 21
Kahumatamamoe, 20
Kahungunu, 21
Kahungunu tribe, 177
Kahurangi, Te, 16 (n), 20, 22, 165
Kahuwera, 122
Kahuwera forest, legend of, 124
Kahuwera, house of learning, 33
Kai Iwi, mount, 215
Kaipara district, 7, 150; tribe of, 143
kaitaka, 139 (n)
Kaitangata, 246, 255
Kaitotehe, Te Wherowhero's pā at, 94
Kaiwhare, defined, 88 (n)
Kākākura, Te, escapes from Te Arawī pā, 81
Kakati, 20, 22
Kakepuku, mount, 122, 233
Ka mārama ake te Ao, 252
Ka mārama te Ao, 252
Kanawa, Te, 20, 22, 50, 55, 59, 60, 150, 195, 269; escapes Ngāti Toa, 62, 79; at Mātakitaki pā, 113, 115; at Haurua meeting, 198
Kanawa, Te Kihirini Te, 211
Kaniatakirau, Te, 177 (n), 183, 184 (n); and kingship, 179
kao, 18 (n)
Kaokaoroa o Pātetere, 129
Kapara, W., 219
Kapiti Island, Te Rangituatea visits, 104
Kapuoterangi, Te, 21
Kaputuhi tribe, 122
Karapiro, power station, 226
Karauria, 183, 184 (n)
Kāretu, killed, 48
Karewa island, 88 (n)
Karewaho, 49
Karioi, mount, 26, 215; Ngāti Koata on, 59
Kati, *see* Takiwaru
Katipa, Te, 157, 168 (n)
Kauae, Te, 49

kauri, 17 (n)
Kauteuri canoe, 49
Kauwhataroa, 21
Kawa, Te, 184
Kawairirangi I, Te, 20, 22
Kawairirangi II, Te, 20, 22
Kawatapuarangi, 20
Kawau, Te (rock), 74, 88 (n)
Kawau island, 143; Te Wherowhero visits, 159
Kāwhia, 15 (n), 26, 32, 50, 56, 164; Ahurei house of learning at, 32; Te Hurinui visits, 35; tribes of, 42, 129; tribal wars over land of, 42-46; Te Rauparaha attacked at, 48; Te Rauparaha gains ownership of, 51; battle of, 58-81; Tirohanga track, 60; Manukorihi arrives at, 93; Te Wherowhero's force leaves, 94; Waikato escape to, 115; Hongi Hika enters, 116; some Ngāpuhi escape to, 120
Kāwhia Harbour, 44, 50, 54, 59, 63, 65, 87; Ahooterangi killed at, 43; Ngāti Toa trespass in fishing grounds, 46; Unuatahu crosses, 49; pā in, 79
Keanuku, 242
Kearangi, 242
Kelly, L. G, 125 (n)
Kent. Capt., marries Ngangiha, 164
Kerehi, Te Herekiekie, 184
kererū, 18 (n)
Keteanataura, Te, as high priest of Tāmaki house of learning, 32
Ketemaringi, 130
Keunga, Te, 44
Kiharoa, 47
Kihikihi, 138 (n), 169 (n); battle of Hurimoana fought near, 16 (n)
Kihirini, Te Kanawa Te, *see* Kanawa, Te Kihirini Te
Kikitai, 20
Kimihia, 38
kings, Māori, Te Wherowhero chosen, 36-37
King Country, 191
Kinohaku, Te Rauparaha's defences at, 56; Maniapoto attacks, 63

Kinohaku gap, 60, 63
Kirikiriroa, 229
Kiritehere, remnants of Ngāti Toa,
  Koaka etc. gather at, 81
Kiwa *see* Pacific Ocean
Kiwi (Waikato chief); 45, 54, 88 (n) ; in
  battle of Kāwhia, 59-62, 63
Kohika, Te, 139 (n)
Kohimarama, 149, 160, 164, 190;
  meeting at, 162-164
Kokuoterangi, Te, 21
Kore, Te, 34, 238, 254
Kore Nui, Te, 254
Kore Parā, Te, 254
Kore Te Whiwhia, Te, 254
Kore Te Oti Atu Ki Te Pō, 254
Korokino, 38
Koropiko, 146
Korotangi, 32
Kukutai, *see* Waata Kukutai
Kupe, 21
Kurahaupō canoe, 20, 34
Kuraimonoa, Te, 246, 256

laments, for Raparapa, 72-74
land sales, 102, 106-107

Maheu, Te, 252
Māhinārangi, 20, 26-28, 33, 35
Mahoenui, 53
Māhoetahi, 220 (n)
Mahuki, 126
Mahutu, Te (Marokapa chief), 20, 50;
  killed, 52
Maketū, 88 (n)
Makomako, 42
Mama, 96, 98, 100, 101, 144, 144; at
  Ōkoki pā, 96-97; dies, 99
Manawakawa., 180
Manawatū, Te Whatanui in, 149
Manawatū river, 185 (n)
Mangahana, 138 (n)
Mangahaua, 'peace track', 50
Mangakōwhai, 48
Mangaohoi stream, 130
Mangaokewa stream, 89 (n)

Mangaorongo stream, 116
Mangaotake river, 53
Mangapiko stream, 111, 112, 113, 169(n)
Mangarorongo stream, 33
Mangatāwhiri, *see* Mercer
Mangatāwhiri stream, 125 (n), 219, 219(n),
  237; Hongi Hika crosses, 120
Mangati river, 122
Mangatoatoa, 169; Waikato tribes
  assemble at, 46
Mangatoatoa pā, of Tūkōrehu, 51
Mangauika pā, Waikato tribes escape to,
  113, 114, 115; Te Wherowhero
  visits, 115; Hongi Hika takes, 116
Māngere, Te Wherowhero resides at,
  149, 159, 164, 187, 189 (n)
Maniapoto, Rewi, 89 (n), 92, 169 (n),
  219; command used by, ix-x;
  kills Houtaketake, 89 (n); British
  confiscate land of, 169 (n)
Maniapoto tribe, *see* Ngāti Maniapoto
  tribe
Manukau, 129
Manukau harbour, Hongi Hika crosses
  110
Manukitawhiti, killed, 48
Manukorihi, 169 (n); runs from
  Pukerangiora to Kāwhia, 93;
  accompanies Te Wherowhero, 97
Manukorihi pā, 94
Māori King Movement, 36, 176-185,
  187, 189; disputes over whom to
  appoint, 181-178; ritual of first
  ceremony, 212-216; coat of arms,
  223-224; motto, 223-224
Māori and—
  sports, 25; traditions, 25; customs
  and traditions, 25-26, 32-33;
  legends —of Te Wherowhero's
  ancestors, 25; of tūī and
  Kahuwera forest, 123; songs,
  27-28, 156-157; culture and
  learning, 32-33; kings, viii,
  126(n), 163, 164, 175-185, l94,
  189; wars, customs, 36-37; wars,
  use of sea forces in, 55-56; king
  makers, 39; presentation of
  huahua, 122-124; wedding
  ceremony, 128-130; land claims,
  149, 152, 153; land laws, 153,
  154; first marriages to Pākehā,

Māori and – *continued*
164; coat of arms, 223-224; theory of evolution from Io, 238-248; world of stars genealogy, 250-252; genealogy of man, 254-256; chants for the dead, 268-273; journey to the underworld, 273-275
Mapiu river, 116
Mapunakiterangi, 246, 256
Marae, Erueti, 15 (n)
Maraeroa, 122, 129
Marangai areare, 74 (n)
Marangaiparoa, 38
Mare, Te, 131
Marokopa, 93, 52
Marokopa district, 16 (n); chief of, 52; Ngāti Maniapoto attacks, 52
Marokopa river, 4, 25, 29 (n)
Maropounamu, Te, wife of Raparapa, 69, 72; lament for Raparapa composed by, 72-74
Martin, W., Chief Justice, 154
Marutehiakina, 26, 29 (n)
Matahourua, 21
Mataipuku, 146
Mātakitaki pā, 118, 120, 121, 143; Te Wherowhero defeated at by Hongi Hika, 110-116; Hongi Hika at, 116.
Matamata district, Ngāti Hauā of, 166
"Matarua", protective garment, 69-70, 75(n)
Mātaatua canoe, 21, 34
Mātaatua point, Waikato seaborne force lands at, 59
Matemateaonge, mount, 177
Mātene Te Whiwhi, 39, 176, 183
Matire, (son of Taepa), 38
Matire Hoahoa, 256
Matire, (daughter of Toka) marries Takiwaru, 142
Matohe, Te, 38
Matutaera, *see* Tāwhiao
Māui, 38, 39
Mauinaina, 143; Te Wherowhero at, 149
Maukuwai, canoe of Ngāti Mahuta, 49
Maungakiekie pā, 16 (n)

Maunganui, mount, (*see* also Maungaroa, mount) 240
Maungaroa, mount, 240
Maungatautari, 16 (n), 144; killed, 53
Maungatautari, 226; tribes of, 42, 52, 80, 129, 130, 145; Te Rauparaha visits, 47
Maungatautari, mount, 230
Maungwhau, 149, 164
Maunsell, Archdeacon, 154
Maunu, 38, 39
Mautara, kills Haunga, 47
Mercer, 125 (n), 226
Mere, 38
Mikotahi, 145
Miringa Te Kakara, school of learning at, 33
missionaries, Te Wherowhero approves 151
miti, 18 (n)
Moanarire, Te, 242
Moanataiaha, killed, 48
Moeatoa, mount, 81
Moerangi ranges, 15, 25; tribe of district, 43, 129
Moerua, Te, Ngāti Maniapoto chief, 50, 54; killed and eaten, 50
Mohi, 42
Mōkaikainga, 59, 60
Mōkau, 26, 49, 52, 56, 64, 103 (n), 169 (n); valley, 50; Te Rauparaha and tribes of, 51; river, 53, 85, 95, 122; Ngāti Toa return to, 71: tribes of, 129
Mokoia, Arawa people defeated at, 47
Momo, Te, 138 (n)
Moreotewhenua, Te, 242
Morgan, Rev. J. (missionary), 214, 230
Mōtai, 20, 22
Motungaio pā, 44, 56; in battle of Kāwhia, 59, 80
Motunui, battle of, *see* Ōkoki pā, battle of
Motuopuhi, Te Wharerangi's pā at, 48
Moturoa 145
Motutāiko island, 131, 139 (n)
Motuwhāriki, 242
Mount Eden, 149

Moutoa, 185 (n)
Muriwhenua, 208
Muriwhenua burial cave, 65, 74 (n), 88 (n)
Muriwhenua clan, 66, 74
Murupaenga, 211

Nanaia, 21
Narungaiho, 20
Nehenehenui tribes, 191 (n), 195, 265
Neko, 139 (n)
New Zealand Company; Te Wherowhero reviews land claims of, 166
New Zealand Land Company *see* New Zealand Company
Ngaehe, Te, 53
Ngai, 256
Ngai Nui, 256
Ngai Peha, 256
Ngai Roto, 256
Ngāi Tai, in Te Rauangaanga's force, 7
Ngana, 254
Ngana Maoe, 255
Ngana Nui, 255
Ngana Roa, 255
Ngana Ruru, 255
Ngangiha, 165, 170 (n); marries Capt. Kent, 164
Ngāpuhi tribe, 53, 142, 157, 167, 168 (n); attacked by Arawa, 47: Te Rauparaha accompanies, 51; Hongi Hika leads to and takes Mātakitaki pā, 110-116; takes Maungauika pā,116; divides, 116; section under Te Huiputea — reconnoitres Ōrongokoekoeā, 118; rests at Ōrāhiri, 116, 118; wiped out at Ōrāhiri, 119; retires to Mangatāwhiri stream, 121; Te Wherowhero routs, 142-145; Te Wherowhero makes peace with, 150; prepares to attack Auckland, 152; attends Kohimarama, 162
Ngāpuketūrua pā, Tūkōrehu's army besieged, at, 93
Ngārauru tribe, 178
Ngarongokitua, 38

Ngāruawāhia, 131, 226, 227, 230; wedding of Te Wherowhero at, 128, 129, 130; captured by General Cameron, 151; crowning of Te Wherowhero at, 212-215; gathering at on Te Wherowhero's death, 268
Ngata, Sir A., 179 (n)
Ngātapa, 51; attacks Tūkōrehu's pā, 51-52
Ngātata, with Te Wherowhero attacks Taranaki, 144
Ngāti Akamapuhia, 58, 63, 81
Ngāti Amaru, 129
Ngāti Apakura, 129, 165, 207
Ngāti Hā, 129
Ngāti Hauā tribe, 129, 130, 167, 204; invades Ngāti Apakura country, 165; at Paetai meeting, 211
Ngāti Hikairo tribe, 15 (n), 42, 50, 129; in battle of Hingakākā, 12; chief of, 54; in battle of Kāwhia, 58, 59, 60
Ngāti Hine tribe, 46, 211
Ngāti Hinemihi, 122
Ngāti Hourua, 55, 129; at battle of Hingakākā, 7
Ngāti Kahu, aid in attack on Mangatotoa pā, 51
Ngāti Kahungunu, prisoners returned to, 165
Ngāti Kahutōtara, 164
Ngāti Koata, 42, 51; join Ngāti Toa, 48, 56; defend Motungaio and Pouewe pā, 59, 81; divide up, 81; after battle of Kāwhia, 81
Ngāti Korokī, 129
Ngāti Māhanga tribe, 42, 43. 48, 54, 55, 165; chiefs of, 49, 70, 76
Ngāti Mahuta, 17 (n), 25, 43, 46, 48, 55, 129; in Te Rauangaanga's force, 7; members of, 43
Ngāti Maniapoto tribe, 35, 54, 55, 56, 83-84, 94, 94, 118, 119, 129, 130, 142, 144, 151, 195, 219, 237; in battle of Hingakākā, 4, 7, 8; leader of, 4, 7; genealogy of, 16 (n); houses of learning of, 33; chiefs of, 46; war with Ngāti Toa, 46; Te Rauparaha's last battle against, 51-52; raids Marokopa, 52; attacks Ngāti Toa, 52; defeats

Ngāti Maniapoto tribe – *continued*
Ngāti Tama, 53; neutrals in war against Ngāti Toa 55.; in battle of Kāwhia, 58 *et seq.*; members saved from Waikawau pā, 59; members saved from Te Roto and Te Kawau pā. 63; attacks Te Arawī pā, 80; hinder Te Rauparaha's escape to Te Kawau, 84-85; march toward Waitara, 92; at Ōkoki pā, 96-97; offer sanctuary to Te Wherowhero, 116; sub-tribes of, 118, 122; obtain firearms, 119; Te Wherowhero with, 122; invade Taranaki, 144; takes Pukerangiora pā, 144; arrival in New Zealand, 190; meet at Haurua, 198-200; at crowning of Te Wherowhero, 212

Ngāti Maru, 129

Ngāti Matakore, 122, 125; pā of, 116, 118; at Ōrāhiri attack, 118-120

Ngāti Mutunga, 102; Te Rauparaha lives with, 94; prepare for invasion by Waikato tribes, 94

Ngāti Nahia, 48

Ngāti Naho tribe, 129, 211

Ngāti Ngāwaero, aid in attack on Mangatotoa pā, 51

Ngāti Pāoa, of west Hauraki gulf, 49, 129

Ngāti Paretekawa, 132, 169 (n)

Ngāti Patupō, 55

Ngāti Pou, 43, 46, 49, 55, 129; gather force to attack Te Rauparaha, 48

Ngāti Raerae, 122

Ngāti Rārua, 55, 56; in battle of Kāwhia. 58, 81

Ngāti Raukawa tribe, 27, 42, 49, 52, 88(n), 128, 148, 176, 183, 191(n), 227; houses of learning of, 34; oppose Te Rauparaha, 47; Te Rauparaha's last invasion into district of, 52; Te Rauparaha plans to join, 80

Ngāti Rehu tribe, 43

Ngāti Reko tribe, 43, 48, 55, 129

Ngāti Ruahine, 145

Ngāti Ruanui tribe, 144, 178

Ngāti Rungaterangi, 121; assist Tūkōrehu's force, 93

Ngāti Tai, 129

Ngāti Tama, 49, 50, 56, 64, 71 80, 87, 101; aid Te Rauparaha, 52-54, 56; chiefs of, 54, 64, 69; at battle of Kāwhia, 71; prepare for Waikato tribes approach, 94

Ngāti Tamainupō tribe, 55, 129; attacked by Te Rauparaha, 48

Ngāti Tamamutu, 88 (n)

Ngāti Tamaoho, 129; in Te Rauangaanga's force, 7

Ngāti Tamaterā, 129

Ngāti Te Akamapuhia, 56

Ngāti Te Ata tribe, 49, 129, 168 (n), 194: in Te Rauangaanga's force, 7

Ngāti Te Ihingarangi, 122

Ngāti Te Kanawa, 122

Ngāti Te Koherā, 129, 131, 138 (n)

Ngāti Te Waiohua, 129

Ngāti Te Wehi tribe, 55, 129; domain of, 42; land of, 43-44; some Ngāti Koata join, 81

Ngāti Tipa, 49, 129, 130, 211; in Te Rauangaanga's force, 7

Ngāti Toa *see* Ngāti Toarangatira

Ngāti Toarangatira, 35, 43, 48, 50, 52, 56, 59, 78, 94; in civil war with Tainui tribes, 36; Te Rauparaha as chief of, 42; battles over land at Kāwhia, 43-46; at war with Waikato tribes, 43-46, 48-49: attack Ngāti Tamainupō, 48; attacked by Ngāti Maniapoto, 52; Te Wherowhero organizes attack on, 54-56; in battle of Kāwhia, 58-72, 79; burial grounds of, 74; defeated at Te Arawī pā, 79-80; escape from Te Arawī pā, 80-82; some Ngāti Koata join, 81; remnants at Kiritehere, 82; remnants leave for south, 82; remnants trek to Te Kawau pā, 83-86

Ngāti Turumakina, 139 (n)

Ngāti Tūwharetoa tribe, 33, 48, 88 (n), 129; raiding in Taupō country, 121

Ngāti Uenuku-kopako, 90 (n)

Ngāti Uru, aid in attack on Mangatotoa pā, 51

Ngāti Wairangi, 129

Ngāti Whakaue, 90 (n), 146, 177

Ngāti Whanaunga, 129
Ngāti Whātua, 7; join Waikato, 143; at Kohimarama, 162
Ngāti Whawhakia, 25, 129
Ngātokakairiri pā, Tautara taken to, 43; Unuatahu killed at, 50
Ngātokawaru, 227; kills Te Putu, 227
Ngāwaero, marries Te Wherowhero, 127-132; at Whatiwhatihoe, 130-137; songs of, 132-135
Ngoki, chant of, 23, 27
Ngongotahā, mount, 177, 215
Nguha Huirama, Te, 29 (n)
Ngunguru, Ngāpuhi defeated at, 143
Niho (Ngāti Maniapoto woman), 52
Noaia, 131, 139 (n)
Nohopapa, 131
North Island, Arawa canoe arrives at, 3
Nuitone, Te, 157, 168 (n)
Nuku, 101; at Ōkoki pā, 96

Ōhāua, Ngāti Toa retreat to, 49
Ōhaupō, 4; battle of Hingakākā fought near, 4
Ōhinemutu, 146
Ohomauri, 241
Ohomuturangi, 241
Ohonui, 241
Ohoroa, 241
Ōkoki, chief of, 38
Ōkoki pā, 102, 103 (n), 164; built, 94; Te Wherowhero's forces attack and capture, 94-98; Taranaki tribes in, 101
One Tree Hill, 16 (n)
Ōngarue river, 33, 122
Ōpārau, tribes of district, 42
Ōpārau river, 60
Ōparure, 'peace track' from, 50
Ōrākau, 92, 169 (n); battle of, 156, 158
Ōrākei-Kōrako, 229
Ōrona, 86 (n)
Ōrongokoekoeā pā, Te Wherowhero arrives and settles at, 116, 118, 122-124; Huiputea reconnoitres, 118; some Waikato and Ngāti Matokore leave, 118-119; remains of, 125 (n)

Ōtaki, Te Wherowhero visits, 149
Otapeehi, Te, assists Te Wherowhero, 116; aids in annihilating Huiputea's force, 118-120; Te Wherowhero guest of, 122, 125
Otiki pā, attacked by Waikato tribe, 49
Ōtorohanga, 4, 17 (n), 50, 116, 118, 119, 125 (n), 142, 195; Waikato escape to, 115; Te Wherowhero near, 115; Pikauterangi's forces near, 4; Huiputea's force annihilated at, 119

Pacific Ocean, 16 (n)
Paerata, Te, 156, 159; song of, 156-157
Paetai, 204, 205, 207, 208, 211
Paewaka, Te, 55, 187, 189 (n), 198
Paikea, 21
pakipaki, 139 (n)
Pamotumotu pā, Te Wherowhero visits, 116
Pā-oneone pā, 89 (n)
Papakura, Te, 166, 252
Papa mea, Te, 252
Papa o Rotu, Te, house of learning, 33, 34, 165; Te Wherowhero attends, 34
Papatatau o Uenuku, 32
Parāone, Tiwai, 223
Pararewa, 71; Tūpoki camps at, 53
Paratui pā, 169 (n)
Parekōhatu (mother of Te Rauparaha), 42
Parekohu, captured by Ngāpuhi, 115
Parerahui, chieftainess, killed, 52
Parctckōrae (Māori poetess of Tainui), 38, 75 (n)
Pātea, killed, 49
Pātea, Tūkōrehu defeats inhabitants of, 93
"Pathway of Tūrongo," song of Ngoki, 27-28
Patu, Te, 42
Peehi Kupe, Te, 56, 81; wife of, 84
Pekapeka, Te, killed, 52
Pēria, 193
Pikauterangi, Tainui chief (the Rebel), 16 (n), 35, 36, 54; in battle of Hingakākā, 4-15; battle song of, 5-6, 16 (n); revenge against army of, 92

Pikia, 54, 55, 58, 59, 60
Pikiao I, 20
Pikimaunga, 77
Pikirangi, 53; kills Te Waero, 54
Piopio, 50, 52; house of learning near, 33
Pipi, 241
Pipiri, 241
Piraunui, 106-107
Piri Kawau, 176
Piro, 255
Pirongia, 15, 116; tribe of district, 42, 129
Pirongia, mount, 60, 110, 113, 116
Pō Āio, Te, 251
Poakai, 47
Pohaturoa, 229
Pohepohe, 167
Pokaitara, Te, 56, 64
Pō Ki Katau, Te, 251
Pō Ki Mauī, Te, 240, 251
Pō Ki Raro, Te, 251
Pō Ki Roto, Te, 250
Pō Ki Runga, Te, 251
Pō Ki Tawhiti, Te, 250
Pō Ki Tua, Te, 250
Pō Kumea, 251
Pō Mā, Te, 251
Pōmare, defeated and killed, 142
Pō, Sir Māui, 38
Pō Nui, Te, 250
Pō Pakō Rea, Te, 250
Pō Pango, Te, 251
Pō Papa Kina, Te, 250
Popoto, 21
Pō Roa, Te, 250
Porokoru, 156, 168 (n), 187, 189 (n), 198
Porokuru, see Porokoru
Porourangi, 21
Pō Ruru, Te, 251
Pō tangotango, Te, 252
Pōtatau, see Wherowhero, Pōtatau Te
Pō tiwhatiwha, Te, 252
Po tuki, Te, 252
Pouewe pā, 43, 44, 56; in battle of Kāwhia, 59, 81
Pouha, killed, 48
Pouheni, 21
Pou kōhatu, 243
Poukura, killed, 48
Pōuriuri, Te, 252
Poutaina II, 38
Poutama, Maungatautari killed at, 53
Pō Whakarito, Te, 251
Pō whakarongorongo Tapairu, Te, 252
Pō Whero, Te, 251
priests, Tainui belief of, 34
Pūhaorangi, 246, 275
Puhianu, 20
Puhiarohia, 20
Puhirere, 21
pukatea, 17 (n)
Pukauae, 43
Pūkawa (see also Taupō Lake), meeting of chiefs at, 188, 189, 190, 214
Pukenui hills, Hou-taketake tribe settles on, 87 (n)
Pukerangi, 143, 145
Pukerangiora pā, 101; Tūkōrehu's force escapes to, 93; besieged, 93, 94, 97; Te Wherowhero relieves, 102; Te Wherowhero captures, 145-146
Pukewhau, 211
Puna, 239-243
Punatoto, 54, 55, 76
Puniatekore, 26
Pūnui river, 4, 46, 130, 138 (n), 169 (n), 219;
Puoho, Te, 56, 64; at Te Kakara battle, 69, 70; leaves battlefield, 71; uses gun; 70; death, 71; as Ngāti Toa leader, 71
Purewa, Te, duel with Tūkōrehu, 92
Putakarekare battle, 44
Putauaki, mount see Edgecumbe, mount
Puti, 60
Putu, Te, 16 (n), 20, 227, 228; assassination of, 227

Rā, Te, 241, 252
Raglan Harbour see Whāingaroa harbour
Rāhiri, 129
Rahurahu, 49

Rahuruake, Te (Te Kanawa's mother), 62, 115; captured, 115
Raka, 20, 22
Rakaherea, Te, 38, 39
Rakataura, 32; names Whāingaroa, 29 (n)
Rākaumangamanga, canoe of Ngāti Mahuta, 49
Rakaumoana, 21
Rakeihikuroa, 21
Rākeiora, 255
Rakeitekura, 21
Rakeiuru, 20
Rangahau, 240
Rangi, Te Nui e Tū Iho Nei, 239-245, 252, 254
Rangiahua, 190 (n)
Rangianewa, 190 (n); killed, 165
Rangiaohia, 4, 165, 190 (n), 207, 211, 231; tribes of 129; agriculture at, 231-232, desc. of, 233; mission school at 233; desc. of surrounding land, 233-234
Rangiātea, school of learning at, 33, 34, 35
Rangihaeata, Te, 39, 56, 63, 104-105 (n); sister of, 43; leads Ngāti Toa, 63; Te Kanawa escapes, 79; escapes from Te Arawī pā, 81; gathers remnants of Ngāti Toa, 81
Rangihīroa, Dr. Te, 38
Rangihīroa I, Te, 38
Rangihīroa II, Te, 38
Rangihokaia, Te, 77
Rangikohua pā, Parerahui killed at, 52
Rangimahora, 16 (n), 20, 22
Rangimoewaka, Te, kills Te Rauparaha's wife, 50
Rangimōnehunehu, Te, 139 (n)
Ranginumia, 64
Rangirangi, 26
Rangipōtiki, 43
Rangiriri, 211
Rangitikei river, boundary of land occupied by Te Rauparaha, 103
Rangitihi, 20
Rangi Topeora, sister of, 43
Rangitoto, 129
Rangitoto ranges, 116

Rangituamatotoru, Te, 131
Rangituatea, Te (Maniapoto chief) 46, 54, 55, 60, 63, 101, 129; assists Te Rauparaha's escape from Te Arawī, 80-81; visits Te Rauparaha at Te Urungaparoa, 83-84; assists Te Rauparaha's escape to Te Kawau pā, 84-86; farewell song to Te Rauparaha, 85-86; meeting with Te Rauparaha, 103-105 (n)
Rangituehu, Te, 21
Rangituke, defeated and killed, 143
Rangiwhakaia, Te, 71
Rapa, 21
Raparapa, 48, 56, 64, 76, 208; kills Unatahu, 50-54; protective clothing of in battle, 70: wife of, 70; at battle of Te Kakara, 69-71; lament for, 72-74; tattooing of, 75 (n); fight with Te Awaitaia 76
Rarohenga (world below), 273
Rauangaanga, Te, 16 (n), 17(n), 24, 25, 33, 94, 97, 100; battle song of, 2, 7-8; son of, 3; at battle of Hingakākā, 4-15; forces in battle, 7; teaches Te Wherowhero, 32, 34; leads Waikato against Ngāti Toa, 44-47; Te Rauparaha copies strategy of, 51-52; at Te Kakara battle, 69; advises Te Wherowhero on attack of Ōkoki, 94-97
Raukawa, 20, 22, 26, 33
Raukawa tribes, arrival in New Zealand, 190 (n)
Raumako, Te (daughter of Tāmehana Te Waharoa), 207
Rauparaha, Te (The Conqueror) 98, 102, 144, 176, 178 (n); parentage, 42; trespasses on Maniapoto territory, 46; war with Maniapoto and Waikato, 46-47; war cries, 47, 57, 66-67; tries to recruit army, 47-48; invades Whāingaroa and repulsed by Waikato, 48-49; became virtual leader of Tainui, 51; attacks Tūkōrehu's pā with Ngātapa, 50-52; escapes capture, 52; Te Wherowhero mobilises opposition, 54-56; defences of, 56; in battle of

Rauparaha, Te – *continued*
Kāwhia, 63-65, 67, 68, 69, 78, 79, 83-86; illness of, 63, 67, 82; wife of, 70; farewell song of, 78, 82-83; brother of, 79; besieged at Te Arawī, 79; escapes from Te Arawī, 79-81; retreats to Urungaparoao, 80-82, 83; escapes to Te Kawau pā, 84-86; with Ngāti Mutunga, 94; tactics of at Ōkoki, 94-97; leads Taranaki tribes against Te Wherowhero, 98-102; meetings with Rangituatea, 104-105 (n); prisoner at Auckland, 162; attends Kohimarama meeting, 162-164
Rawahirua, Te, 35, 38, 42
Rawharangi, son of, 76
Rehetaia, 38
Reid, Rev. A., missionary, at Te Kōpua, 233
religion, chants, mythology and ritual of, 235-263
Remuera, feast to entertain Fitzroy at, 166
Rereahu, 20, 22, 34, 89 (n)
Rereahu tribe, 122, 124
Rī, 241, 245
Ria, 38
Rimurehia, 242, 244
Rina, 38
Riupawhara, Te, 139 (n)
Riutoto, Te, 119
Rīwai, Hēmi, 219
Riwhenua, 242
Rongoroa ranges, tribes trapping birds in, 122; legend of tūī in, 124
Rongo (god of peace), 190, 243
Rongokako, 21
Rongomaiwahine, 21
Rongorito, Te, 33
Roore, Erueti *see* Erueti, R.
Ropi, 157, 168 (n)
Rota, 71
Rotorua, 90 (n), Te Rauparaha visits, 47, 54
Rotorua district, 146
Rotoaira, lake, 177

Rotoaira tribe, 48
Rotokākahi lake, 90 (n)
Rotorua lake, 177
Rotu, establishes house of learning, 33
Ruaihono, 21
Ruaimoko, 244
Ruapehu, mount, 226
Ruaputahanga, 21
Ruataraongo, 241
Rungaterangi, 20, 22
Rurutangiao, 241
Rutu Pahū, 256

Selwyn, Bishop, 154, 193
Smart, H. D., 107
songs, battle of Rauangaanga, 2; Pikauterangi, 5-6; farewell of Te Rauparaha, 78, 82-83; of Rangituatea, 85-87; of Ngāwaero, 132-135
Stanley, Lord, 166
Sutherland, E., 108

Taepa, 38
Taharoa, 45, 54, 56, 60, 63, 67-69, 71, 208; battle of, 63-65, 75 (n)
Taharoa hills 60
Taharoa lake, 60, 62, 75 (n), 79
Tahatiti, 255
Tahaunui, 21
Tahingaotera, 21
Tahiti, Arawa canoe arrives from, 3; canoes arriving from, 34
Tahuriwakanui, 42
taiaha, 74 (n); defined, 29 (n); chief proficient at, 46, 48
Taieti, and Māori King Movement, 189 (n)
Taihuru, 38
Taikiharau, canoe of Ngāti Pou, 49
Taiko, killed, 48
Tainui canoe, 20, 29 (n), 32, 33, 35, 88 (n), 168 (n), 190; Hoturoa commands, 22, 190
Tainui tribe, 4, 36, 43, 54, 55, 87 (n), 98, 129, 144, 146, 209 (n); chiefs of, 4, 16, 17 (n), 76; legends of and Tūrongo, 26-27; songs

Tainui tribe – *continued*
of, 27-31; culture of, 32; art, 33; houses of learning, 32-34; teachings of, 34-37, 270-272; search for inscribed emblems of, 92; beliefs of priesthood of, 36; customs of, 50; poetess of, 75 (n); as seaborne force in Kāwhia battle, 55, 59; make peace with Tūhoe, 92-93; invade Taranaki, 93; at Pukerangiora pā, 93-94; at Ōkoki, 94; attend Te Wherowhero's wedding, 129; Sir G. Grey lives with, 151

Taipōrutu, Te Wetini, 219, 220 (n)

Taka, 47

Takerei Te Rauangaanga, 157, 164, 169 (n)

Takerei *see* Wētere

Tākitimu canoe, 21, 34

Takiwaru, (Kati, brother of Te Wherowhero), 24, 102, 106-108; kills Te Whakataupōtiki, 79; marries Matiri, 142

Tāmaki, 129, 143: house of learning at, 32

Tāmaki isthmus, 7, 169 (n), 237

Tamakiterangi, 255

Tamangenge, 21

Tamatea, 21

Tāmati, Hone, 178

Tamatekapua, commander Arawa canoe, 3

Tāmehana Te Waharoa, 133, 165, 176, 178 (n), 190 (n), 204, 205, 207, 213; and King Movement, 193-195, 211; Tāmehana, Wiremu *see* Tāmehana Te Waharoa

Tāmihana Te Rauparaha, 176; and kingship, 177, 178 (n)

Tāne (the orphan-maker), 190 (n)

Tāne (god of forests), 123

Tānemahuta, 243, 244

Tānepukurua, 241

Tangahoe river, 144

Tangaroa, 243

Tangimoana, 20

Tangi Pahū, 256

Tanirau, 198, 199, 200

Tao, Te, 252

Tao werohia Apo, Te, 252

Taoho, 21

Tāpātai, 255

Tapaue, 20, 217 (n)

Tapihana, Te, 216 (n); ritual of at crowning of Te Wherowhero, 212-216

Tapirimoko track, 58

Tarahape, 44

Tārai, 241

Taranaki, Tūkōrehu enters, 93; tribes of attack Tūkōrehu, 93; defence against Te Wherowhero, 94-103; land settlements with Fitzroy, 102; copy of deed of sale by Te Wherowhero to Clark, 106-107; peace terms with Te Wherowhero, 144; Te Wherowhero invades north, 144-146; land claims, 166

Tarapeke (Ngāti Toa chief), 46, 48

Tarapīpipi, 167-168

Tararua range, 215

Tarawera, 90 (n)

Tarawhakatu, 21

tattooing of Te Rauparaha, 75 (n)

Tau Ana Te Marama, 250

Tauhara, mount, 87 (n)

Taui Wētere, 15 (n)

Tauke, 214

Taumatakanae stream, 56, 63, 64, 72, 75(n), 76

Taumatamaire hill, 58

Taumatamaire track, 52

Taumatawiwi, fishing grounds at, 46

Taumauri, 21

Taungawai, first to fall at Ōkoki, 103 (n)

Taungawai (brother of Te Rauparaha), killed, 78

Taupiri, tribe of, 43; Ngāpuhi at, 121

Taupiri, mount, 94, 183, 227

Taupiri, Kuao, mount, 227

Taupō, paramount chiefs of, 1; Te Rauparaha visits, 47-48, 54; district, 129

Taupō, Lake, 88 (n), 226

Taupō tribe, *see* Ngāti Tūwharetoa

Tauranganui, canoe racing at, 25

Tautearahi, canoe of Ngāti Mahuta, 49

Tauteka, 139 (n)
Tautara, 42
Tauwhara, mount *see* Tauhara, mount
Tawakemoetahanga, 20
Tawatutahi, 242
Tawatawhiti, 150; Ngāpuhi defeated at, 143
Tāwauwau, 242
Tāwhaki, 245-246, 256
Tāwhao, 20, 22, 26, 29 (n); establishes Rangiātea house of learning, 33
Tāwhiakiterangi, 16 (n), 20
Tāwhiao (Te Wherowhero's son), 126, 208, 265; baptised, 159; steals money to visit Auckland, 159-160; with Gov. Grey, 161; returns to tribe, 160; initiated into Tainui sacred bouse of learning 165; as Māori King, 224
Tāwhirimātea, 243
Te, for names of persons prefixed by Te, e.g. Te Wherowhero *see* under Wherowhero, Te
"Te A" *see* Tāwhiao
Te Ahahiaroa, canoe of Ngāti Te Ata, 49
Te Arawī pā, 103 (n); Te Rauparaha retires to, 63, 71; siege of, 79-78; Ngāti Toa escape from, 79-82
Te Aroha, mount, 215
Te Awamutu, 169 (n); mission station at, 232
Te Haupeehi pā, Huiputea at, 118
Te Ikaaranganui, 143
Te Kaawa swamps, 122
Te Kakara, Ngāti Toa defend, 64; battle of, 67, 69-76
Te Kawau pā, 49, 56, 65, 71; Ngāti Toa retreat to, 64, 67, 71, 83-87; Te Rauparaha at, 63; falls, 72
Te Kōpua, 233
Te Kūiti, 89 (n), 126 (n)
Te Kumi, Tāwhiao at, 126 (n)
Te Maika beach, 79
Te Maika inlet, 45
Te Maika pā, Kiwi to attack, 59; Toa evacuate, 62
Te Maika peninsula, 60, 88 (n); Waikato occupy, 62
Te Maika point, 60, 63; Kiwi lands at, 60; burial ground near, 65

Te Mangeo, 4, 18 (n); chosen as battlefield, 5
Te Marae o Hine (Te Rongorito's home), 33
Te Mataotutonga, 227
Te Matau, 139 (n)
Te Moata canoe, 131
Te Motu island, 88 (n)
Te Papa o Rotu *see* Papa o Rotu, Te
Te Motu, 65
Te Ngako, greenstone tiki, 131, 132
Te Paerata, Te Hoariri dies at, 156
Te Rapa, 131, 139 (n)
Te Raro, 138 (n)
Te Rauamoa, Waikato and Maniapoto army at, 46; Te Wherowhero at, 60; Hongi Hika passes through, 116
Te Raupō, 52
Te Rongoroa, 130
Te Rore, Pōmare defeated at, 142
Te Roto pā, 56, 64; Ngāti Toa retreat to 71
Te Ruaki, 144
Te Ruaki pā, 144
Te Taharoa, lake, 56
Te Tiroa, 122, 130
Te Titimatarua, retreat of Te Rauparaha *see* Te Urungaparaoa
Te Tōtara pā, 44, 45, 47, 60, 63; Te Rauparaha attacked at, 46; Te Rauparaha's defences at, 56; Kiwi to attack, 59; besieged in battle of Kāwhia, 60-63; evacuated, 63
Te Tōtara peninsula, 63
Te Urungaparaoa, stronghold of Te Rauparaha, 56; Te Rauparaha retreats to, 81-82; Te Rangituatea visits, 81
Te Wahakaikuri, canoe of Ngāti Pāoa, 48
Te Waruhanga, war canoe, 45
Te Whaanga, 26
Te Whāiti, Tūkōrehu passes, 92
Te Whara hills, 191 (n)
Tiaia, pleads with Te Rauparaha, 84
Tihirahi, Te, 55
Tikawe, 144
Tiki, 255

Tikiāhua, 240, 249
Tiki Ahu Mai i Hawaiki, 255
Tikiapoa, 240, 249
tiki, 131
Tiki Te Pou Mua, 255
Tiki Te Pou Roto, 255
Tiororangi, 241
Tipi, in battle of Hingakākā, 6, 7, 11, 15
Tiramanuhiri, 22
Tireke, catches Raparapa's weapon, 76
Tiria, 165
Tiritiri o matangi peninsula, Hikuparea pā on, 46
Tiriwa, in battle of Hingakākā, 6-10
Tirohanga-Kāwhia track, 60, 87 (n); summit, 89 (n); Hongi Hika uses, 116
Tīrua point, 56, 58, 81, 103 (n); Te Rauparaha retreats to, 81-82, 83, 85
Titiokura, mount, 215
Titiraupenga, 129, 138 (n), 155
Tītokowaru, 178
Tiwha, 181
Tiwhakopu, 38
Toangina, 42
Toarangatira, 35
Tohi, ceremony, 125 (n)
Tohuroa, 38
Toi, 255
Toitoi, 38
Toka, Ngāpuhi chief, daughter of, 142
Tokaanu, 139 (n)
Tokerau, 21
Tokerau hill, 139 (n)
Tokohihi, 24
Tokomaru canoe, 20, 34
Tongameha, 245
Tongapōrutu river, boundary of land sold by Te Wherowhoro, 102, 106-107
Tongariro, mount, 177, 226; district, 129
Tongariro river, 226
Topeora, 39
Topia Tūroa, 176, 177, 178; and Māori King Movement, 189
Torea, Waikato defeat Ngāti Toa at, 48

Toroa, 21
toroa, 17 (n)
Totoia, killed, 48
Totorewa, Moerua's wife at, 50
Totorewa pā, Te Wherowhero visits, 116; tracks, 60; peace —, of Ngāti Maniapoto, 50
tribes, *see* individual tribes under Ngāti Maniapoto etc.
Tuaka, 21
Tuakau, home of Ngāti Pou, 48
Tuaropaki, 129, 131, 138 (n), 155
Tuata, 16 (n), 20, 227
Tuatangiroa, 21, 26
Tūheitia, 165
Tuhi, Te, 49
Tuhi, Pātara Te *see* Taieti
Tūhoe tribe, 88 (n); make peace with Tainui, 92
Tūhoro, 195; at Haurua meeting, 198
Tūhua, 38
tūī, legends of, 124
Tuiri, Te, 139 (n)
Tūkaitaua *see* Tūmatauenga
Tūkanguha *see* Tūmatauenga
Tūkariri. See Tūmatauenga
Tūkāroto (Te Wherowhero's son), *see* Tāwhiao
Tū Kau Whata Rangi, 252
Tūkiakina, 242
Tūkohunui, 241
Tūkōrehu (Raukawa-Maniapoto chief), 46, 51, 54, 55, 74 (n), 132, 136, 138 (n); attacked by Te Rauparaha and Ngātapa, 51-52; mobilises Maniapoto to oppose Te Rauparaha, 54; in battle of Kāwhia, 58-59, 63; duel with Te Pūrewa, 92-93; besieged at Pukerangiora pā, 93, 94; Te Wherowhero relieves at Pukerangiora pā, 102; daughters of, 128; presents huahua, 136-137
Tūmatakeueue *see* Tūmatauenga
Tūmatauenga, 244, 245, 254
Tūmatawhāiti *see* Tūmatauenga
Tumukerekere, 252
Tungia, 81

Tuotauwha, 21
Tupeotu, Te, 99, 100
Tūpoki, Ngāti Tama chief. 52, 53, 56, 71; defeated and killed, 53; sister of, 69, 71
Tūpurupuru, 21
Tūrangawaewae pā, 230
Turata, 130, 131, 138 (n)
Turaukawa, 144
Turi, 21
Turimataoneone, 21
Turimataorehua, 21
Tūroa, Topia see Topia Tūroa
Tūrongo, 20, 22, 26-27, 34, 35; song about, 27-28
Turton, H. H., 108
Tūtaerere, 46, 83, 103 (n)
Tutangatakino, 243
Tū Te Kuku Rangi, 252
Tuterangiamoa, 241
Tutonga, killed, 48
Tuwhareiti, 38

Ua Haumene, Te, names Tāwhiao, 126 (n)
Uata, Pāora Te, 219
Ue, 20, 22, 157, 168 (n)
Uehae, 21
Uehoka, captured and killed 48
Ueko, 242
Uenuku, 38, 194, 244, 246, 247, 249
Uenukumairarotonga, 20
Uenukutuhatu, 21
Uerata, 20
Ueroa, 21
Uira, Te, kills Te Hurinui, 35, 42, killed 43
Umukiwhakatane, Te, 16 (n)
Unuatahu, Te, 54; pursued by Raparapa, 49; killed, 50, 75 (n)
Uoko, 242
Urenui district, 94
Urewera district, Tūhoe tribe of, 87 (n)
Uruhapāinga, 165
Uruhina, 20, 22
Ururangi, 20
Urutonga, 255

Victoria, Queen of Great Britain, Te Wherowhero's letter to, 153-154; and Māori King Movement, 189

Waahi district, 7, 15 (n); home of Ngāti Mahuta, 49
Waahi Lake, 25
Waaka, Te, 139 (n)
Waata, 144
Waata Kukutai, 124, 137 (n), 158, 169 (n), 208
Waero, Te Tūpoki's daughter, 53-54; killed. 54
Wahanui (son of Irohanga), 16 (n); in battle of Hingakākā, 4-11, 15; at battle of Hurimoana, 16 (n)
Wahanui (son of Waiora), 53-54
Waharoa, Tāmehana Te see Tāmehana Te Waharoa
Waharoa, Te, 129, 146, 157, 165
Waiata (wife of Te Wherowhero), 128
Waihora, 131
Waikanae, chief of, 38
Waikarakia, house of learning at, 33
Waikare, lake, 25
Waikato, Pikauterangi invades, 4-15; Tainui houses of learning in, 33; Hongi Hika invades, 110; British confiscate land in, 169
Waikato heads, Ngāti Tipa of, 49
Waikato river, 116,185 (n); tribes from, 7; Hongi Hika canoes on, 110; desc. & history of, 226-229; desc. of land surrounding, 229
Waikato tribes, 54, 56, 144, 98-103; war chieftain of, 3, 4; in battle of Hingakākā, 4, 7, 9, 18; at war with Ngāti Toa, 43-46, 48-49; in Te Wherowhero's force, 54; mascot of, 67; in battle of Kāwhia, 58 et. seq.; at Te Kakara battle, 67-71; march toward Waitara, 92; called to Tūkōrehu's aid, 93; Te Wherowhero leader of, 94; attack Ōkoki pā, 96-97; defeated at Mātakitaki pā, 110-115; introduction to firearms, 110-116; first guns owned by, 111; assist in annihilating Huiputea's force, 118-119; raiding in Taupō area, 122; attend

Waikato tribes – *continued*
Te Wherowhero's wedding, 128-130; defeat Ngāpuhi, 142-144; peace made with southern Taranaki tribes, 144; take Pukerangiora pā, 144-146; invade Taranaki, 146; peace with Ngāpuhi, 150, at Kohimarama meeting, 149; arrival in New Zealand, 190; at Paetai meeting, 205-209, 211; at crowning of Te Wherowhero, 212
Waikawau, 122
Waikawau pā, 55, 74 (n), 92; defeated, 58-59
Waikawau river, 58
Waikohika, 22
Waimate pā, 144
Waimiha river, 33, 122
Waiora, 22; son of, 53
Waipā, 111; tribes of district, 42
Waipā range, 230
Waipā river, 110, 111, 114, 115, 116, 122, 233, 237
Waipari stream, 118
Waipā-Waikato river junction, 226; Pikauterangi goes toward, 4; district of, 4
Waipunahau, 38
Wairarapa, Tūkōrehu passes through, 93
Wairau massacre, 162
Wairere, 129
Wairere falls, Ngāti Tama camps at, 52
Waitangi, killed by Raparapa, 75 (n)
Waitangi, Treaty of, Te Wherowhero & Heuheu do not sign, 147
Waitaoro, 39
Waitapu 49; killed, 43
Waitara, 92; Āti Awa tribe of, 88 (n); Tūkōrehu defeated near, 93
Waitara district, 178 (n)
Waitematā harbour, 143-190
Waitetuna, 129
Waitohi, 39, 48
Waitōtara river, boundary of land sold by Te Wherowhero, 102, 106-107
Waiuku, 7, 49, 194
Wakaiti, Te, 17 (n)

Wāka Nene, 167
Wakefield, Colonel, 166
Waotu, 129, 229
Wariwariotu, Te, 241
Waru, Hōri Te, 198
weapons, pou-whenua, 17 (n); used in battles, 66, 70, 71, 76
Wehi, Te, tribe of claims land, 42
Wellington, Te Wherowhero accompanies Hobson to, 166
Wellington harbour, Te Rauparaha occupies land as far as, 104
Werawera, 38, 42; killed, 80
Wesleyan Mission Committee, 154
Wētere, 157, 166, 168 (n)
Weu, Te, killed, 49
Whaaro (of Ngāti Maniapoto), attacks Ngāti Tama, 52
Whāinga, Te, 52
Whāingaroa, 208; tribes of, 55, 76, 129; Kiwi's force at, 59
Whāingaroa harbour, 26, 129; naming of, 29 (n); Te Rauparaha at, 48
Whaititiri, 255
Whakaawi (wife of Te Wherowhero), 114, 125; birth of son of, 116
Whakaete, Te, kills Te Arawaka, 79
Whakairoiro, 49; home of Te Hiakai, 43
Whakamaru (Maniapoto chief), 46; killed by Te Rauparaha, 46
Whakamarurangi, 16 (n), 22
Whakaotirangi, wife of Hoturoa, 191
"whakarewa" (Te Wherowhero's *mere*), 145
Whakataupotiki, Te, killed, 79,
Whakaue-Kōpako, Arawa confederation, 90 (n)
Whanganui, Tūkōrehu at, 93
Whanganui tribes, 176, 177, 178
Whangape, lake, 25, 143
Whāngārā, 178 (n)
Whāngārei, Ngāpuhi tribe from 47; Ngāpuhi defeated at, 143
Wharauroa, 38
Whare, Te, 138 (n)
Wharekauri, *see* Chatham islands
Wharengori, Te, kills Tarapeke, 47; killed, 48

Wharepuhi, Te, 44; sister of, 44, 74; killed, 48

Wharepuhunga, 129

Wharepuhunga district, 131; tribes of, 42, 52, 81

Wharerangi, Te, Te Rauparaha hidden by wife of, 48

Wharetiki, farewell song by, 82-83, 87 (n); used by Te Rauparaha, 82-83, 87 (n); executed, 87

whare wānanga, defined, 32

Whata, Te, 49; killed, 43

Whatakaraka, Te, 89 (n)

Whatanui, Te, 139 (n), 185 (n); refuses Maungatautari lands, 149

Whatawhata, house of learning at, 33

Whatihua, 26, 29 (n)

Whatitiri, 246

Whatiwhatihoe, Maniapoto tribes meet at, 130-138

Whauwhaunganui, Te, 242

wheat, 231

Whenuatupu, house of learning at, 33

Wheoro, Te, 208

Wherowhero, Pōtatau Te, 3, 4, 32-37, 46, 52, 76, 79, 93, 94, 95, 120, 122, 146-147, 165, 169 (n), 175, 184 (n), 190 (n), 193, 198, 205, 219, 236, 265; childhood of, 24, 25, 33; attends Papa o Rotu school, 33, 34; and Māori King Movement, 36-37, 176, 187, 193-195; leader against Te Rauparaha, 54-56; in battle of Kāwhia, 60, 63, 71; at Te Kakara, 69; brother of, 80; called to aid Tūkōrehu, 94; defeated at Ōkoki, 96-98; in retreat, 97-98; kills many of Taranaki's best warriors, 98-101; sale of land by, 102-107; defeated at Mātakitaki pā, 110-114; at Mangauika pā, 116; visits Pamotumotu 116; settled at Ōrongokoekoeā, 116, 118; helps annihilate Huiputea's force, 118-120; as guest of Te Otapeehi, 122-124; marries Ngāwaero, 128-130; at Whatiwhatihoe, 131-137; defeats Ngāpuhi, 142-144; invades south Taranaki and makes peace, 144; captures Pukerangiora pā, 144-146; relationship with Te Arawa, 146; makes peace among tribes, 149-151; approves missionaries, 151; attitude to British, 152-162, 165; at Kohimarama meeting, 162; song of refusal, 187-188; notes on song of refusal, 190-191; speech at Waiuku, 194, 196(n); song of sorrow, 200-201; notes on song of sorrow, 209; proclaimed king, 211-216; desc. of, 233; death of, 268-271

Whetū, Te, 249

Whioi, 185 (n)

Whiriaiterangi, 242

Whiritaura, Te, 242

Whirotetupua, 255

Whiwhi, Mātene Te *see* Mātene Te Whiwhi

Wī Neera, 38

Wiremu Tāmehana, 158, 169 (n)

Wī Tako, 176, 178 (n)

Index to Genealogical Tables

Ahitumuaki, 38
Ahooterangi, Te, 171, 202
Ahumai, 171
Airini, 180
Akanui, Te, 171
Akuhata, 181
Amohau, Te, 181
Aorangi, Te, 184
Ariariterangi, 181
Atainutai, Te, 180
Atairangikaahu, Te, 228
Ataiwhanake, Te, 258

Hapaikura, 256
Hāpuku, Te, 180
Hau, 184
Hauāuru, 202
Hauiti, 184
Hāwea, 180
Hekemaru, 181, 257
Hehiri, Hitiri, 171
Herewini, 181
Heuheu I, Te, 171
Heuheu II, Te (Tūkino), 171
Heuheu III, Te (Iwikau), 171
Heuheu IV, Te (Patatai), 171
Heuheu V, Te (Tūreiti), 171
Heuheu VI, Te (Hoani) 171
Heuheu VII, Te (Hepi), 171
Hīkaka, 202
Hikawera II, 180
Hineiteumu, 181
Hinekura, 184
Hinemapuhia, 171
Hinepare, 171
Hinera 181
Hineturaha, 184
Hinewai (Maniapoto chieftainess), 202, 263
Hingangaroa, 184
Hitaua, Te, 180
Hone Teri, 171
Horahora, 184

Hore, Te, 171
Hotomatapu, 257
Hotuope, 257
Hoturoa, 256, 257
Hotu Wai Ariki, 255
Houmaitawhiti, 256
Hourua, 202
Hurinui, Te, 263
Hurinui, Te (the author), 202, 263

Ihingarangi, Te, 171
Ihutarera, 181
Io (Māori God), 249, 250
Irohanga, 202
Iwipupu, 184

Kahoki, 171
Kahukuranui I, 184
Kahukuranui II, 184
Kahumatamomoe, 181, 257
Kahungunu, 180, 184
Kahurangi, Te, 171, 180, 184, 202, 258
Kanawa, Te, 171, 180, 184, 258
Kaniatakirau, Te, 184
Karauria, 180, 184
Karera, 184
Karewa, 258
Karihimama, 184
Kauru, Te, 180
Kawairirangi I, Te, 171, 180, 184, 257
Kawairirangi II, Te, 171, 180, 258
Kawatapuarangi, 181, 257
Kauwhata, 258
Kāwhia, 171
Ketekura, Te, 258
Kikoreka, 171
Kokuotepo, 256
Korokī, 171
Kōtare, 258
Kuraataiwhakaea, Te, 228
Kurī, 171

Māhinārangi, 180, 184
Mahuta, 171, 181, 257
Maniaihu, 258
Maniapoto, Rewi, 20-21, 22, 38, 171, 180, 184, 257
Manutangirua, 184
Maroro, 184
Marukawhiti, 184
Maungatautari, 22, 202
Māwakenui, 257
Māwakeroa, 257
Māwaketaupō, 257
Moeroro, 171
Momoirawaru, 171
Mori, 180
Mōtai, 257
Muera, Te, 181

Ngaiwiwera, 171
Ngarokitepo, 184
Ngarue, 202
Ngātokawaru, 228
Ngātoroirangi, 256, 257
Numiaiterangi, 180

Oneone, 180
Oro, Te, 171

Paerata, Te, 171
Pahura, 184
Pakaruwakanu, 258
Pāora, 181
Parekaihewa, 171
Parekawa, 171
Parengāope, 171, 180, 184, 202
Parengāope I, 20, 22, 258
Parengāope II, 258
Parepounamu, 257
Pareraumoa, 258
Paretekawa, 171
Paretekōrae (Māori poetess of Tainui), 202, 263
Peehi Tūroa, 180
Pikauterangi, 38, 39
Pikiao I, 181, 257

Pikiao II, 181
Piungatai, Te, 180
Porourangi, 184
Poutama, 202
Poutama II, 202, 263
Pūkaki, 181
Pukauae, 171, 202
Puraho, 171
Purangataua, 171
Putu, Te, 181, 228, 257

Raka, 257
Rakaipo, 184
Rakauri I, 256
Rakeihikuroa, 180, 184
Rakeihopukia, 171
Rākeipoho, 257
Rangiaho, 171
Rangihopuata, Te, 180
Rangiita, Te, 171
Rangikaianake, Te, 180
Rangikamangumangu, 180
Rangikawhiua, Te, 180
Rangimahora, 171, 180, 184, 202, 258
Rangimakiri, 171
Rangitakumu, 257
Rangitapu, 256
Rangitaumaha, 180
Rangitihi, 257
Rangitu, 256
Rangituehu, Te, 180, 184
Rangitumamao, 184
Rata, Te 171
Rauangaanga, Te, 20-21, 22, 180, 181, 184, 202, 228, 258
Raukawa, 171, 180, 184, 257
Rauparaha, Te, 38, 39
Rauti-Hauā, 171
Rereahu, 171, 180, 184, 257
Ruamuturangi, 256
Ruapakura, 184
Ruawehea, 257
Rungaterangi, 171, 180, 184, 258

Tahinga, 257
Takihiku, 180
Takinga, Te, 181
Takoro, 184
Tamakari, 181
Tamatekapua, 20, 181, 256, 257
Tamiuru, 181
Tangihia, 257
Tangimoana 171, 257
Tanirau, 202
Tapaue, 181, 257
Taraia, 180
Tarao, 256
Tarawhaene, 256
Taringa, 171
Tauaha, 184
Taumatua, 256
Taunga, 256
Tautini, 184
Tawakemoetahanga, 181, 257
Tāwhaki, 256
Tāwhao, 257
Tāwhiakiterangi, 181, 228, 257
Tāwhiao (Te Wherowhero's son), 171
Teehi, Te, 181
Tiaria, 171
Tikiorereata, Te, 258
Tini, Te, 171
Tokerau, 184
Tokohihi, 258
Topia Tūroa, 180
Toreheikura, 228
Tuaka, 180, 184
Tuata, 181, 228, 258
Tuhera, 171
Tūhourangi, 181
Tukuoterangi, 180
Tunaeke, 181
Tunohopu, 181
Tupahau, 38
Tupani, 184

Tūpurupuru, 180, 184
Tūrongo, 257
Tutaepena, 184
Tutakamoana, 38
Tūtānekai, 181
Tutetawha, 171
Tuturu, 171
Tūwhakahautaua, 258
Tūwharetoa, 171, 257
Ua-te-awha, 180
Ue, 257
Uenuku-kōpako, 181
Uenukumairarotonga, 181, 257
Uerata, 181, 257
Ueroa, 184
Umukiwhakatane, Te, 202
Upokoiti, 180
Uruhina, 171, 180, 184, 258

Wahanui (son of Irohanga), 16 (n), 22
Waharoa, Te, 171
Waiheketua, 256
Waitapu, 180
Wakahuia, Te, 171
Wakatotopipi, Te, 180
Wano, Te, 263
Wano, Te Hurinui Te, 263
Wawahanga, Te, 180
Wehiwehi, 258
Weka, 180
Whakamarurangi, 202
Whakapapa, 184
Whakatatari, Te, 184
Whakaue, 181
Whakinga, 184
Whatumairangi, 181
Wherowhero. Pōtatau Te, 20-21, 171, 180, 181, 184, 202, 228, 258
Wiki Tahutahu, Te, 180
Wiremu Tāmehana, 171